Holly has written the definitive strategic marketing manifesto. She has shared the scar tissue you get only by living and breathing the ups and downs of building a business and has described those lessons in a straightforward, digestible, and fun read. As one who has reviewed thousands of business plans and hundreds of board plans, Holly nailed it. You must keep your eye on the horizon lest you go off course, but you better pay maniacal attention to the details that are driving to that horizon. Holly's sage advice acts as a rudder and should be absorbed by every B2B CEO trying to balance their ship.

TED SCHLEIN
Former managing partner, Kleiner Perkins
Founder partner, Ballistic Ventures

Rollo's advice is a lifeline for those preparing for a major transaction or going through a pivot. If you're ready to turbocharge your software business and find hidden value, *Power of Surge* is an indispensable guide.

DAVID LANG
Partner, KKR

Refreshing and powerful. Rollo's insights about how to use strategic marketing as a value driver are helpful and impactful. She not only diagnoses root causes hindering results but also offers actionable remedies that CEOs can put to work immediately. The framework she lays out in this book can help companies set themselves up for long-term success.

BETTY HUNG
Managing director, Vista Equity Partners

Holly Rollo's new book is a must-read for any investor or CEO in the B2B software space. Her decades of marketing leadership success at important companies have given her the ideal perspective for crafting a tight, actionable framework for creating a competitive advantage. All of this is combined with a highly accessible narrative style. What is not to like?

SEKSOM SURIYAPA
Partner, Upfront Ventures

Today more so than ever, a B2B software CEO needs the skill to navigate sudden and unexpected changes in the business climate. *Power of Surge* offers actionable insights to leverage marketing as a source of strategic advantage and maximize the value of a business at exit. It is very clearly a practitioner's rendition and presents this advice in a refreshingly relatable and compelling way. It's a great addition to any CEO's bookshelf!

ROHIT GHAI
CEO, RSA

What a wonderful opportunity for CEOs to learn the uncensored truth about marketing in our uncertain roller coaster of a world. Holly Rollo generously shares her relentlessly practical, no-holds-barred experience as a CMO. She reveals how small businesses can avoid fumbling their fortune, achieve better results, and become resilient by capitalizing on how marketing really works.

KATHLEEN SCHAUB
Marketing management strategist
Former IDC CMO advisory practice leader

HOLLY ROLLO

POWER OF
SURGE

FIVE WAYS TO SUPERCHARGE
YOUR **B2B SOFTWARE
BUSINESS** AND UNLEASH
HIDDEN VALUE

Published by Advantage Books, Charleston, South Carolina.
An imprint of Advantage Media.

ADVANTAGE is a registered trademark, and the Advantage colophon is a trademark of Advantage Media Group, Inc.

Printed in the United States of America.

10 9 8 7 6 5 4 3 2 1

ISBN: 978-1-64225-811-0 (Paperback)
ISBN: 978-1-64225-810-3 (eBook)

Library of Congress Control Number: 2023924598

Cover design by Analisa Smith.
Interior design by Wesley Strickland.

This publication is designed to provide accurate and authoritative information in regard to the subject matter covered. It is sold with the understanding that the publisher is not engaged in rendering legal, accounting, or other professional services. If legal advice or other expert assistance is required, the services of a competent professional person should be sought.

The opinions voiced in this material are for general information only and are not intended to provide specific advice or recommendations for any individual. All investing involves risk, including loss of principal. No strategy assures success or protects against loss.

Advantage Books is an imprint of Advantage Media Group. Advantage Media helps busy entrepreneurs, CEOs, and leaders write and publish a book to grow their business and become the authority in their field. Advantage authors comprise an exclusive community of industry professionals, idea-makers, and thought leaders. For more information go to **advantagemedia.com**.

To my children and my greatest teachers, Emily and Jake, and to my husband, Stephane, for his impassioned encouragement.

How inappropriate to call this planet
Earth, when it is clearly *Ocean*.

−ARTHUR C. CLARKE

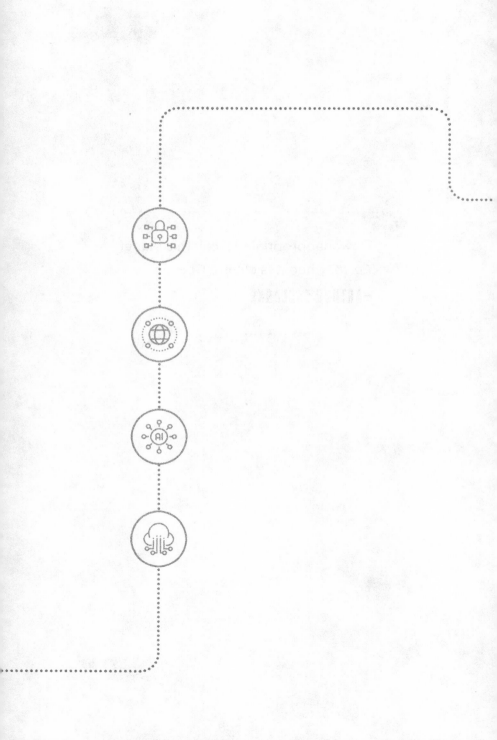

CONTENTS

FOREWORD xiii

ACKNOWLEDGMENTS xix

INTRODUCTION: SURGE 1

SECTION 1: THE STORM 9

1. VALLEY OF TRANSACTIONS 21

2. SO ... YOUR CMO STINKS? 39

3. TRENDS AND IMPLICATIONS 63

4. MARKETING TRANSFORMED 87

SECTION 2: THE POWER OF SURGE 107

5. STRATEGY 113

6. UNITY 135

7. REPUTATION 167

8. GAINS 193

9. EFFICIENCY 217

SECTION 3: SMOOTH SAILING 241

10. THE MARKETING INVESTMENT 247

11. FINDING AND KEEPING A STELLAR CMO 275

12. STAYING ON COURSE 299

13. ADVICE 325

CONCLUSION 361

ABOUT THE AUTHOR 375

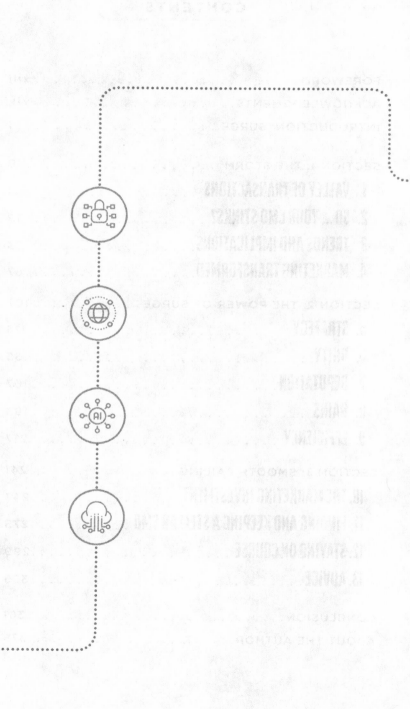

FOREWORD

IN THE EVER-EVOLVING and fast-paced B2B software industry, CEOs need to not only survive its storms, but also harness its intensity to drive increasingly ambitious outcomes. The need for more strategic, customer-centric execution is critical because companies no longer have the luxury to experiment and evaluate results—they must anticipate conditions and make brave decisions. Knowing how to best leverage marketing to drive strategic outcomes can seem elusive, especially as compared to product development and sales execution, which have well understood frameworks and playbooks. Strategic marketing is arguably the biggest untapped opportunity and remains largely uncharted territory for most organizations.

I have known and worked with Holly Rollo for over a decade and am grateful that with this book she is bringing her deep expertise to a broader audience. I am lucky to have worked side by side with her, watching her implement the principles she lays out in this book and the powerful outcomes they can drive.

Small to midsize B2B software CEOs and investors continue to struggle with the *CMO problem* and the impact strategic marketing can drive across the entire go-to-market (GTM) motion. It's not always clear how to best achieve aggressive growth targets using today's digital-first models. Facing bigger competitors with bigger budgets requires new paradigms, a unified strategy, and more modern methods that only a fraction of companies have figured out how to do well. Having been in the trenches with Holly Rollo, I have experienced her deep and intimate understanding of these challenges which she has now crafted into this transformative guide that promises to help CEOs get the results they deserve and the ROI they expect.

As a friend and colleague of the author, I have had the privilege of witnessing the passion, dedication, and effort poured into defining a practical guide for how to get results in *Power of Surge: Five Ways to Transform Your B2B Software Business and Unleash Hidden Value.* Her approach is a combination of proven best practices, new insights, and decades of transformational leadership experience in the B2B software industry.

This isn't your typical business book with generic advice; it's full of concrete specifications that help you make actionable decisions today. Written by a seasoned strategist who has faced the same headwinds at B2B software companies of all sizes, she provides a framework that you can apply to match your unique situation whether your goal is to scale, transform, turnaround, or position yourself for a future transaction. This book delves into the dangerous embedded assumptions that are holding you back, how to get alignment across sales, marketing, product, and customer success, and how to drive accountability and execution across the customer experience. *Power of Surge* empowers CEOs, founders, and investors to finally address their biggest GTM disconnects and rewrite their destinies.

This book should be used as navigational aid for companies who are racing to win, looking to not just adapt but surge ahead. The central premise is that if you are a B2B software company operating today, facing financial headwinds and the possibility of acquisition are practical certainties. However, depending on your unique business situation, you can design a strategy to use these conditions to your advantage.

The digital-first era demands not just adaptability but a sound marketing strategy that keeps pace with the rapid technological advances and dynamic shifts in buyer behavior. Random, tactical marketing programs are likened to sailing blindly through this digital landscape—they can do more harm than good. This book emphasizes that, while the past taught us valuable lessons, doing things the same way we are accustomed to is holding us back and we must reprioritize customer experience, digital modernization, and strategic positioning. Companies that embrace these priorities not only weather tough times better but also become more attractive to potential acquisition targets.

B2B technology buyers are emerging as techsumers with generational expectations for engagement that changes when, where, and how they consume information. Organizations that differentiate themselves based on customer experience and align their operations with the customer journey statistically enjoy higher success rates so designing for this is key. In addition, strategic positioning is not just a marketing afterthought; it directly influences adoption, conversion rates, and, consequently, growth and market share, so it must be a business imperative at the onset.

In this book, a new definition of B2B marketing is proposed—one that recognizes the expectation of always-on digital engagement in our connected world. The customer journey is explored as no longer linear but interconnected and complex, disrupting traditional GTM models and sales motions. This paradigm shift necessitates a fresh perspective on marketing and its role in driving business value in radical unity with sales and customer success.

Using a sailing analogy, the central question posed is whether businesses are merely cruising or racing. For those aiming for the latter, the book introduces the five Power of Surge Principles: Strategy, Unity, Reputation, Gains, and Efficiency (SURGE). Each principle is not just a theoretical concept but a practical, actionable step toward transformative success.

The book culminates by addressing the importance of smart investing, sound leadership, and avoiding organizational decisions that seem like good ideas on the surface but over time can lead you astray. It offers insights into deciding what marketing programs to invest in, the foundational importance of digital stacks and always-on activities, and the critical role of a great CMO in achieving success. It concludes with additional advice from other seasoned executives across the industry.

I can attest to the authenticity of Holly's insights and the practicality of the solutions presented in this book. This is not a detached observer pontificating; this is a fellow traveler sharing lessons learned the hard way from being on many journeys with companies of all sizes. *Power of Surge* is a strategic companion for CEOs, founders, and investors alike. It provides a roadmap to not only stay afloat but to surge ahead, leveraging the transformative principles of SURGE to unlock hidden value and achieve sustained success in the digital-first era.

May your voyage be filled with discoveries, may your business soar to new heights, and may the hidden value within your organization emerge as a force to be reckoned with.

NILOOFAR RAZI HOWE

Senior operating partner, Energy Impact Partners; technology executive; entrepreneur; investor; board member

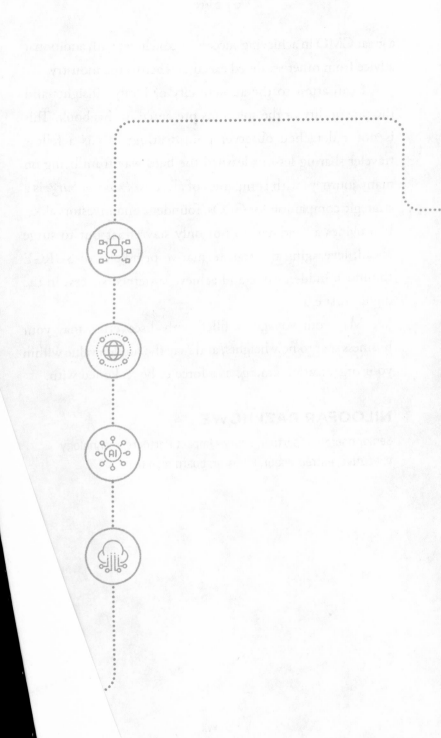

ACKNOWLEDGMENTS

THIS BOOK WOULD NOT have been possible without the resilience and determination of the women in technology with whom I have had the pleasure to work with over the last thirty-plus years. Your courage to be gracefully disruptive has pushed me through my darkest moments of self-doubt and hesitation. To these extraordinary women, as well as all the allies who advocate for our interests, I would like to express my heartfelt gratitude for boldly striving to advance this industry every single day.

SURGE

WHEN I FIRST started sailing, I mostly tried not to die.

I started by gleefully hopping on boats and acting like I'd been there before, but at one point I realized that with only two people on the boat, if someone else fell off, it was curtains for both of us. I hauled my brain begrudgingly inside a classroom to conquer the basics of sail theory and navigation. Then, under supervision, I confronted the moody conditions of the San Francisco Bay and tussled with the soggy blob of fog that appears out of nowhere and makes oncoming cargo ships deadly. After a few years of barely avoiding bashing my brains in with the boom doing accidental jibes, my instructors finally awarded me the coveted silver sticker that gave me the authority to skipper on my own—then fled the docks before I asked them to join me as crew.

Years into it I was improving, but I felt like an impostor because up to that point, I hadn't done a proper offshore

1

passage other than a three-day stint off the coast and carefree bareboat charter trips in the British Virgin Islands and Belize. I wanted to do true blue-water sailing before I called myself a sailor. So I secured a position as crew on a boat sailing from Key West to Bermuda, which is roughly the distance between Los Angeles and Dallas over eight to eleven days, depending on the conditions. I wanted to see what I was made of, and this trip did not disappoint. We sailed nonstop day and night through an equipment failure, lightning storms, and a medical situation with one of our crew, and we pounded upwind for days at a twenty-degree heel, which meant we got clobbered by the boat every time we went to use the bathroom. Also, I had to manage an annoying tickle in the back of my head reminding me that I volunteered to put myself on a boat in the Bermuda Triangle.

There were magical moments too. Embracing the night sky each evening was truly a religious experience, aside from one day in a storm. This was a bit more chilling in more ways than one. We sailed through miles of fields of Portuguese men-of-war and were visited by joyful dolphins. At one point we stopped our boat and plunged into water a mile deep. Minutes later, after rambunctiously giggling about it back on board, we saw what we thought was a shark swim past that was at least half the size of our boat. None of us spoke a word for the next hour.

Since then my husband and I have embraced the goal of a multiyear circumnavigation and have spent years enjoying the wonder of the ocean's alien sea life. We have also witnessed the fury of Poseidon amassing his posse to prove who is in charge. As you might imagine, one forms a unique relationship with weather systems, wind conditions, and the behavior of coastal waters and delights in the mesmerizing and ever-changing shape of the water. Sometimes it's smooth and enchanting as the wind practices pirouettes above it. Sometimes it's violent and threatens to take no quarter—a reminder that having a healthy fear of the ocean's power helps keep us humble and using its conditions to seek an advantage can help keep us safe.

One season we were attempting to make it from the northern side of France on the Atlantic, crossing the notorious Bay of Biscay around and through the Gibraltar Strait, across the Med, under the southern boot of Italy, and into the Adriatic Sea to Montenegro. We had a limited time to get there before my visa expired, but because we puttered around early on with lingering boat projects, we got a late start leaving. While eating authentic Sicilian pizza, an unexpected storm started to develop in the area. We found ourselves in a situation where we had just a couple of days left on our visa and an unpredictable storm system forcing our hand.

If we stayed, we risked getting caught in the southern Italian immigration and legal system. (This was during the pandemic, so the immigration policies were confusing, even for the people trying to enforce them.) If we left, we risked challenging conditions and only had a brief window to decide. We decided to go for the Adriatic crossing and tucked into the safety of the bay in Montenegro just in time to secure ourselves from the forty-mile-per-hour winds that came within just thirty minutes of docking. Had we spent any more time deciding, debating, or hesitating, we would have had a very bad situation on our hands. Indecision would only have made it much worse and would have limited our options altogether.

I've come to believe two things about sailing: Being a true master seaman/woman would take many lifetimes; you simply can't know everything and prepare for everything. After that it's a vicious mental rivalry between fear and courage happening between your ears. My initial mindset was to sail with caution to protect my existence, but now I understand there is danger in operating this way. It leads you to overthink and second-guess yourself, leaving you paralyzed when you need to be decisive and mentally clinging to the dock with your attention in entirely the wrong direction. Half measures never produce a good sailing day, and challenging conditions are a gift that pushes you to either dig deep or find a way to use them to your advantage. After proper preparation, you need to go with gusto toward your next destination, where success welcomes you to shore with a pink lei and a sparkling lemonade. Truly, the best way to sail—the way that delivers the most rewarding and safe experience—is with purpose and moxie. But that shift in mindset takes work.

As my husband and I sailed together over the years in our coveted spare time, I was also deep into my professional career, helping lead B2B software companies through various flavors of business transformation. What I've observed is that there are marked parallels between sailing and achieving successful business outcomes in this crazy industry, and your approach and mindset will define your outcome before you even cast off. More importantly, you can take advantage of conditions in which others are busy just trying to survive and achieve results that others wouldn't dare to imagine.

This is where the *Power of Surge* comes to life in a business context. It happens when you face a challenging situation and find ways to use it to your advantage by combining the perfect blend of intensity, speed, and approach to create a powerful and often underestimated force that demands attention, makes a statement, and doesn't ask for forgiveness.

The legendary waves of Nazaré, Portugal, have a unique surge that the rarest of souls try to conquer. It is notorious for having monstrously high and wild breaking waves due to its deep underwater canyon that affects the currents and surrounding sea state. It is in this powerful place that Garrett McNamara surfed a seventy-eight-foot wave and set a world record, which Sebastian Steudtner broke later—an eighty-six-foot tower, to prove that extreme conditions can lead to extreme outcomes. It takes courage to ride a surge like that. And in the context of business, it takes those with the willingness to embrace the Power of Surge to achieve what others can't even imagine.

Surge: [sərj] *verb, to move suddenly or powerfully upward or forward*

It is not only possible to use conditions to create unimaginable results; it is also possible to create conditions that generate a surge to get specific outcomes. I've spent years refining the

Power of Surge using strategic, modern marketing methods to drive growth, scale, and transformation that have also led to many transactions, and here are the basic elements:

By taking a strategic approach to modern marketing, you can massively increase the value of your company, either over the long haul or leading up to a transaction. In this book I will outline five ways you can get a strategic, competitive advantage starting today. Using these proven, practical approaches, you can increase the value of your business and tap into the potential hidden right in plain sight.

Many of the ideas shared in this book will show how to create the Power of Surge so it's there precisely when you need it. However, to execute a surge-worthy strategy, you need to conquer your mindset and ask yourself if you are simply trying to survive, clinging to old beliefs and paradigms, or if you are ready to dig deep to create a much bigger opportunity for yourself and your company.

If you are ready, let's do this!

THE STORM

ARE YOU A CEO or senior executive at a small to midsize business-to-business (B2B) software company that wants to grow but questions the value you are getting from your current marketing program? Perhaps you have already had a couple of false starts at it, and you are wondering whether you need a new chief marketing officer (CMO) or a new marketing model altogether.

Here are five possible reasons your current marketing program isn't living up to your expectations:

1. You are expecting modern results but are executing against old paradigms.

2. You hired a head of marketing whose skills are a mismatch for what you need.

3. You have trust and alignment gaps with your CMO on what should be done.

4. You have a strategy problem.

5. All of the above.

The good news is that these things are solvable and directly within your control. In this book, I'm going to break it all down and cover how you got here, what needs to change, and what you can do next. You will finish with a path forward that will help you surge past your competition, achieve the upsides you are looking for, and unleash hidden potential for you and your investors that may be sitting right under your nose. With the right insights and best practices, you can grow, turn around, or transform your company and get the impact from marketing that you want within the time horizon your investors expect.

Whether you are in your early stages and just getting started, striving for scale and hypergrowth, or are running a company in distress, strategic marketing is critical to your success. With the speed, scope, and scale of the customer-led digital experience, it's more important than ever to be deliberate and precise about how you leverage marketing in this hypercompetitive, overcrowded, and ever-changing B2B software space. Also, because you are constantly looking for ways to fund new innovations while adequately managing cash flow, you need to be confident your marketing spend will deliver the best return on investment (ROI) for the business.

Today's modern marketing is a complex system based on a rapidly evolving and monumentally fragmented web of technology and capabilities that has taken on a life of its own.

It is highly operational and data-driven, requires discipline to map your solution to the customer's deepest needs and desires at precisely the right time, and requires a bespoke formula of art, science, strategy, and talent to get right. Understanding all the modern methods and tools is arduous, with thousands of new technologies, complex data privacy regulations, rapidly evolving AI algorithms, cybersecurity and integration implications, news cycles that last hours instead of days, and buyers with the online attention spans of hummingbirds.

Intuitively, you may already sense that your company could be doing a better job at marketing, but no matter what experience, degrees, or technical credentials you have as a CEO, a founder, or an investor, it would be a stretch to expect you to have a deep understanding of what it now takes to deliver a strategic marketing program with impact. Marketing has fundamentally changed from what it used to be, and staying current is a challenge for those of us who do it for a living. So while your intuition is probably right about the problem, you will need more than that to solve it.

Because of the competitive pressures, economics, and nature of how marketing has evolved, I can also state with confidence that most B2B software CEOs and investors grossly underestimate the impact marketing can have in driving higher value, higher multiples, and higher personal success. A stellar modern marketing program has the power to completely alter your trajectory if you can properly put it to work and get results you may not have begun to imagine.

The B2B software industry has enjoyed some incredible success stories involving companies that seem to have shot to stardom overnight, and they are as glorious as they are rare. This industry is intensely transactional and frothy, with only a tiny percentage of software companies making it to the coveted market leadership quadrant. Everyone else will spend years trying to achieve their full potential, enjoy the adventure of getting bought or sold, or turn into zombies at a painfully slow rate.

I've worked at and consulted with many companies, from start-ups to multinational corporations and everything in between, so let me share an all too familiar story:

> Company X's journey has been a roller coaster of hits and misses trying to get the product right. It was either not the right market fit, not the right use case, or not the right market timing. Finally, because of either organic development or a clever acquisition, the new version of the product was ready, and everyone was banking that it would propel the company to its next stage of growth. The team believed in it with unwavering faith, but despite the best efforts of the sales team, they struggled to get people's attention and drive momentum. Desperate to turn the tide, they hired even more salespeople, but old or nonexistent market perceptions kept getting in the way.
>
> The sales team found themselves explaining and educating prospects endlessly, with no early funnel to cultivate or fall back on. Every quarter was a grind. Quotas

were missed, salespeople started quitting, and investors grew restless, demanding to see results.

So what was the answer?

Better marketing—because that would fix everything! Except there was no foundation in place; no clear view of customer and prospect behavior; outdated or nonexistent technology to reach a digital-first audience, which should have been addressed years earlier; and a lot of half-built bridges from stop-and-go activities of the past.

They decided to hire a new CMO, who came in and managed the conflicting opinions about what should be done, scrambled to build a high-performance team, and implemented a modern tech stack. Yet progress was slow, not because of budget but because of friction. They couldn't make changes fast enough because of the colossal difference of opinion about what *good* marketing looked like and how to get there. Expectations varied from all sides, lines of accountability and authority were muddy, and legacy perceptions about marketing methods of the past clouded the CMO's ability to progress in modernizing for scale and speed.

Despite their best efforts to make progress, conversations kept going in circles back to the immediate needs of the present quarter, which stalled major decisions to drive the changes necessary to break the logjam. No one could agree on where to direct marketing investments.

All of this unfolded quickly after years spent evolving the product strategy and even transforming the sales model. Given the current trajectory, with cloud economics and growing customer acquisition cost (CAC), it would now take more money and time for them to deliver the return that investors expected. Regret settled in as the executives all realized they had waited too long to prioritize marketing and weren't fully confident in the path forward, which by now had become convoluted and contentious.

Now the stakes are high, and forecasts are softening. The CMO, once determined and focused, is frustrated and resentful. The CEO is aggravated, the board is disappointed, and investors are baffled.

While this is a tragedy, it is completely avoidable!

Scenarios like this play out *all the time*. But they don't have to.

Unfortunately, marketing is where all the silos, blind spots, dangerous assumptions, and unintended consequences collide in this dizzying digital world we are all functioning (or not) in. On this hyperintelligent, intensely competitive super-highway, marketing is the roadkill when business fundamentals are askew. While modern marketing has been the fastest-evolving area, it has the lowest level of shared understanding among executives, investors, and boards for how it actually works. Today's marketing function is rife with misconceptions, competing priorities, misaligned stakeholders, a bubbly talent pool, and a sea of technologies without the budget or luxury of time for incoherent or convoluted mandates.

Small and midsize software companies are competing with bigger companies with bigger budgets, and today's progressive CEOs yearn for a more aggressive marketing posture that can match the new pace of evolving buyer expectations. Yet they can't get faster outcomes by applying legacy methods that worked beautifully … a decade ago. To be competitive means applying strategic marketing earlier and more assertively than in years past, but this can't be done if there is no alignment on what success looks like and what's required to get there.

Why I Wrote This Book

After more than thirty years in B2B technology specializing in major transformations and transactional moments—including turnarounds, hypergrowth, carve-outs, and pre- or post-equity transactions—I've been through a lot of ups and downs and have seen business plans work brilliantly, fail miserably, and even succeed miserably with varying degrees of human suffering.

This book puts three decades of learnings into a framework so you can walk away with a clear playbook for getting the marketing your company deserves. It focuses on solving marketing issues that you uniquely face because, all things being equal, I believe this is where the greatest competitive advantage exists for you. If you could get the strategic marketing right, your imagination isn't big enough for what awaits on the other side—I promise you!

Over the years, I have seen many of the same problems reemerge precisely because there wasn't a shared understanding of the root cause of the problems and how to avoid them, so history keeps repeating itself for those of us who have been around long enough. As an industry we need to stop cutting corners and debating proven methods and get on with the business of progress. As such, in some areas I will go a bit deeper to unpack the root cause of some of the biggest problem areas, and I encourage you to fight the urge to skip to the punch line. Understanding how you got there helps you understand what to really fix instead of chasing red herrings that lead to the wrong outcomes.

If you are a founder, a CEO, or an investor in a small to midsize B2B software-based company, this book is for you. Every software company is unique, of course, so not every example in this book will apply to everyone. However, this book is for you if your company delivers products or solutions in the following ways: software as a service (SaaS), platform as a service (PaaS), infrastructure as a service (IaaS), serverless computing, managed service provider (MSP), virtual desktop infrastructure (VDI), containers as a service (CaaS), integration platform as a service (iPaaS), Hybrid SaaS/on prem, open source, freemium, crowdsourcing, ad supported, or tech enabled.

If you are in B2B software segments such as cybersecurity/access/risk management, business applications, integration/orchestration, business intelligence, artificial intelligence (AI), project management, storage/backup/recovery, collaboration/communication, fintech, martech, sales tech, customer experience, e-commerce, content management, human resources, etc., you will gain valuable insights.

Simply, if you sell software to businesses versus consumers, this book is for you.

This book provides a roadmap that drives ruthless focus and swift execution. What it *isn't* is a detailed, deep dive into the specialized functions within marketing, such as how to execute account-based marketing (ABM) or how to use search engine optimization (SEO) better. There are other books for that. What I will cover is how to approach marketing strategically from here on out so everything you do after that has both a bigger impact and a higher ROI.

Before we continue, I'm making you the following promises:

- The advice I'm giving you is based on proven methods that are practical, immediately actionable, and risk-free.

- You will walk away with a prescriptive approach on how to use marketing to unlock hidden value for your company that investors will care about, particularly if a transaction is in your future.

- You will finish this book with a clear idea of what a marketing strategy looks like and what you can expect from a modern marketing engine.

- You will have a clearer idea of what kind of CMO you need and how to keep them.

- You will know what situations and dangerous assumptions to avoid.

- You will gain insights and perspectives from legendary marketing and GTM leaders across the B2B industry in addition to my own, so you know what I'm sharing isn't just one person's experience and opinion.

Soon, with the hypergrowth of the software industry and countless software companies emerging, there will be countless software CMOs! A secondary aim of this book is directed at the next generation of software marketing leaders in their quest for glory. By fixing the many disconnects outlined in the book, my desire is to make their jobs just a tiny bit easier.

> ### GO TO MARKET (GTM)
>
> → For the purpose of this book, GTM includes sales, marketing, and customer success/service functions that create face-to-face, virtual, or digital customer touchpoints.

CHAPTER 1

VALLEY OF TRANSACTIONS

UNICORNS. Everyone wants to create a company that becomes a blockbuster brand in the proverbial hot minute. You know the ones. They fly over the chasm with zeal, straight into the coveted leadership quadrant. These newly established leaders do the impossible, surviving hypergrowth and the toils of scale. Now these companies, which exist as lasting brands and are too big to buy, are busy defending their position and customer base from competitors coming at them from all sides.

Depending on what sources you read, there are roughly a thousand tech unicorns standing worldwide each year. These companies boast an average valuation of $3 to $4 billion with eager investors salivating for that coveted acquisition or a $10 billion initial public offering (IPO). If the past is any indicator, only a handful will ever make it there.

And then there's everybody else.

The rest of the industry lives in the *Valley of Transactions*, where deals are inevitable, as it's often more appealing for investors to sell than to go public, because of either the timing of payout or the actual percentage of return. For others, the path is much more complex, and for the companies that linger, growth and scale are the right ideas, but the path can be, let's say, elaborate. Some companies go on an acquisition spree of their own, go public, go private, and then get bought themselves.

FireEye is a great example of a company that enjoyed the full experience of what the Valley of Transactions has to offer. FireEye was founded in 2004, and in 2013 it acquired Mandiant for $1 billion and went public, raising $304 million from the offering. The company's stock price surged on the first day of trading, making it one of the most successful IPOs of the year with a valuation of $2.3 billion. Over the course of a handful of years, they made various acquisitions, including nPulse, iSIGHT, X15, Respond Software, and Cloudvisory, adding up to over $600 million in acquisitions. In 2021, FireEye was split out and sold to a private equity (PE) firm, Symphony Technology Group, for $1.2 billion. With the split, Mandiant reemerged as a stand-alone company. A year later Symphony Technology Group merged FireEye with McAfee and renamed the combined entity Trellix.

Then one year after that, in September 2022, Google acquired Mandiant for $5.4 billion, a decent outcome for Mandiant in the end. FireEye/Mandiant was a company in the right place at the right time as the cybersecurity industry popped off, and in addition to a bunch of people making money, the bonus gift was that everyone involved got to experience the full range of human emotions, I'm sure.

For some companies such a saga can be an exciting linear adventure. For others it can be full of unexpected plot twists. Goals can get intricate, and focus can go asunder as shares trade hands or as various executives take the helm in search of new ways to achieve progress, deliver on customer commitments, and drive value for investors. As if that wasn't hard enough, things get gnarly when economics shift since the technology industry is highly sensitive to downturns due to pressures on discretionary spending and dependencies on a dynamic global economy.

The Valley of Transactions was born exclusively on the premise of exploring innovation, and it evolved over decades mostly on the backs of willpower, optimism, and luck. By *luck* I mean that in some of the segments, companies could make money simply by being open for business, which created an industry full of loose habits and shiny objects. So while innovation and good timing lead to rapid growth and excitement for many, as an industry we didn't get to fully practice being sustainable, profitable, adaptable, and resilient. Instead, we became highly competent at being impulsive, reactive, and hopeful, and we also came to believe that growth was a strategy. More on this later.

In this business, there can be a lot of mania for many reasons that might include binging on opportunities in every direction, trying to rebound competitive moves, endless firefighting within the customer base, and making fast deals or executing creative financing to make the numbers all work out. It can be easy for strategic lethargy to set in, and long-term planning can fall overboard without anyone ever missing it. This can become the default operating rhythm, and the company can get lulled into believing they are playing the long game when, really, they aren't doing that at all. Some companies want to win long term, and they talk about it a lot, but they are operating simply to survive the next quarter or fiscal year. With all eyes on the quarter or the close of the year, tough choices can be kicked down the road that may otherwise create a meaningful competitive advantage when the world gets wonky.

In good times growth can happen without a business strategy, and problems can be solved by throwing people at them. The fixation on the short term may work for a while, but it stops working when times get tight and can turn into a rash effort to spread cuts and layoffs across the company to protect EBITDA (earnings before interest, taxes, depreciation, and amortization). This can inadvertently trigger a series of events that cause a contraction that now needs a rescue and recovery mission.

The good news is that while the technology industry is sensitive to downturns, it can also play a vital role in driving economic recovery if vendors take advantage of opportunities presented in those times. Modernization initiatives in these cycles often become catalysts for growth, as many businesses seek deeper efficiencies and unity. Yet it is ironic that many B2B software companies that serve these businesses remain strategically clumsy and operationally shortsighted while at the same time evangelizing how their technology supports long-term success for customers by creating efficiencies, alignment, and productivity—since that's the fundamental nature of what software does! But I digress.

Having a thoughtfully curated business strategy helps you focus on what matters most, grow quickly when times are good, and continue to prosper when others struggle. It allows you to position yourself to surge out of a downturn to your intended destination, not simply react to a bad storm.

We have seen this play out historically. Those that pursue intergalactic world domination in earnest make a deliberate decision to do so over time and have a prevailing strategy for how to get there. I'm referring to those tech founder-CEOs that everyone either wants to emulate or loves to hate. However, they share common attributes that include having a bold vision, an unwavering passion, an extreme commitment, and a maniacal focus that also meant they burned a lot of boats that would otherwise be used to fling them off course. But just as a reminder, they represent the 1 or 2 percent of companies that ever make it to this scale and are typically led by some of the most bold, ambitious, and sometimes stubborn founder-CEOs of our time.

This industry is more unpredictable than ever with more start-ups, more advanced innovation, and more complex global dynamics, so we should expect much more volatility on the horizon. A solid strategy can withstand gale-force winds and anticipates the probability of a transaction, which happens much more often than it doesn't. In times of unpredictability, organizations with solid business strategies will have a better chance of delivering earnest value creation, perhaps in addition to, but not exclusive to, investor returns.

Wait ... what does all this have to do with marketing?

The fundamental premise of this book is that you can't use marketing strategically if you don't have a business strategy that suits your situation and the conditions ahead of you. You can't have phenomenal marketing if you are just doing tactics and activities that are random and one-off; you won't get the multiplier effect with any meaningful impact. So if you want to use marketing to instigate more dramatic value creation, you must be willing to use it as a strategic function, which first requires you to have a business strategy for it to anchor to.

> *You will never get great marketing if you don't have a business strategy.* **Period.**

Being Strategically Rudderless Means You Are Adrift

Many companies I've worked with stress that growth is their strategy. *Growth is not a strategy; it's an outcome.*

What I've seen time and again is that companies set the financial plan based on assumptions of the previous year or quarter and sprinkle in some risk and some growth aspirations, and this becomes the baseline financial plan. Puts and takes go here and there, and out pops the annual budget, which becomes the plan of record (which is a spreadsheet, not a plan). In truth, growth is just how many nautical miles you do in a day toward your destination—it is not your destination. It's like rowing feverishly around with your buddies in circles, trying to convince them you are getting somewhere and having fun. I know you and your investors want to see growth because it's a measure of momentum and predictability. It's proof that whatever you're doing is working, but it doesn't demonstrate long-term sustainability and value. It could just as easily be evidence of luck.

The common mindset among executives is to show investors top-line growth as quickly as possible. The belief is that this will provide more options for how to exit the business down the road. The challenge with this thinking is that no small or midsize B2B business is ever able to grow at all costs. You need a North Star and a logical path to get there.

It's difficult to generate meaningful, predictable growth and showcase value creation in a transaction, which might include evidence of a reduction in customer churn, a reduction in the cost of customer acquisition and service, market leadership momentum, and operational discipline, without some kind of thoughtful strategic focus. Without a larger strategy, aspirations of growth can stall because of a lack of market fit; it can start costing too much because you are going in too many directions, it can get too difficult because you are in a segment with too many competitive barriers, or you just aren't set up for good execution. If you want sustainable growth, you need a sound strategic plan—and it's not your annual budget.

Having good software is dope, but the tech industry is littered with products that were good, even great, but are no longer around. This is also why a technology roadmap is not the same thing as a sound business strategy.

There are companies that have products that are just okay or good enough but have found a way to be compelling and enduring. What makes these good-enough products winners is that they have a business strategy that forces them to maintain focus. They have asked themselves the tough questions:

- What is my destination, and how will I get there?

- What customers are most important to me, and why?

- What makes me so different that customers can't live without me?

- What guides decision-making and prioritization on a daily basis?

- What needs to be in place for me to execute well?

They have found a way to achieve growth because they have a holistic strategy with an endgame that is the guiding force when hard decisions need to be made.

Plan for What's Probable, Not for What's Possible

It's possible you will effortlessly achieve market leadership overnight either because your product is that awesome or because you are lucky—but that's not what's probable. If your product is good and you have decent leadership, two things are more likely at some point: you will face financial headwinds (macroeconomic or self-imposed), or you will get bought, or both.

If these two things are highly probable, would it change the path you are on today? Here's what such a path might look like:

It means having a strategic vision, operational discipline, orchestrated execution that's watertight, and a resilient immune system with top talent. What I'm suggesting is to game the probabilities by picking a multiyear window to prove out your value story and win in specific beachheads. Start with what you want that story to say and work backward about what you need to do to get there. Pick a strategic playbook that fits the business situation you are in (more on this later), that you can execute on no matter what conditions you face, and fiercely focus and execute with urgency against that timeline. Make the hard decisions as if your life depended on it, early enough for it to make a difference in a transaction. It means your business deserves thoughtful preparation to compete with an ambitious strategy in a finite amount of time and resources, with intense focus, and with decisive execution using the conditions (or creating conditions) that give you the Power of Surge.

What do you have to lose? The worst-case scenario is that you end up with favorable outcomes but no transaction—meaning you will still be farther ahead than you would have been just cruising along.

Strategic Considerations

Let's talk about the following three major considerations when building a surge-worthy strategy: (1) you should plan for a transaction with a financial buyer within a multiyear timeline, (2) you should plan for a downturn, and (3) marketing is no longer your lifeboat for controlling expenses.

PLAN FOR A TRANSACTION WITH A FINANCIAL BUYER

We already discussed the probabilities of getting acquired in this business. If you aren't already a market leader, or unless you are on a path to nowhere at all, the chances of this are high. Most companies want to be bought by a strategic buyer, but you will be more valuable overall if you have multiple parties interested, so it's best to plan for a financial buyer as a core assumption. Strategics want to buy you and see you as a possible fit for what they want to accomplish, but they have many hills to climb once you are over a certain size. However, financial buyers make up the majority of investors overall, so they have the odds.

As you know, there are three things financial buyers look for when they consider purchasing a B2B software company. The first is a recurring revenue model with high gross margins. The second is a large addressable market. And the third is a competitive advantage around the core product or service that isn't stretched all over the place—the legendary moat. When PE firms are looking to invest in a B2B software company, it's important that you have a good narrative and demonstrated metrics in all three of these areas. *Spoiler alert: Strategic marketing can help you in every single one!*

PLAN FOR A DOWNTURN

There are three rules in sailing: (1) don't fall off the boat, (2) reef well before you need to, and (3) always have a plan B.

Every ocean sailor will tell you that a plan B (or a risk management plan) is critical because something always goes wrong, and it's always in the middle of the night, in bad weather. The idea behind a plan B is that you are freed up to sail with verve and optimism, but a plan is there that accounts for what's most critical to get done when things go sideways. The business version of this is deciding how you would operate and prioritize based on the assumption that there could be downward financial pressure. It might come from an actual downturn, or it might come because the growth you expected leveled off because of a lack of sales execution or poor planning.

If you consider recent years to predict what you may face in the future, it's helpful to learn from other companies that faced major challenges in crises. We can look backward at what happened to companies in previous downturns to understand why some were hit hard and others came out on top. Historically, what we know is that downturns expose flaws for some and create focus for others. You want to be the latter.

Bain & Company executed the Bain's Sustained Value Creators analysis, looking at what happened in the last financial crisis.[1] They examined a group of almost 3,900 companies worldwide as they headed into the last major economic downturn of 2008 and determined who posted double-digit earnings growth in the five years leading up to it. What Bain observed was that winners did things differently and fared better as a result. According to Bain's analysis, as soon as the storm hit, performance diverged sharply, and *winners* grew at a 17 percent compound annual growth rate (CAGR) during the downturn, compared with 0 percent among the *losers (their words not mine)*. What's more, the winners locked in gains to grow at an average 13 percent CAGR in the years after the downturn, while the losers stalled at 1 percent. What did they do differently?

---

1   Tom Holland and Jeff Katzin, "Beyond the Downturn: Recession Strategies to Take the Lead," bain.com, May 16, 2019, https://www.bain.com/insights/beyond-the-downturn-recession-strategies-to-take-the-lead/.

Here's what the research suggests as it relates to building a modern GTM engine today:

1. Plan for cuts, but don't cut line-item expenses across the board. Instead, cut in places that would create headroom to invest in modernization to fuel future growth.

2. Focus on the core of the business to improve business processes, operate more efficiently, and cut low-priority activities.

3. Maintain marketing and prioritize improvements to the customer experience by investing in modern digital capabilities.

Notice the focus put on core strengths and directing investments in modernization, customer experience, and the creation of an engine for scale and growth, not just cutting everything. Even in bad times, companies that want to succeed despite hardship double down on marketing and customer experience. Unlike their competitors, winners lean into these things instead of dialing back.

If you plan conservatively and build on top of it, versus planning optimistically and cutting in the year, you have the upper hand in making sure you are growing revenue, growing value, and building a sustainable growth engine. There's an opportunity to apply these learnings to your own plans so your business strategy has risk management built in, and you can execute effectively.

Why is planning this way a good idea? I can honestly say that through the length of my career, there have probably only been a handful of times the business has come to marketing to give us extra money at the end of a quarter. Mostly, the business comes to marketing as the lifeboat for managing expenses due to some kind of financial pressure that should have been planned for originally. Most B2B software businesses underinvest in marketing to start with, so further cuts create deeper problems. These cuts are felt more acutely in marketing, cause stops and starts, and are likely why you aren't getting what you need out of marketing.

MARKETING IS NOT A LIFEBOAT

In the olden days, CEOs and investors were able to get away with looking at their organizations' marketing program as a line-item expense versus a long-term investment because in the past, marketing would mostly spend money on things such as trade show booths, paid placements, nifty campaigns, and big PR firms—all things that would be easy to do less of in a bad year. When they hit a bad quarter, that was an easy bailout option. Today, that line of thinking doesn't work.

In today's digital-first model, marketing is the electricity that powers the customer-led experience, and it is how your customers and prospects engage with you 24/7.

Cutting marketing now can have disastrous consequences in a world where the customer experience is always on and driving demand, user traffic, and pipeline. Modern marketing is about creating a customer experience that's ever-present, always learning, responsive, and personalized. It can no longer be thought of as a transactional expense that delivers discre-

ıary tactics. It's now become the cost of doing business
ınable you to dynamically shift investments around as
 market changes. Market downturns or tough times are
:cisely when you should lean into spending on modern
ırketing and strategic positioning, not when you should
ıll back. Yet pulling back is exactly what many B2B software
ompanies default to. Consequently, they manifest the
utcome they most feared: irrelevance in the market and an
nability to grow.

Creating a resilient company requires an investment
in modernization, customer experience, and the creation of
an engine for growth, which requires time, discipline, and
resources to do right. This is where expectations on ROI can
go awry. Determining ROI can be a challenge in companies
where marketing is still in its infancy and where the foundational engine and data analytics haven't been created yet. For
these organizations, it's challenging to track impact end to
end, let alone predict buyer propensity in the virtual buyer's
journey. That's why your marketing might seem like a black
box to you—because there's no foundation in place that
exposes what is and isn't working.

If you have an earnest desire to truly create customer
value over the long haul, marketing is an investment in a
business system that fuels your customer experience. In this
model, you mustn't think of marketing as day trading but as
building for the long game that you and a potential buyer will
value. In such a model, there's an understanding that while
the market will fluctuate, over time the strategy will create

value based on the combination of decisions that were made to offset market conditions outside your control.

If you can think of marketing as an investment, you have a chance at growing at a winner's pace of 17 percent in a downturn—so just think about what's possible when times are good.

Summary

The Valley of Transactions is quickly evolving from an open ocean of endless exploration, where just being on the water makes you a success, to a place where the unprepared will simply sink into the depths of irrelevance. Mergers and acquisitions (M&As) are inevitable, as are downturns in some shape or form. Having a quarter-to-quarter mindset is no longer sustainable because the market will get increasingly volatile, and luck and optimism alone won't help you create a valuable business.

Being a successful B2B software business is not just about having an aspirational idea about the future and having a great product. You also need to anticipate and plan for alternative scenarios that both keep you safe and deliver positive outcomes despite downward financial pressure. To thrive, you must commit to a strategic, ambitious path, but consider the probability of being bought by a financial buyer looking for a predictable, operationally sound investment. With good planning and a sound strategy, you can make quick decisions, position yourself for success, and avoid months, and maybe years, of unnecessary woe.

Marketing has evolved to become the central nervous system for how you engage digitally with your customers and prospects, and you can no longer rely on cutting it when times get tough. Having a clear strategy sets the foundation for you to use marketing as a competitive advantage to get the impact and ROI you are looking for, in good times and bad.

In the Valley of Transactions:

➜ The days of easy money and creative deals are over; the focus must be on creating sustainable value by executing a thoughtful business strategy that takes a longer-term view.

➜ If you are in B2B software, it's highly probable that you will get bought, so plan for it.

➜ Executing with urgency toward a probable transaction helps drive focus and gives you a better chance of thriving versus hedging or cruising to survive.

➜ Marketing is no longer your cash lifeboat because it's how customers engage with you.

➜ In downturns, those that emerge healthier are those that invest in customer experience, digital modernization, and strategic positioning as a best practice.

➜ A strategy that accounts for a downturn or a transaction in one to two years must be considered so you can be in the best position if your intended journey takes an unexpected twist.

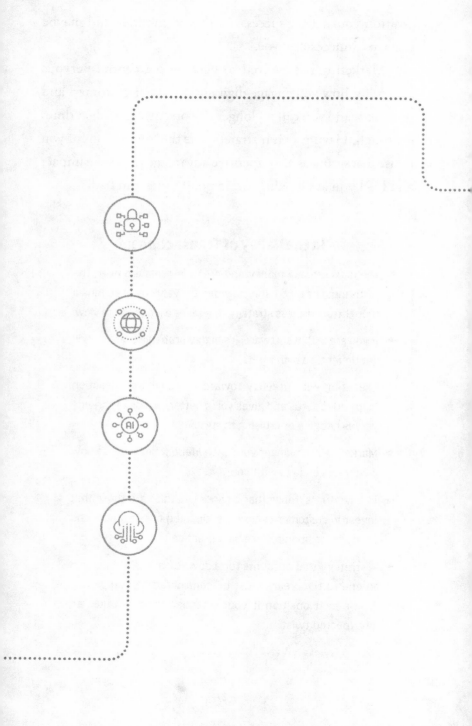

CHAPTER 2

SO ... YOUR CMO STINKS?

I FREQUENTLY GET calls from CEOs struggling with marketing and frustrated with their current CMO. Here's a flavor of what I hear quite a bit. One had been through three CMOs in three years but couldn't figure out why none of them seemed to be able to deliver impact. Another had compensation constraints, so he hired a high-potential product marketer but wondered why they couldn't see ROI. Another ran through two heads of marketing who both insisted the focus be put on awareness instead of in-quarter deal flow. Others claimed it was a poor cultural fit.

The most common thing I hear is (and I'm kindly paraphrasing), "Our last CMO just wasn't very good."

In truth, the CMO can only be successful if they are on the same page with the CEO about three things (1) what success looks like and what the priorities are, (2) how to best apply modern strategic methods in the context of the company's situation, and (3) a sound strategic marketing plan—which can't happen without a sound business strategy, which I beat to death in the last chapter.

Now let's talk about the difference between incrementalism in marketing and playing to win and outline some dangerous assumptions that might be holding you back from getting the marketing you want.

Are You Cruising or Racing?

What is your current approach to marketing? I'm not talking about just surviving, doing more things, or shifting small tactics such as buying more digital media, doing more online events, or executing ABM. I'm asking if you have a strategic approach to how you target, what you say, and where you spend your money for the biggest market impact—from generating demand to creating a conversion pipeline to engaging customer advocates who do the selling for you.

Competing in today's high-velocity world requires you to do more than just putter around. In theory, many CEOs and investors understand this. But focusing mainly on the product and sales motion and using marketing as a *nice to have* to do a bunch of activities is like having a great boat and a strong crew but not having any sails. If you are cruising, you would just turn on the engine when you needed to, wasting time and a lot of money on diesel. If you are racing to win, everything is thought through and executed with precision, which includes being weight conscious and superefficient.

The great news is that getting the marketing you need and deserve is absolutely within reach. It's not some elusive formula you stumble upon through trial and error or being lucky to land a good CMO. You may not have to hire for it or spend a whole lot more money than you already do. It's completely available to you today. In fact, marketing might be your biggest opportunity and your biggest untapped strategic weapon if you are open to a new perspective and open to doing things differently.

I've also seen firsthand how making a few strategic changes in the approach can have a profound impact on results. I've seen software businesses navigate through the storms of change and cultural complexities, and as a result, I've formed some strong opinions about how to achieve the outcomes everyone wants while avoiding self-inflicted torment and fiscally ridiculous decision-making. If you could crack the code to execute customer-led, accretive marketing, you would be a force to be reckoned with.

> **Most companies like yours are also struggling with marketing, so if you can nail this, you will have a massive competitive advantage!**

Just functioning as a healthy software company is hard enough, but at some point, the time arrives to prepare for a transaction or a major funding round. It takes a monumental effort to prepare for this, not just to clean up the books but to clean out the bilges to get the deal room ready. Executives have to get their story straight to pass the red-face test and produce the right data that somehow rationalizes where they are and why they did what they did. I've found these moments to be a lot like a couple trying to hastily anchor their boat in a crowded anchorage—it's where all the dysfunction and baggage come on deck for the world to see.

Through these transaction experiences, I have seen many CEOs and investors become frustrated about how to deliver the best narrative for growth, ROI, and predictability given what all the data and charts are saying. While there may have been a lot of activities and improvements, it's often hard to demonstrate how the company can deliver repeatable pipeline or user flow and dependable conversion rates, particularly in today's dynamic and digital environment where the customer controls the buying cycle and the product is increasingly supposed to be selling itself.

What went wrong? Let's explore some dangerous assumptions that can get in the way.

Dangerous Assumptions

1.) ASSUMING INCREMENTALISM IS PROGRESS

It's generally estimated that there will be more than a million software companies on the planet in just a few years. This means if you are in this business, you're in the race of your life, and you can't afford to confuse tangible progress with incrementalism and half measures.

It's easy to disguise incrementalism as progress, as people get comfortable with self-induced limitations or poor planning. Incremental progress and tangential activities don't get the job done in an environment of urgency or in a twelve- to eighteen-month window leading up to a transaction event. However, that's all that's left in the end when you get multiples that are just *meh*.

You can certainly have a lot of activity but with barely noticeable differences in the end aside from price increases and longer-term contracts. *Progress* is a word used to make ourselves feel better because incremental change is better than none, and it helps us justify the effort and personal sacrifices along the way. Unfortunately, this kind of progress is what you get when you aren't serious about winning, and let's face it: Who here considers delivering incremental progress a victory?

This was never truer than in B2B marketing. Getting small improvements can be appealing, and this is what is expected by much larger and more mature organizations that are left to tweak their marketing programs to get any optimizations they can muster—but this is not you. For you, it is a red flag that you could be avoiding major decisions or transformations that give you much more significant gains. In the rapidly evolving business landscape, where competition is fierce and customer demands constantly evolve, your marketing demands bold and strategic moves that disrupt the status quo, seize emerging opportunities, and drive meaningful change.

By embracing a more transformative mindset, you can quickly create a program that allows you to adapt to market shifts, reach new audiences, and outpace your competitors who sit stuck and idle in their own complacency.

2.) ASSUMING YOU ARE SELLING SOFTWARE

First, you are not selling anything; customers are buying things. Second, you are not selling software; customers are solving problems. Pain motivates change. You can only control what the customers' experience is as they try to get some pain relief. Gone are the days of the linear sales process, where you control the message and dated paradigms about how the pipeline works. Customers want solutions, and ideally, they don't really want to deal with salespeople unless they absolutely must.

The way customers research and scope how to solve a problem is through a complex and organic digital system of networks and connections, not through a sales process or a directed path you put them through. They will chat with virtually everyone else possible before they call you in an effort to avoid getting trapped in your database purgatory, which they must now spend the next decade opting out of. They prefer to get a free trial, a usable demo, some case studies, or a peek at your code somewhere. Then they will seek out all the reasons not to buy you from forums you didn't even know existed. Finally, when they have satisfied themselves that you are a legit option, only then do they want to engage with you.

So many companies are so focused on the sales motion, sales commissions, sales forecasting, sales operations, and quarterly growth that they completely miss what is important to customers. Customers don't care about your processes, who their sales rep is, or that they need to sign the contract by

Friday. They care about whether you can help them solve their problem without a lot of drama and unnecessary effort and expense. They want to be able to get help without talking to anyone, if possible, and they want the least amount of friction when dealing with you. None of these things have anything to do with your internal operating rhythm or who your head of sales is.

What you control is how you articulate your value proposition in terms they care about, in places they care about, from people they care about, and how you deliver a Zen-like customer experience as they try, buy, and use your product.

3.) ASSUMING GREAT PRODUCTS ARE ALL THAT MATTERS

You could have the best product with the deepest feature set of anyone in your category. That used to matter, but more and more customers prefer the vendor with the best overall brand experience from end to end. By *brand experience* I mean the combination of your reputation in the market, ease of doing business, great support capability, and overall value you provide in solving their problem.

Many software companies are taking a product-led approach as a path to paradise, but that doesn't mean that the sole requirement is that the product works. (The exception to this might be if you are serving developers with a freemium business model; then yes, maybe your code is all that matters—assuming people can find it.) For everyone else it means the entire company should be focused on the customer experience as a whole, including product, marketing, purchasing, sales, onboarding, support/success, expansion, and renewal. Cool product features get increasingly less cool if customers need to wait two days to get a call back on pricing, if their billing is confusing, or if your digital support center puts people in an endless phone tree spiral of death.

Your company is your product; your actual software product/service is just a feature.

4.) ASSUMING THE SOFTWARE SERVICE YOU DELIVER IS YOUR BIGGEST TECHNOLOGY ASSET

The following are the three software platforms you have as a company:

a.   The software or software-based services customers buy.

b.   The back-end software or software services you use to run your company, such as financial, payroll, HR systems, internal collaboration, development, workflow, document sharing, etc.

c.   The software you use to deliver your digital customer experience (CX), which includes customer relation-ship management (CRM), marketing automation, chat, content management system (CMS) or web platform, and a bunch of other digital tools to drive targeting, content, scoring, interactions, engagements, support, and communication.

If you agree with the two previous assumptions already mentioned (about solving problems not selling software and the importance of delivering a frictionless experience), you will immediately understand why the software platform you use to enable your digital customer experience is arguably the most important one for driving business value and differentiation.

How many resources are dedicated to each of these three platforms in relation to the others? If you can't quantify what resources are dedicated to your digital customer experience, know what the tech strategy is and who is accountable for it, know what data you have and where it is, or have an idea about what your roadmap is for it, you are already behind. Think of the digital customer experience platform as the code base for your business. Get that right, and you will rule the world.

5.) ASSUMING MARKETING IS A DISCRETIONARY, PROGRAMMATIC EXPENSE

We talked about this already, but let me add a few points. While marketing often gets a bad rap, it's one of the most valuable and underleveraged assets in most B2B software companies today. Great marketing has the power to change minds and shape industries. And now, due to the blistering speed of digital adoption and online customer experiences, marketing has moved closer into sales and customer success territory than ever before. Also, in today's modern business, marketing is now a technical function by nature, executing engagement moments through a cloud-based web of tools and services that has been assembled mostly under the radar.

Customer engagements are served virtually through real-time placements, digital journeys, and automated workflows. The marketing budget that once could be cut at the end of a quarter if things didn't look so hot has become directly linked to the way customers interact with you on a 24/7 basis. There's no cutting that. In fact, a large part of your marketing budget should probably be categorized as IT operating expenses (OPEX) if you want to get precise about it.

With so many methods and technologies available today that span market education, trying, buying, onboarding, and using, there is a lot of confusion about where the budget should go. What was once a tidy functional silo—where marketing was a discretionary expense and sales and support were mostly made up of headcount—is no longer the case. It can be difficult for executives to understand how to prioritize the right mix and what proportion of spend should be directed toward the distinct functions when the end-to-end experience is (or should be) tightly intertwined.

Having the right investment to attract and engage buyers in the market begins with an understanding that today's B2B customer demands digital sophistication—you need to be able to give them what they need, where they are, when they want it.

6.) ASSUMING MARKETING IS ON A NEED-TO-KNOW BASIS

As mentioned before, there's a belief that growth alone provides options, and closing deals is what matters, so there's no sense in spinning everyone up on a possible transaction plan until we get there, so why talk about it?

This growth-centric mindset works in the context of sales because selling is about closing deals. You set a revenue target, there are quotas, you sell things, and you grow. You don't need to worry about a transaction outcome to successfully book a deal. However, at some point, to become more relevant and to get more at-bats, you need a marketing engine to influence buyers to encourage engagement, secure their share of mind, and persuade them to think and do things differently. For marketing to do that, there needs to be some prioritization on where the growth should come from, not strictly in sales territory terms but in customer needs and customer segment terms where you can have a competitive advantage, shorter sales cycles, and a lower cost of acquisition.

Marketing needs to make investment decisions about the most important levers to help you get the most business value over a certain time frame. Those decisions might be different from what you have them currently focused on in a quarter-to-quarter or transactional aperture. A probable acquisition can profoundly change priorities, strategies, and funding mix.

Also, many executives believe that the CMO doesn't need to know about a probable transaction because if they did, they might choose to leave. This could not be further from the truth! If you are a CMO in software today, you expect to go through many transactions in your career. It's a thing. This isn't why CMOs leave.

Everyone knows CMO tenures are some of the shortest in the industry. Based on my own quantitative research on this topic with B2B tech CMOs, here are the five reasons they leave, in order:

1. Misaligned expectations about what marketing can deliver within the budget envelope

2. Interest to pursue a better opportunity because of compensation/potential upside

3. Not aligned with CEO/founder

4. Post-transaction decision (M&A, PE buyouts, etc.); exits or opt-outs

5. Lack of authority to make decisions/changes necessary to achieve goals

With certainty, I can say that the reason a CMO would leave would not be because you told them your potential transaction was the endgame and asked for their help with that. CMOs don't leave out of fear of a transaction happening. CMOs leave because of misalignment that comes from not knowing what the plan or strategy is, not having alignment on what a good strategic marketing looks like, not being able to make the decisions needed to be successful, and having appealing options to go elsewhere.

Fundamentally, CMOs need to know they are contributing to driving value for the business, not just doing a bunch of tactics. If you want your marketing to be more strategic, you need to include it in the strategic conversations.

Unintended Consequences

The source of many of the problems and shortfalls that exist in marketing is due to years of accumulated misunderstandings, disconnects, and a lack of both information and alignment that have evolved over time. Many CMOs, despite their best efforts at clairvoyance, can't help you if they don't know what you are thinking—whether you have a clear idea or you are still germinating. When CMOs aren't aware the company could be headed for a transaction and strategically aligned with you, it can create unintended consequences that will continue to get in the way of greatness and a great valuation. Let's talk about them.

UNINTENDED CONSEQUENCE 1: WRONG PRIORITIES

Marketing cannot execute with full focus on the right set of priorities if they don't have a clear understanding of how their efforts help or hurt the business in *both* the near and long term. So while the CEO and the board may be clear in their own minds on the exit timeline and what the books need to look like, the marketing teams are breathlessly running for growth, building for scale, and applying methods mastered by those that aspire for long-term market dominance. Therefore, their priorities and tactics may not be the best methods for a company that aspires to have a favorable exit in a given time frame.

UNINTENDED CONSEQUENCE 2: QUESTIONABLE DECISION-MAKING

When there's a misalignment in strategy, marketing decisions are made without consideration for what will be valued by an acquirer when the time comes. This can lead to bad investment decisions that reflect poorly in due diligence. It can also create a lot of backward engineering, a narrative about why certain decisions were made at the negotiation table. For example, an acquirer may want to look at the strength of the customer base and lifetime value (LTV) as a priority—but marketing was too busy focusing on net new lead generation and funnel building based on *growth*—and come deal time, there's no real evidence of opportunity for expansion and retention aside from a couple of lucky big whale deals.

UNINTENDED CONSEQUENCE 3:
INSTABILITY AND FALSE STARTS

When marketing doesn't understand the strategy or desired endgame, the result is misaligned incentives and unnecessary turnover. If everyone is focused on net new logos as quickly as possible but performance bonuses are incentivized based on EBITDA, it can lead to a lot of confusion. It can be frustrating to the marketing team that is executing on the thesis of *growth as a strategy* that assumes marketing is a critical component, but efforts can be abruptly halted for no apparent reason. CMOs and teams won't complain about budgets and resources if they understand the *why* of it all.

They can't understand the why if they don't have a financial understanding of the business and a strategic understanding of what you are trying to achieve. Yes, they may be trying to seek it out; however, a lot of CMOs continue to struggle with being included in conversations that might both enlighten them and help them better explain inconsistent behavior to the broader team, who might be at the end of their rope. Instability and unnecessary turnover can cause multiple false starts with multiple marketing leaders and delay results by months, or sometimes even years.

UNINTENDED CONSEQUENCE 4:
REDUCED AGILITY AND SUNK COSTS

The investment plan in marketing is different if the desired outcome is a favorable transaction in eighteen months versus building for growth and scale over five years. Marketing initiatives are planned and paid for well in advance and often carry contracts that span quarters or years. When plans are made and resources are allocated, they are typically set based on the strategic goals over a longer-term horizon versus an imminent exit. Once set, it's difficult to make changes should the need arise without dramatic consequences, such as mass layoffs or cutting initiatives midstream (further incurring sunk costs). This can result in terrible optics at transaction time because you will need to explain why cuts were made in places where money *could have been* moved, not where it *should have been* moved, because of contract constraints.

UNINTENDED CONSEQUENCE 5:
MISALIGNMENT ON WHAT GOOD MARKETING IS

Finally, it's important for everyone to be on the same page about what good marketing looks like. There is a lot to do on this front because there are huge gaps among what CMOs aspire to, what executives think and expect should be done, what is possible, and what should actually be done.

Most marketers are groomed to understand that successful marketing means building an iconic brand powered by a sophisticated growth engine. All the marketing case studies, marketing thought leaders, authors, and even CEOs use

Google, Salesforce, Adobe, Workday, Apple, and the like as the bar for good marketing. Marketeers are conditioned to understand that achieving this kind of scale and brand value over a longer time horizon *is what defines success in their careers*. With this as the context, compounded with the direction they may be getting from you to seek growth, they are working toward building an epic brand and growth engine to scale the company beyond billions of dollars in revenue—which may not be the right play for you.

On the other hand, what CEOs often expect to be good marketing is usually one of these things: what they see their competition doing, a program they have seen work before at a previous company without an appreciation for how mature the operational capabilities were that were underneath it, what they intuitively think should be done, or what they think other market leaders or legendary companies have done in the past. Also, they expect it to be done in a fraction of the time and cost.

Meanwhile, what should actually be done is a very focused subset of activities that neither the CMO nor the CEO has alignment on but that the company desperately needs. I believe this gap around what defines *good* is at the center of why many CEOs are so profoundly confused and dissatisfied with their company's marketing efforts.

> In truth, executives, investors, and boards are focused on growth on the *path to an exit*. Most CMOs and marketing teams are focused on growth on the *path to building a sustainable brand*.

The Silver Bullet

The silver bullet isn't some magical marketing program or cutting-edge AI tool. The silver bullet is starting early.

Often, executives are focused on some kind of product pivot to the cloud or to a platform, rebuilding source code, addressing sales execution, or managing customer churn. Only after these things are underway do they realize they must address market perceptions and create demand. At this point you are already at a disadvantage because it's likely there's no marketing plumbing in place yet to build upon.

It takes just as long to develop great marketing capability as it does to develop a great product because of how technical modern marketing has become. It's an old paradigm to think marketing is something you do at the end as an afterthought. Just as with product development, creating a modern marketing engine takes nine to twelve months, give or take (plus however long it takes you to onboard a CMO). It's highly likely that by the time you realize you have a marketing problem and need a new approach or are in that tight window before a transaction target date, you are behind. I'm not saying nothing else can be done in the meantime; I'm just saying it's not like turning a spigot on and expecting water to instantly blast out on the other side. Modern marketing requires you to build the plumbing first in order for it to work.

What happens next is soul-crushing for your existing marketing team because in an effort to get to the heart of the matter, CEOs will blast them with questions about why no one can show ROI and what actual revenue the team is driving. These are all great questions that everyone wants to be able to answer, but at this point either there is no hose or there are holes in it with water shooting everywhere because they haven't yet been able to modernize the engine or finalize closed-loop reporting with sales to connect proper attribution. You can't expect to identify the marketing problem and have it miraculously fixed the next day.

The opportunity here, in sailing terms, is to reef early. When you are thinking of transforming either your company's product roadmap or its sales model, that's also the time to consider what you are going to need on the strategic marketing front. Don't wait until later when the wind gets violent, and your crew is in a panic to manage the situation.

Strategic Marketing Only Works If It's a Strategic Function

The pace of change today requires strategic marketing more than ever. As a function, it is on the bleeding edge of change and innovation all the time. It is precisely because marketing changes so rapidly that we need to take a strategic approach to it. This is an absolute requirement if we wish to connect the value of our activities to business outcomes more directly, and it starts with making sure the CEO and CMO are 100 percent aligned on the endgame and how to get there. There are just too many things to do in an ever-shrinking time frame, and no one has time anymore for distractions or random acts of marketing that deliver nothing.

Central to any good strategy is defining success measures beyond generic lead goals and conversion rates. To do this, CMOs need to have a seat at the table and a voice in determining what decisions need to be made for a successful GTM and how to prioritize for the best ROI. You can't have great marketing if you see it solely as a service function or simply to create leads for your business. By using marketing strategically, not only do your chances of market impact improve, but it would also alleviate the need for the CMO to waste huge amounts of time creating a business case the size of *War and Peace* to get funding every quarter. It also eliminates the need to build a business case in quantum terms to convince the technology leaders of the best path forward. If this is happening today, it is a symptom that marketing is already too far removed from the ongoing conversations and shared understanding of how the business is approaching the market.

With the rapid digitization of pretty much everything in our lives, we don't have the luxury of time to incubate or evolve a shared understanding of what it means at a foundational level to connect and engage our customers to drive progress. We have evolved our business models, we have evolved how we develop software, and the business tools used for customer experience are evolving in days, not years. It's now time to evolve how we think about marketing and the role of the CMO. We need to get on with the business of solving increasingly harder customer problems that require the scale, scope, and speed of digital, which is catapulting everyone into the next phase of innovation and evolution as a species.

For Start-Ups

If you are the CEO/founder of a start-up, you have the same version of the marketing challenge but with fewer resources and more fidgeting. It's likely you are the primary driver behind some of the marketing initiatives, with a small number of more junior-level marketing people just trying to do a good job but not delivering the results you want. You also need to deal with more stakeholders or investors that weigh in on how you should be marketing the company, what your message should be, and who you should be targeting. For you, clarity of focus is even more critical. You don't have a dollar to waste and must use speed as your ally to execute a highly focused set of priorities that are clearly communicated across your team.

I've also observed that the time a small company needs a CMO's help defining a plan and putting in a foundation is precisely when they can't afford one. This can lead to a lot of unnecessary restlessness and experimentation. In section 2, I will cover how you can get on the right path with the team you have now.

It Can Be Done!

I've seen many success stories over the years, but I wanted to share one where impact came swiftly because there was unity of purpose and a clear outcome.

I joined a portfolio company for a large, well-known PE firm as the CMO, and the transaction outcome was made clear to everyone. I was given a very specific mandate to reinvigorate and reposition the company, create industry interest, and help package the company for an ultimate exit. The board and CEO understood the potential for marketing to make a difference; they were committed to being aggressive in decision-making to speed the process, and I had the full support of the CEO and the board.

While the company was rapidly pivoting to a SaaS business model, I worked with the head of products and the head of sales to define a strategy based on where the market was going, not where it was. Our budget was very conservative, and there were hurdles to hiring quickly, but we had some good ideas on how to break through the noise if we acted fast. We created a business case and marketing strategy to help the company transform to a cloud model, modernize its market position, pivot to a platform product strategy, evolve its narrative, and transform its brand from legacy to modern.

We presented the strategy to the board for approval, and seventy-two working days later, we launched what looked like a brand-new company with a progressive, competitive strategy into the market. There was more work to do to continue to evolve the product roadmap and transform the sales organization, of course, but from a value creation standpoint, marketing had played its role and created noticeable momentum seventy-two days from the day we got board approval on the plan. The company later enjoyed a successful acquisition.

My Challenge to You

Collectively in this industry, our bias for action can make us myopic. It's easy to get stuck swirling in the currents, making only mild progress toward the shore, blaming bad conditions or a navigational error by the person in charge. Soon, what we focus on (which is usually in-quarter shortfalls) gets bigger, which can make us shortsighted and tactical, missing opportunities to make meaningful adjustments because we are too focused on details that we can't measure or fixing problems that are just distractions.

Over the years I've seen many companies fall into the trap of shortsighted thinking or fixed assumptions based on practices that worked before at someone's previous company. It's humbling to admit that the rules have changed, the sea state is different, and assumptions should always be pressure tested, so it's paramount for us all to have a learning mindset in this business.

> Trying to use modern methods while still applying last-generation paradigms doesn't work.

While the cloud software market is estimated to have grown five times in the last ten years, how we think about marketing is stuck, which is both the problem and the opportunity. And it's no secret that marketing has a brand problem of its own, loaded with a thousand different meanings and misunderstandings that make it difficult to agree on how to get things done. My challenge to you is to approach marketing with a learning mindset, free from dangerous assumptions or baggage from the past.

Just as the ocean is full of ways to die, the software industry is full of reasons to fail, but clumsy marketing should not be one of them.

Summary

As a sailor, it goes without saying that knowing where you want to go is a good idea, and setting proper expectations and having clear communication with the crew aren't just nice to have; they are safety issues. Everyone in the boat has an important role to play and can best contribute if they know what is expected of them and why it matters. It's also critical when there's rough water so everyone can operate the boat safely and avoid discussions when everyone should be focused on execution.

Based on the goals of your investors, how likely is it that you will face a transaction event in the future? Are you prepared to explain why your company can get higher valuations (because of its position in the market)? If this is likely, it's critical that your CMO and marketing team have a playbook for creating the best transaction outcome, that you are aligned with and support it, and that you are confident you have the right marketing resources in place to execute.

This will include the following:

➜ Clearly communicating your aspirations and expectations to your CMO so they can help you

➜ Understanding what dangerous assumptions you might have about marketing and how they have the potential to create unintended consequences that work against you

➜ Having a shared idea of what good marketing looks like for your company uniquely

➜ Ensuring you have a strategic marketing plan in place early enough for it to make a difference either as a competitive advantage or to unlock hidden value leading into a transaction

➜ Moving as quickly as you possibly can

CHAPTER 3

TRENDS AND IMPLICATIONS

IN THE 2000 AMERICA'S CUP, the average boat speed was around eight to ten knots. In 2017, it was over thirty knots, thanks to the hydrofoils, which played a huge role in this massive increase in speed. The 2021 America's Cup saw boats reach speeds of *fifty knots* or more because of rapid changes in sailing technology.

In just over twenty years, new innovations made the boats faster, more maneuverable, and more efficient. The use of composite materials, computer-aided design, and simulation advances in data analytics and sensor technology have allowed teams to gather real-time data on the boat's performance and make strategic decisions during the race. These technical advances have transformed the America's Cup race from a primarily physical and tactical competition into a high-tech battle of engineering and innovation, where the ability to adapt quickly can make all the difference. It's still a boat, and it's still sailing, but the racing will never be the same.

So it is with marketing. Some innovations have been gentle evolutions made over the years; others are entirely disrupting how we operate. To call what we are facing today *modern marketing* is where you might hear the faint sound of every B2B tech CMO doing a collective eyeroll. There's really no such thing as *modern* per se (although I'll refer to it as that for the sake of readability in this book). The marketing we do today changes tomorrow, and that's how it's been for decades—it's always modern; whether you're using it that way is an entirely different matter, and we will focus on that next.

There are some dramatic shifts happening in the industry that make it more important than ever to adopt a modern way to apply marketing or risk being left behind. There are also some important trends that have implications across the business and are not just confined to marketing alone. Some trends are disruptive in nature, and some are more of an evolution that becomes increasingly urgent and complex the longer it's left unaddressed. Let's cover some of the biggest requirements in today's ever-more modern marketing environment and how they might impact the way you need to monitor, anticipate, and rapidly adjust to meet your buyers and customers where they are.

Adopting an AI-Powered Digital Engine—A Disruption

Artificial intelligence (AI) has already made significant strides in marketing, transforming the way companies can engage and interact with customers and prospects digitally. From chatbots that provide instant customer engagements to predictive analytics that help make data-driven decisions in real time and help create personalized content with tailored messages for individual types of customers, AI has and will continue to revolutionize marketing. The potential of AI is mind-numbing, and the future promises even greater integration of AI into execution and workflow, resulting in increased automation, deeper insights, more personalized experiences, and changes to how work gets done across marketing, sales, and customer success.

As more companies continue to digitally evolve, AI will handle repetitive and time-consuming tasks such as data analysis, lead nurturing, automated funnels, and campaign optimization. It will do this with unparalleled efficiency and accuracy and promises to help marketing focus on more contextual aspects such as crafting compelling messaging, ideating creative campaigns, and building more compelling customer engagement strategies. Since garbage in is garbage out, this will mean product marketing will need to be much more strategic and get even closer to the in-product experience, which will require more alignment than ever with the product teams.

AI also continues to provide increasingly valuable predictive insights. In the not-too-distant future, AI-powered analytics will basically eliminate the need for analytics provided today by marketing operations and RevOps teams. These insights will come faster and trigger optimization and refinements that improve targeting, conversions, and ROI as the action is happening. Many organizations have gotten by with less-mature practices in sales and marketing operations, workflow, and process, but AI can't work well if the process and data structures aren't also considered.

Personalization is something marketers have been trying to get done for years, but AI is a massive game-changer. Now data analysis is happening at the individual level to both create and serve up highly personalized experiences as the person clicks the button. With AI, marketing teams can create dynamic and contextually relevant content, offers, and recommendations tailored to each customer's unique needs, interests, and stage in the buying cycle. This level of personalization (while a little creepy) can also significantly enhance customer engagement and loyalty, ultimately driving revenue growth. But to have personalized content to digitize the buying process and speed conversion, this transforms our old ideas about *sales enablement* and will shift them more to *buyer enablement* and conversion, which will be a new capability.

AI is enhancing the customer experience with engagements placed at precisely the right time in the customer's digital experience. As it's becoming more sophisticated, the interactions are becoming more difficult for people to discern what's human and what's not. AI-powered chatbots can handle complex customer inquiries, provide product recommendations, and offer personalized promotions, all while providing 24/7 support. Not only does this provide a greater customer experience, but it also helps drive down the cost to both acquire and serve customers and transitions the customer support model to digital first. Chat interactions that used to happen in silos (one method on the website, one method in the product, and one method for help desk) need to be seamless and unified so the customer experience is consistent all the way through.

AI will completely transform the way we engage and deliver our products and services, and it makes the changes necessary in the entire GTM model both thrilling and savage!

The Rise of the Younger B2B Techsumer—An Evolution

As consumerization of technology continues, the buyers of technology are behaving more like consumers than tech buyers in the early interest and consideration phases of the buyers' journey. This has no doubt changed how you think about your GTM model, but there are larger implications.

Traditionally, there were technical buyers that bought technical things to go with other technical things. It was an engineer talking to an engineer about how to solve a problem. They could get super geeky and get into the weeds, where speeds and feeds were king. This is ideal for a more high-touch motion. On the B2B software side, the cloud products are getting more consumable, easily configurable, and easier to use, with integrations built in and subscription-based pricing. A customer can ramp down usage over the course of a contract, adopting a competitive service, often without you having any idea that they have no intention of renewing until they just don't.

Marketing now must consider this new consumer-buying orientation arising from decision-makers who aren't always technical or inside the product. It must also contend with strong internal stakeholders with deep affection for their own technology who want to see specs splashed all over your company's homepage. As buyers act more like consumers, the sales cycle is getting shorter, and the proof of concept is becoming a relic of the past. Buyers expect the product to work as promised and want to use free trials to kick the tires. In some cases, a video describing use cases and screenshots is enough. The new normal is to create an account and a password and get after it.

This means you need a more low-touch motion and potentially elements of a product-led growth (PLG) model. But wait! You can't go down the PLG path and still have your die-hard technologists solely produce technology-centric interactions, which is great for a technical buyer but not so great for everyone else. In fact, a lot more of the *everyone elses* are now involved in the buying decision and don't have a technical orientation, nor do they use the product every day. Everyone else wants to understand the benefits and the ROI, who else has used it, and if the company can credibly deliver on all the promises it's making *before* they have a technical conversation or download a trial. A PLG model alone won't fix this if the people defining the PLG journey don't understand the expectations of the evolving *techsumer*. You must have a unified PLG strategy, not one isolated to the product teams alone. We will cover this more in section three.

Also, the majority of B2B technology buyers are now between the age of twenty-five and forty years old. This means that the next generation of B2B software buyers have totally different expectations than some of us who have been around a while might be used to. True digital natives grew up swiping and tapping apps and have a whole new set of expectations of how software is supposed to work. They grew up with consumer technologies that are easy to use and are always available. They are used to getting what they want, when they want it, and they expect the same from a business service like yours.

This also means that they are not going to put up with a software service that is hard to use or takes a long time to get up and running. They will quickly move on to something else if they feel that they are not getting what they need from their current vendor. These customers expect and demand a much more hands-on, personalized approach but are also completely comfortable browsing more online and talking less to a human. Therefore, marketing is increasingly playing a larger role in the digital buyers' journey than it once did, demanding a completely new take on how sales and marketing function.

Research shows that next-generation buyers place more value on popular brands and peer opinions than the generation before them. If you have great reviews, brace yourself for them to jump into your arms. A decreasing percentage uses analyst rankings and reports. I must admit, I secretly do cartwheels inside thinking about how changes are afoot for technology analysts after the shakedowns some of them have put us all through.

All of this may cause you to reconsider your existing assumptions and GTM strategies to be sure you are focused on providing a great customer experience at every stage of the buyer's journey. It means making sure the product is backed up by positive peer reviews, being operationally prepared to deliver quicker buying cycles, and having a strategy in place to swiftly upsell and cross-sell these customers once they have made their initial purchase. Then there's everything needed to codify the relationship to drive loyalty, expand usage, and encourage evangelism.

The old way of marketing, selling, and supporting even the newest software won't work. A whole next-generation experience needs to be there. If you can appeal to this new generation of buyers across all aspects of your business, then you will be well positioned for success in the years to come.

Shift to Social Influence—An Evolution

The shift away from traditional PR and news toward social media and the prevalence of misinformation has had a significant impact on how information is created, managed, disseminated, and consumed in B2B technology. The likes of X (formerly Twitter), Discord, and other platforms have challenged the influence of traditional gatekeepers in the tech and business media, but they're also plagued with misleading information aimed at manipulating broader opinion or used as clickbait. Product reviews and online opinions can be gamed, and people care less about facts than they do about drama. Traditional tech media no longer cares as much about products as they do about IPOs, M&As, or CEO follies, so strategic communication has completely changed.

The function has flipped from mostly PR with a little bit of social to mostly social with a little bit of issues management. A robust social program can showcase opinions and thought leadership, help customers share stories, and engage in conversations that were previously inaccessible. Moreover, companies can leverage social channels to directly engage with their audiences, bypassing traditional editorial gatekeepers. Influencer and creator marketing and brand advocacy have risen in prominence to shape perception and drive interest. Social listening and proactive reputation management have become critical, and participating in video, podcast, and other social methods is now mandatory.

Unfortunately, there's no such thing as free coverage anymore since most of it either costs money to do or is pay to play. While it presents challenges in terms of information credibility and breakthrough, it also opens new possibilities for engagement, creativity, thought leadership, and direct customer communication. Striking a balance between the benefits and drawbacks will be crucial in navigating the complex information landscape well into the future.

There is so much on this topic, but the core point is the communications portion of your marketing program has completely shifted from traditional PR/AR to social influence, which doesn't come free or without thoughtful effort.

Obsessing over Customers— An Evolution

This is an age-old concept, but it's still surprising to me how few companies are authentically customer-obsessed. My friend Jack Mandelbaum has a big, fat brain as a mathematics major at MIT, an MBA in finance and accounting from Babson College, and a PhD in business analytics from a combined program from Boston University and Harvard Business School. (That's a mouthful.) I started working with Jack years ago, back when infrastructure software was sexy. At the time he had a budding research business (Management Insight Technologies) founded out of a profound curiosity about why technology companies win or lose in B2B tech and has since had the privilege of working with some of the biggest software brands on the planet. Over the years we've collaborated on many highly strategic projects aimed at understanding what is required to position and win in finicky B2B technology markets.

What I've learned working with him over the years are the following:

1. You can reduce a lot of risk by studying your prospects and customers.

2. If you study the right things, you know exactly what to do.

3. If you do items 1 and 2 above but don't like the answer or don't execute against what needs to be done, failure is mathematically predictable.

Strategic marketing minds have done their homework through market analysis and have concluded that the best method for delivering meaningful results and driving company value is obsessing over customers. Based on decades of B2B tech research that Jack has done over three decades with the biggest software companies in the world, here's what the data shows:

COMPANIES THAT ARE CUSTOMER-OBSESSED TEND TO PREVAIL LONG TERM AND CAN SUCCEED IN MULTIPLE RELATED MARKETS.

However, it is extremely difficult to do because most companies like the idea but are really profit and loss (P&L) obsessed. Based on his research, those companies tend to be shorter lived and often sell for less.

CUSTOMER-OBSESSION ONLY MATTERS IF IT'S MEASURED.

It means decisions should be based on doing the right thing for the customer, creating measures for it, and knowing when to make appropriate decisions.

BEING CUSTOMER-OBSESSED IS HARD TO DO.

It adds no value if you can't deliver on it and still be profitable or show a path to profit. Having the right team with the right motivation and solid executive leadership is key.

BEING CUSTOMER-OBSESSED IS WHAT DEFINES YOUR BRAND.

It defines your positioning relative to other companies in the same market, which is the ultimate measure of short- and long-term success. Also, strong brand positioning almost always reflects a company that is also customer-obsessed.

BRAND POSITIONING IS USED DIFFERENTLY BY CUSTOMER-OBSESSED COMPANIES AND P&L-FOCUSED COMPANIES.

Customer-focused companies look to brand positioning as a measure of how well they are meeting customer needs and constantly seeking improvement, which rewards them with a great reputation. P&L-focused companies look to brand positioning as a measure of how well they are focusing on areas of short-term strength or current market perception.

EVEN CUSTOMER-OBSESSED COMPANIES CAN'T HAVE IT ALL.

There will be customer segments aligned with your company's value proposition and customer segments that are less aligned. It's important to have a segmentation strategy that accounts for your strengths and your ability to influence those segments. Brand measures can create laser-like clarity for the company's leadership team to track penetration and decision-making against the segmentation model.

FINALLY, HAVING A STRONG CUSTOMER-OBSESSED CULTURE AND STRATEGIC POSITIONING MATTERS TO LONG-TERM COMPANY VIABILITY, AND IT CAN BE MATHEMATICALLY PREDICTED.

With the right insights, there is a 100 percent chance a business can see where it stands in the market, what is likely to happen, and what can be done about it.

> **Being customer-obsessed means understanding that the customer experience you deliver is the most valuable feature you have.**

In B2B software there is *so much noise*! More new software companies are putting up a proverbial shingle than ever before, and you have no doubt seen this in your own market share projections as well. That translates to a lot of B2B software companies doing a lot of marketing!

When buyers fail to see an obvious difference between products, the next most important thing to consider is what it is like to engage with you. Whether your company is in the first phase of accumulating users on a free service or you already have thousands of paying customers, it's critical to be laser focused on customer experience and an end-to-end program around it. We all know that it's cheaper to keep a customer than it is to acquire a new one—and the numbers prove it. It's been well established through the Net Promoter System created by Frederick Reichheld that there is a direct correlation between retention and increasing profits. Yet it seems only the big, established software companies measure their executives on retention and expansion versus net new logos. Just something to consider.

That aside, when we talk about customer experience, we are really talking about the way customers perceive their interactions with your company as a whole, not just in customer success or service. This includes every touchpoint, from the first time they hear about you to when they make a purchase to how they are treated throughout the life of the relationship. Let's face it, software has bugs and is never perfect, so there are bound to be frustrations and issues with your products. That's a generally accepted idea for anyone using software. What's important is creating a great customer experience every step of the way, including flawless communication and easy troubleshooting. When you leave them feeling good, they come back.

People won't leave if the product is good enough and the experience is amazing. They will leave if your product is good and the experience is terrible; it's as simple as that. So make sure you are investing in both your code and in creating the experience around it.

Brand Positioning—An Evolution

The reader gasps in horror. *Did she just use the B-word?* Before you indulge in the sudden urge to gag, let me define what modern brand positioning is and the three reasons why it's important for you to reconsider it as a core element of your marketing strategy. In B2B software, branding today doesn't mean what it once did back in the day—with flashy ad campaigns and fluffy jazz fingers. In our industry the very word *branding* has its own brand problem. But let me try to clear some of that up.

Brand positioning does not mean flashy ads or logos on mugs. Brand positioning means the following:

- Having a compelling customer value proposition that is unique in the market and backed by customer success stories

- Having a consistent customer experience that aligns with your core value proposition

- Establishing your company as a thought leader on a pain topic your market cares about

- Having a consistent message that people can understand in under seven seconds (give or take) that motivates them to want to learn more

- Showing up in relevant digital places to give your seven seconds a chance to be seen

- Implementing strategies that capture a meaningful engagement or trial that people want to opt in to

- Engaging in strategic communications across social and influencer channels

We've established that the tech buyer is behaving more like a consumer. When you add this to the fact that B2B software is maturing with more noise than ever on social media platforms and in online forums (now powered by AI), the industry is starting to adopt dynamics and attributes that are very consumer-like, and this is the headspace we need to be in when we apply marketing principles to get the results we want.

The more mature and commodity-like a product is in the consumer market, the more branding can help it differentiate. The more noise in the market and the more fragmented the market is, the more halo the better brands get, which drives preference and consideration. The younger the buyer is, the more brand reputation and customer success matter. The more price pressure there is, the more the brand value and lack of friction in their digital interaction help garner a premium price.

We are going to dive a little deeper into this topic, and I'm taking you with me whether you like it or not, so buckle up. What follows is critical context for you to appreciate before you reject the idea of brand positioning altogether.

B2C BRANDING PRINCIPLES CAN BE APPLIED TO B2B WITH MATHEMATICAL RESULTS

In a study by LinkedIn's B2B Institute,[2] they found that B2B companies can benefit from the same B2C best practices that have been used over the last fifty years. They concluded that there is a quantitative relationship between a brand's share of voice (SOV) and its rate of growth. Feel free to explore the paper, but here's what the research says:

> **The higher the share of voice, the higher the rate of growth.**
> **The higher the rate of growth, the higher the share of market.**

---

2   Les Binet and Peter Field, "The 5 Principles of Growth in B2B Marketing," https://business.linkedin.com/marketing-solutions/b2b-institute, accessed October 27, 2023, https://business.linkedin.com/content/dam/me/business/en-us/amp/marketing.pdf.

Based on the research, B2B brands appear to benefit from SOV gains at the same rate as B2C brands. If you think about applying this to how you currently allocate funding, this means you can be statistically confident in getting the results you want, even though you might refuse to believe solid brand investments might help you.

The challenge is that because B2B tech companies rarely allocate funding to multiyear initiatives such as SOV, thought leadership, or positioning activities, it's hard to show consistent execution to measure the gains. Often, these types of things tend to get sacrificed first over sales activation initiatives, making ROI data collection difficult. Unfortunately, tech companies struggle to get a meaningful uplift that comes with doing both because they rarely, if ever, do both together for long enough for it to make a difference. It's hard to break out of the noise if you don't invest in breaking out of the noise.

Their data, and any CMO, will tell you that marketing works best when brand and activation work together. In fact, the same study suggests that maximum budget efficiency happens when there is roughly an even investment in both brand SOV and sales activation. Granted, brand SOV spend typically costs more than activation, but this should not at all mean that you should do less activation than you are today. It's more likely you just aren't doing the brand activities at all, or at least ones with meaningful investment.

Another compelling model that is mathematically well-known in the consumer space that can also apply to B2B and is one of the most cited laws of marketing that has been applied by B2C for many years is the Bass diffusion model.[3] It's also covered in the same study but has been known in marketing circles for years.

In the simplest terms, this equation is used to calculate adoption. For any innovation, there is a pool of potential adopters who will adopt on their own with some level of probability. Other adopters will imitate them with another level of probability. By applying this model, one can calculate the number of new adopters at any given time.

$$n_t = (p + q N_t)(M - N_t)$$

| New adopters | Proportion who will adopt their own | Proportion who will imitate | Cumulative adopters |

Figure 3.1

The Bass diffusion model helps forecast adoption and predict sales.

When you combine brand activities with sales activation activities to amplify the success of momentum of early adoption, you can get faster overall adoption and growth than if you did one or the other alone. If you increase brand and SOV spend early, you can influence the number of new adopters who tell more people, which increases those who imitate the purchase/use in a shorter period of time. This sounds like common sense put in these terms, but in B2B tech, we have a hard time investing this way.

---

3   "Bass Diffusion Model," Wikipedia, October 16, 2023, https://en.wikipedia.org/wiki/Bass_diffusion_model.

> When looking at these models and the research and applying the data, it can be concluded that B2B companies tend to do the *exact opposite* of what they should be doing and what is statistically well-known in the consumer world.

Instead, most B2B software companies focus on sales activation, with minimal brand and SOV spend; they don't benefit from early market capture and sustained growth. In fact, the typical approach follows the quarterly motion of lead generation without uplift, which results in staying flat or only seeing marginal increases, seasonality, and price changes notwithstanding. However, if you do both over time and nothing else, the math says your adoption volume will come quicker, and quarterly results will get increasingly better over time. I'm just saying.

Data Privacy, Cyber Threats, and Targeting Policies—An Evolution

Data privacy, cyber threats, and data regulations have already ushered in a profound transformation we all got a taste of initially when the General Data Protection Regulation (GDPR) in Europe and the California Consumer Privacy Act (CCPA) in the United States took effect and compelled marketers to reassess their data collection, data usage, privacy policies, and security practices. This was just the beginning.

With the increasing digitalization of businesses and the widespread collection of customer data, concerns surrounding the privacy and security of personal information have escalated. Increasingly complex regulations will continue to emphasize transparency, consent, and the rights of individuals over their data. As a result, marketers are required to obtain explicit consent for data collection, provide clear privacy notices, and offer opt-out mechanisms. This has led to a more personalized and permission-based approach to marketing, with strange results. Some users are becoming more cautious about sharing their data and are demanding greater transparency and control, while others don't care at all and just hit the accept button everywhere they visit.

To balance personalized advertising and user privacy (given that users now have more control over their data and browsing experience), Google intends to phase out third-party cookies and opt for other methods that are yet to be rolled out. For many, Google targeting and search are the main components of how they drive traffic and leads. The full picture of the impact is yet to be seen, but companies have been slow to reassess a first-party data strategy.

Finally, the rise of cyber threats and data breaches has forced marketers to consider how to manage such events because companies now understand that a breach not only jeopardizes sensitive information but also has the potential to undermine brand reputation and erode customer confidence, no matter how big or small the event is. Marketing programs must now consider crisis-response planning, cybersecurity protocols, access management, and data-protection measures in partnership with their risk, security, and IT teams.

Summary

Buyer expectations have changed, and old engagement and delivery models no longer work. Having a great brand position and being customer-obsessed have been statistically proven to increase adoption, profitability, market share, and value. With the rise of AI, we can take our businesses to places we couldn't imagine before, but with the good comes the bad. Crime has gone virtual, and digital risk has shot through the roof, ushering in an onslaught of complex regulations and data-privacy requirements. Also, because of the organic nature of the online experience, social networks, and the digital hive mentality, we now have less control over the customer experience and our reputation than at any time since we started talking to B2B customers online.

> **Knowing how to adopt and use modern marketing methods isn't the challenge. Adapting effectively across the entire business to take advantage of modern methods is the challenge.**

It's likely you are already considering the implications of many of these quickly evolving or disruptive trends. The point is that marketing alone can't take advantage of the opportunities they present or solve many of the new challenges that go along with them because they require taking a whole new look at your customer experience, GTM models, and IT/data security priorities altogether. It does no good for marketing to adopt new tools and methods to help address the changing dynamics if the company isn't prepared for the broader implications that go along with them.

If you are sailing in increasingly less predictable conditions in a faster, more modern boat, you have less time to respond, less margin for error, and bigger consequences. That means you need to carefully track minute changes in the conditions to anticipate what needs to happen almost instantly. Likewise, to compete in today's rapidly evolving digital business environment, you must adapt to the changing requirements or risk being left behind.

Disruptive and evolving trends that will most impact your marketing efforts include the following:

➜ AI will evolve the scope of marketing's impact on the customer experience with more personalization, real-time optimization, data analytics, and AI-powered interactions. If you aren't using it by now, you are already behind.

➜ Gone are the days of controlled PR activities and free coverage. Social influence programs are critical, as are issues and reputation monitoring and management.

➜ B2B technology buyers are changing; they expect a more consumer-like experience with interactions where, when, and how they want them.

➜ Companies that are customer-obsessed in how they differentiate and execute have statistically predictable success and create a customer-centric experience that is their most valuable competitive differentiator.

➜ The strength of a B2B's brand positioning is directly related to growth rate and market share and creates uplift for sales activation at the same rate seen in consumer products, but most B2B companies rarely see this benefit because they rarely do both brand positioning and activation activities at the same time.

➜ With more software companies competing, those that adopt an integrated approach will accelerate growth, get higher margins, and garner more forgiveness for product deficiencies.

➜ Data privacy, complex regulations, and cybersecurity threats will continue to evolve and must be considered across all customer engagement channels.

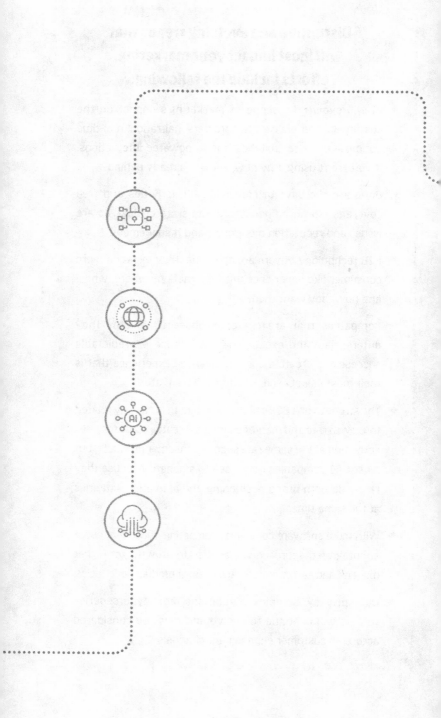

CHAPTER 4

MARKETING TRANSFORMED

THE SAYING GOES, "Sailing is the most expensive way to get somewhere for free, heading exactly in the wrong direction." As anyone who has been on a sailboat knows, you don't go straight. In fact, often, the quickest way to get somewhere that may be directly ahead of you in the distance requires zigzagging many times depending on wind direction, the sea state, the design of your boat, and how good you are at sail trim. On rare occasions, you can sail dead downwind surfing the waves, which is every skipper's idea of a dream day—but it's not something you can depend on.

All this to-ing and fro-ing happens because you can't control the elements. The same is true with the customer journey that has evolved into a complex system defined by changing conditions and customer whims. In this chapter we will explore what that means and what is changing, and we will redefine marketing so we are all on the same page about what modern marketing can do for you.

First, I want to introduce you to Colton. Colton is from Acme Company and has a problem you might be able to help him solve.

This is the buyer's journey you want Colton to have:

Colton visits your website, downloads a free trial, calls to discuss pricing, and signs a contract.

This is Colton's actual journey:

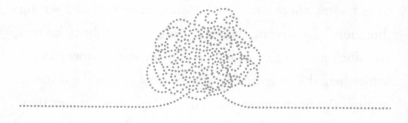

Colton goes everywhere else before talking to you.

Customer behavior has made a wholesale shift to digital. What started in marketing as a slow adoption of new technology accelerated to a breakneck pace, not because it's free and fun but because marketing had to go where the buyers are. Buyers and customers are seeking all kinds of information from all corners of the internet before they even speak to you.

As touchpoints go digital and techsumers take control of their digital journey, a broader and deeper set of digital engagement and experiences are required to support prospects and customers along the way. The customer's journey has changed from a linear process to an interconnected system of omnichannel interactions that quite frankly, can be a hot mess.

Marketing Is a Complex and Messy System of Engagements

Today's marketer can now take advantage of an astounding number of technologies and tools available. We are shifting from what was an intuition-based art form (combined with a linear sales model) into a modern organism fueled by technology, data, and process. In the most mature technology companies, marketing as a department is the biggest consumer of technology. It's used to capture, score, manage, nurture, append, correlate, analyze, entice, promote, demo, convince, personalize, close, provide, enable, syndicate, and socialize anything a company has to offer.

According to the most recent Chief Martec Landscape report, there are over ten thousand marketing and CX solutions as of 2023[4] that are intended to simplify the work of creating frictionless digital interactions. It's honestly created a colossal amount of work. Last I checked, the average company uses ninety-one of these tools—ninety-one!

---

4   Scott Brinker, "2023 Marketing Technology Landscape," Chief Martec, https://chiefmartec.com/2023/05/2023-marketing-technology-landscape-supergraphic-11038-solutions-searchable-on-martechmap-com/.

With a tremendous sense of urgency, marketing is trying to adopt these solutions, manage requests for proposals, repurpose existing licensing agreements, and negotiate contracts to try to build the best customer experience engine possible to show results before the next budget cycle to prove its value—on top of their day jobs. Most of the new services are cloud-based and user-configurable because tech founders from these companies also know that CMOs don't typically have dedicated IT support. In most cases, for small to midsize companies, IT resources are strapped themselves, managing uptime, securing the network, or updating core business applications for the company, which means third-party cloud tools aren't often a key priority.

With so many types of digital marketing tools and customer engagement services available and very little IT support, marketing teams try to quietly solve problems on their own. They have often created shadow IT, made up of outsourced IT services, hired technical experts in marketing operations or within web teams, or contracted agencies (who have engaged their own contractors), to help integrate the different systems. Assuming all these tools have been through a third-party risk assessment, marketing teams are well on their way to building and managing a virtual infrastructure that many executives may not even know exists. Herculean efforts in marketing have been made in the background to track and include marketing attribution to revenue in their quarterly business reviews so they can attempt to tie investment spend to quarterly revenue to protect their budgets.

> Depending on your organization's level of marketing and IT maturity, you may be thinking of this technology as a set of tools, or perhaps you're well on your way to seeing it as a strategic technology platform that deserves more attention.

Silos Are Where Opportunities Go to Die

As mentioned earlier, you likely have three software platforms that matter to your company. The third one is the software you use to deliver your digital CX. This platform is sometimes referred to as the CX or sometimes the martech stack, but it's generally the same thing in a small to midsize software company. As a reminder, it includes capabilities such as CRM, marketing automation, chat, a CMS or web platform, and a bunch of other digital tools to drive targeting, content, scoring, interactions, engagements, support, and customer/ prospect communication.

Broadly, the terms "martech stack," "customer relationship management," and "CX platform" are sometimes used interchangeably to explain very similar things, so let's ground ourselves. Martech was used to stand for technologies that focused on activation and omnichannel demand generation for new and existing customers and began their adoption in the marketing function and sprawled outward. CRM has been around for decades but has also spread out in sales operations to include things such as forecasting tools, activity tracking, account scoring, and so on. CX has come into use over the last few years and is used to include technologies that span the entire customer life cycle as the technology has exploded. To make it more confusing, CX is also used by companies as a term to describe initiatives focused on customer management and often includes or is exclusive to customer success, so that's not helpful. It's also common for each company to define it differently depending on who is responsible for what.

The reason for all this is that historically, the systems and tools were adopted and used in silos based on who adopted them and how they were used over time; marketing adopted marketing automation and content management tools, sales adopted CRM and forecasting tools that sometimes marketing used or integrated with, and support and services adopted help-desk or knowledge-base tools or built their own. The challenge today is that many of these systems are in silos and maybe have bidirectional feeds, but the processes aren't necessarily built for the unified customer experience; more often they are built to support a series of tasks, reports, or functional workflows internally. The fact is, the legacy nature of these systems may be holding you back!

For our purposes going forward, I will refer to the entire tech stack supporting an end-to-end customer experience as the CX platform.

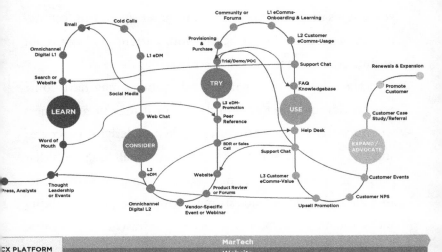

Figure 4.1

In today's digital world, a unified customer experience platform is fundamental to being able to effectively compete as a modern B2B software company.

Do you know what state your customer experience platform is in? Do you know how it works, or has someone shown you demos? Do you have an owner for it? Is anyone responsible for securing and monitoring it and the APIs connected to it? How much budget do you allocate to it?

The success and scalability of your marketing program depend on the maturity of your customer experience platform and determine how customers perceive their overall experience with you. If your company is just getting started in its marketing investments or has underinvested in marketing for years, it is safe to assume that you have yet to put this foundation in place. It could also be that your current platform is not optimized or, worse, is badly outdated.

The CRM system you are using today may have some capabilities to deliver certain things, or it may be a hot mess with inconsistent data structures, broken underlying processes, and bad data. Or you may have dozens of small SaaS tools that people seem to pay for or have acquired in pieces over time, and some functions (such as marketing) may not be talking about them as part of a larger virtual infrastructure because they themselves may just think of them as tools or trials. While these SaaS services work just fine separately, they are connected with APIs that your IT team may not be looking at, which, as a cybersecurity enthusiast myself, is terrifying to say the least.

Technology is only part of the solution. Getting the platform to work right takes dedicated focus and commitment to workflow and process changes across marketing, sales, and services. It requires a technology roadmap and an investment strategy for the long term, or not at all.

HERE ARE A FEW REASONS TO INVEST IN A CX PLATFORM AS A STRATEGIC BUSINESS PLATFORM:

➔ If you want to deliver a compelling, competitive, and engaging experience that meets the expectations of today's prospects and customers

➔ If you want end-to-end reporting that helps you begin to understand customer cost to acquire, cost to serve and ROI across marketing, sales, and customer success

➔ If you want to be able to precisely target accounts with personalized messaging and automated conversion, making every dollar act like $3

➔ If you want the real-time ability for marketing to turn dials to help fill pipeline gaps that creep up on a monthly or quarterly basis

➔ If you want to understand gaps in value delivery with your customers that give you the highest LTV

➔ If you want to quantify and correlate strong brand positioning with customer loyalty

Conversely, if you are six months away from a transaction, don't bother building one because it's too late. But be ready for all the pipeline and conversion questions that may not be automated in your company's current state because you don't have this fixed yet.

Blurred Lines

It used to be that marketing could function on its own island, managing corporate marcom, PR, certain aspects of the website, and major events while generating leads to hand over to sales. That was possible until the explosion of marketing technology and the move to digital engagements as the preferred method by customers and by companies adjusting to SaaS and cloud economics in general. Marketing is doing more digitally than what had been only done previously by sales in a face-to-face context.

Figure 4.2

Digital-first motions have driven marketing into sales territory.

By trying to shorten the sales cycle and get customers to try, buy, and use the product as quickly as possible, it changed the funnel dynamics, as the buyer's journey went from high touch to low touch to, in some cases, product-led. See variations in figure 4.2 below.

Either accidentally or on purpose, marketing has quietly taken on more of the sales function and has gotten both deeper and much wider in scope. It's doubtful many B2B sales organizations see it this way since their functions haven't required an evolution at the same pace. To prove value and go where the glory is, marketing has often willingly taken on more responsibilities within the sales process, as they do their best to optimistically deliver on what sales sees as important and demonstrate alignment with the sales organization.

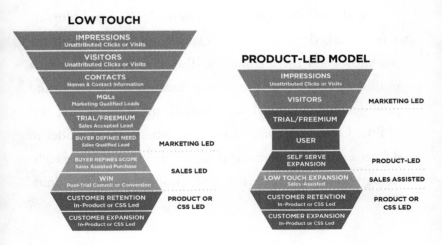

Figure 4.2 *(continued)*

With urgency to prove value and unity with sales, they have contorted themselves into traditional sales processes and systems that were built for better sales reporting and forecasting but not for the attribution across customer journey in the first place. Often, they would change their workflow to match an inefficient process (often within the CRM system) rather than change the process to fit the new requirements. This can happen either because of internal dynamics, a lack of funding, or an inability to drive change.

Now CMOs are asked to deliver the same thing that sales leaders are asked to deliver, except with a very limited technical foundation, little authority to drive sales to follow up on opportunities, constant budget instability, misaligned expectations at the top, and inequity in incentives, since typically, marketing has no commission structure. But who's complaining?

With today's digital-first motion, the lines are blurring across marketing, sales, and customer success on both the workflows and the technology. The spirit behind having a unified CX platform is to deliver meaningful customer and prospect experiences in real time, all the time, online and offline. Once you commit to a customer-centric model to deliver a unified customer experience, you must adopt a technology strategy to enable it to be frictionless across functions.

Marketing Is Not a Vending Machine

A friend and former colleague of mine, Kathleen Schaub, wrote an influential white paper titled "Marketing Is Not a Vending Machine: Rethinking ROI for the Complex Digital Era." Schaub is a career strategic marketer and has spent over a decade at IDC leading their CMO Advisory practice. The paper is a must-read, but I've included an important section from her paper to set the stage for how to rethink marketing and how it's measured.

> Businesses long for marketing that works like a vending machine. Put your money in, and out pops your desired outcome, guaranteed. Unfortunately, marketing behaves more like stock markets or weather than predictable machines. The good news is that science explains marketing's capriciousness, and companies will gain a more effective playbook if they rethink return on investment (ROI) through the lens of marketing's unpredictable reality.
>
> Markets are what science calls complex adaptive systems. Interactions between individuals and enterprises produce feedback loops resulting in volatility, uncertainty, and ambiguity. Digital technology has only increased and accelerated these interactions, compounding complexity's effects. Time is an especially confounding adversary: gaps between marketing actions and measured outcomes allow for increased interactions and thus greater change.

These characteristics make measuring predictable ROI challenging. Marketers understand the importance of ROI. Yet, despite advances in technology and improvements in operations, useful financial information for making marketing decisions remains out of reach for most. The vending-machine perspective blinds management to what is needed for change, so they are unwilling or unable to give marketers the necessary tools.

Marketers lack sufficient data and analytics capability. Outdated management models and organizational structures inhibit reaching objectives. These deficiencies lead to unfit ROI practices, such as rules-based attribution and a short-term focus, causing flawed decisions, frustration, and mistrust. To improve marketing ROI measurement, businesses must reduce dependency on the machine model.[5]

Mic drop.

It's Time to Transform Our Definition of Marketing

It's been my experience that every CEO, investor, or banker has a different definition of marketing and how it works. I'm not alone. I asked ninety B2B tech CMOs to rate various parties in the transaction process on their level of understanding of marketing as a function, how it works, and requirements for success. CEOs/founders and bankers/deal team

---

5   "Marketing Is Not a Vending Machine," squarespace.com, January 2022.

ranked the lowest across all the executive functions when it came to understanding how it works. This is not good, people.

But today is your lucky day because we are going to redefine it right now.

MARKETING REDEFINED:

In our interconnected world, technical buyers and customers expect a different level of digital engagement with B2B software companies. Marketing exists to build meaningful customer engagements and relationships through compelling, always-on experiences that measurably increase the value of the business. The foundation for its execution is built on a sophisticated web of technologies that deliver that engaging and holistic customer experience end to end.

THESE ARE THE ATTRIBUTES THAT MAKE UP A MODERN MARKETING PRACTICE:

Strategic: Marketing has moved from reactive, internally driven execution against tactical, short-term metrics to decisive and deliberate execution toward a defined outcome with value and ROI metrics. It defines the competitive brand position in the market where the company can differentiate and win.

Solution Focused: Marketing has moved from a product-centric to a customer solution-and-benefit orientation, where the focus is on identifying and targeting the unmet needs of specific customer segments. The solutions include the products, but in today's world, the services, support, and overall experience are all part of the solution that solves for these unmet needs across the customer life cycle.

Pervasive: Marketing organizations have moved away from activity-based tactics to an integrated, always-on approach that meets customers where they are with relevant and compelling content at the point of action or decision.

Customer-obsessed: Marketing has shifted from just delivering leads to delivering experiences for specific segments, constantly testing and learning to optimize the customer experience to close the gap between what customers expect and what they receive at every touchpoint.

Powered by a Unified CX Tech Stack: Marketing is powered by a sophisticated web of technologies that drive meaningful relationships and act as the foundation for customer experiences that are bidirectional.

THESE ARE THE SKILLS AND ABILITIES THAT MAKE UP A HIGH-PERFORMING MARKETING TEAM:

Speed: The ability to rapidly develop, test, and execute customer experiences; deploy them at scale; and be able to get there before the competition.

Focus: The ability to ruthlessly prioritize activities and programs that will deliver the biggest customer impact and highest ROI for stakeholders.

Agility: The ability to respond quickly to changes in the market, competitive moves, and customer requirements to take full advantage of opportunities that arise unexpectedly.

Precision: The ability to identify the right targets, touchpoints, and messages and deliver them at the right time with accuracy based on advanced analytics and enabling technologies.

High-Performing Talent: The ability to attract, retain, and inspire high-potential talent that delivers their best work either inside or as an outsourced cohort.

These are the new requirements for today's marketing organizations based on the evolving and disruptive trends that are pushing B2B software companies to a digital-first customer engagement model.

Summary

New sea conditions can call for a new approach to how you have been operating and what kind of equipment and skills you need. When it comes to sailing, there are two types of sailboats: cruising boats and performance boats. Cruising sailboats are like floating homes—they're built for comfort and to carry as much stuff as you think you might need and then some. They've got plenty of space and amenities, and you won't need to be a sailing pro to enjoy the journey, but you won't be winning any races either because they are slow or heavy.

Performance sailboats are designed to more efficiently and quickly slice through any sea condition. They're light and agile, with sails and rigging that can take a lot of power in high winds and maintain great speed averages in light winds. However, sailing one of these babies takes more skill and training if you want to operate it safely and get the optimal performance out of it.

If you are looking to create a competitive advantage for yourself, it might be time to reconsider your approach to marketing overall and ask yourself if you have the right boat for your voyage. Do you want to carry a bunch of legacy stuff you don't use or need and work around the complexity because you don't mind going slow? Or, if you want to go fast with impact, you might need to streamline, simplify, and change a few things.

Here are some things to consider:

The customer journey has changed from a linear process to an interconnected, complex system that no longer works like a vending machine.

➜ Modern customer requirements mean workflows and technologies can no longer sit in silos and require a technology platform with equivalent attention to investment and planning as you would give your product roadmap.

➜ Marketing is now engaging customers and prospects digitally the way sales used to do in person, upending traditional GTM models and blurring lines of accountability.

➜ New dynamics require us to transform our definition of marketing and change old vending machine paradigms for how it works.

➜ Modern marketing exists to build meaningful relationships through compelling, always-on experiences that measurably increase the value of the business.

THE POWER OF SURGE

THE BOAT ALWAYS WINS.

The first time my husband and I sailed on our first boat together, I felt the same way I did when I brought my daughter home from the hospital. I thought, "Whose idea was this to leave us unsupervised with this amount of responsibility?" As a rookie parent, any daily lack of forethought typically only tenders you with either an overabundance of wailing or trauma to the ego. With a large sailboat, neglecting daily contemplation of anything ordinary can lead to sacrificing limbs and inviting a consequential amount of water in places it should not be. If a line snaps in the wrong conditions, maybe the sail will just violently flog, or maybe the line will whip around and transform itself into a guillotine.

What I quickly realized the first time we took our boat offshore was that no amount of muscle could tame a boat if there was a difference of opinion about what you wanted to do and what it wanted to do. To douse a sail, halt it from lunging wrongly into large objects, or coax it to go in a certain direction, the secret was in working with the conditions, not in trying to put more muscle into it. With an eight-pound baby, a bumbling parent can somehow achieve victory every day; with a fifteen-ton baby, the boat always wins.

As a CEO, you are the skipper of a large vessel with many souls aboard, and every day you navigate seas and weather conditions that can change at any moment. There may be days when you ask yourself whose idea it was to leave you with this amount of responsibility, and in truth, it was probably yours. By improving how you contemplate the ordinary, you can master the art of strategy to find ways to work smarter, not harder and to devise an approach that helps you conquer any condition as it comes.

This applies to marketing strategies as well. With proper consideration given in key areas, you can capture the Power of Surge and incorporate proven practices into today's transactional and highly competitive environment. Through proper planning and discipline, you will not only maintain the integrity of your mission and stay focused as you lead your team into racing mode, but you can also keep your decks clean to reduce unnecessary risk and unintended consequences. The following are the five key principles that you can use to create the Power of Surge in your business.

S - STRATEGY

Know yourself and commit to a course.

It's critical to have a crystal clear idea about your business situation, where you honestly sit in the market competitively, and what customer segments best fit with what you can deliver. Only with an honest, informed assessment of your situation can you hope to succeed. Yet, this fundamental principle can be elusive while chasing growth. With a sober view of your situation, priorities become obvious, which is half the battle. With careful consideration of your options and a commitment to your course, it's easier to determine where and how to focus to achieve your goals, even if it means walking away from ambitious opportunities that salespeople are excited about.

U - UNITY

Create radical unity for aligned execution.

The best leadership is unified around one mission and strategy and tightly aligned to a set of metrics that drive accountability and execution. There must be organizational discipline at the top to provide structure and order, while each functional commander is given discretion and decision authority that allows for flexibility, innovation, and variation based on their unique situational awareness. Radical unity is the shared mission, but there should be tightly aligned command and delegated authority at the point of action.

R - REPUTATION

Define your unique advantage and consistently deliver on it.

To compete successfully, you must identify the right context in which to compete, capitalize on your strengths in a compelling way, and position yourself advantageously in relation to the other alternatives. Just as important is to consistently deliver on your promises to your customers, building a lasting trust in your company that keeps them coming back and referring you to others. By positioning yourself strategically, you have a better chance of creating momentum and building a valuable brand reputation in the market.

G - GAINS

Unlock hidden value in new ways.

Company visions should be ambitious, but when goals are set too high or gains are seen as only coming from a maniacal focus on sales execution, you may miss achieving gains from hidden corners of your company that are otherwise just sitting there idle. By expecting and collecting gains as small victories in many places, such as in marketing, you might create new streams of profit and value that may surprise you. By rewarding small wins in many places, your people will build both confidence and desire to contribute.

E - EFFICIENCY

Move swiftly and effectively and with impact.

Speed and efficiency are essential to take advantage of opportunities as they arise. It's no longer about getting to market; it's about getting to the right person at the right time with the right message through the right methods that matter. Precision targeting, agile execution, and meaningful engagement can only be done if you have a clean foundation for process, data, and accountability.

In the following chapters, I will outline each of these elements in detail and provide practical next steps to help take you where you want to go.

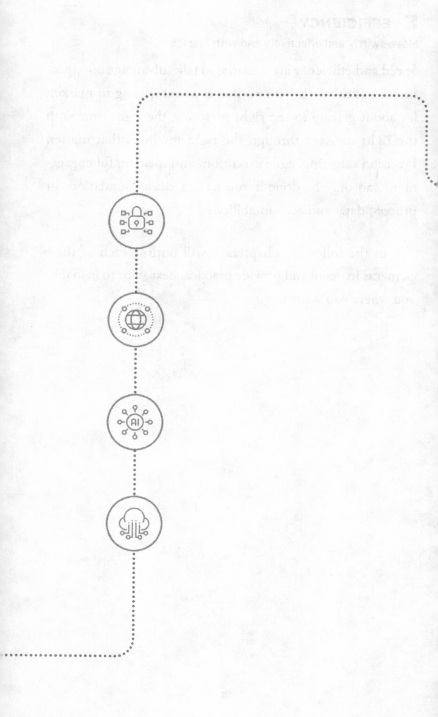

CHAPTER 5

STRATEGY

NEVER LEAVE THE DOCK WITHOUT A PLAN.

A question I get a lot is, "Aren't you afraid of sailing offshore?" My answer is always "Yes, yes, I am," because the ocean is always trying to kill you. You don't just get up one day and sail a straight line into the horizon with an idea and only a hunch about the weather.

When you are planning a long voyage, you look at weather conditions, route, trade winds, currents, average boat speed, wave height, wave period, potential risks, and the condition of your boat and crew. Then you plot your course, decide what kind of sails you will need, estimate how long it will take you to reach your intended destination, and pack whatever you think you might need on your journey, from peanut butter to toilet paper to bandages. You also prepare for alternative scenarios, so you have provisions, medical supplies, and spare parts to get yourself out of a bad situation. You operationally prepare for the worst conditions, but you mentally prepare for the best.

Any good strategy is a lot like a good passage plan. It is a structured approach that helps you achieve your goals within the boundary conditions you have and puts you in an advantageous position before you even turn the engine on to leave the harbor. Having an overall plan to go along with your goal is necessary; otherwise, your actions will be arbitrary and often futile.

Creating a marketing strategy is the same. It involves creating a blueprint to support the company's overall business strategy and then executing it in an efficient and coordinated way. It's true that many marketers can often jump in and start doing a bunch of tactics without a commercial understanding of the business to order to quickly demonstrate value. It's also true that doing a lot of things is often the expectation of those above them seeking immediate results in the current quarter.

Strategic marketing is especially important in B2B software, where the market is noisy and many companies often seem to be delivering similar products or services. To be successful, you must start with a deep understanding of your own weather conditions—your customers' needs, a sober assessment of where you are against your competitors as a vendor, and how you will manage risk or unexpected conditions that arise.

Do you want to be the best company in a particular niche? Do you want to be a platform? Do you want to define your own category? You want to get acquired by someone big, and if so, who? All these questions can be hard to answer if you haven't already considered them. It's helpful to have some kind of framework to make decisions and set priorities.

Strategy is about knowing yourself and committing to an intended course. An effective marketing strategy for a modern B2B software company will include the following two things:

1. Choosing a strategic marketing playbook based on your company's specific situation

2. Defining a market segmentation to contextualize a unique positioning strategy

Often, companies spend millions of dollars and months or years creating the technology but completely neglect the time and effort required to effectively bring it to market. By taking a strategic marketing approach up front, a company can understand the right market segments to go after, how to properly position the company, and how to prioritize the right beachheads. By taking the time up front as the product is being developed, everyone can execute together to create the biggest impact possible. In an ideal world—and I'm speaking mostly to founder CEOs who may still be in the early stages—it is important to consider your marketing strategy before the product is complete. Much work can be done to define the market, create demand, and educate the market if needed. This way, when the product is ready, the buyers are ready too.

Create a Strategic Marketing Playbook

To create a strategic marketing playbook, it's important to take a thorough and honest inventory of where you are and what you are really trying to achieve. It's important to also understand and agree as a leadership team on what your customers need from you in a way that helps you set priorities and stick to them.

WHAT IS THE TRUE CONDITION OF THE BUSINESS IN ITS CURRENT STATE IN THE CURRENT MARKET?

Not the product portfolio, *the company*. Is it a transformation, a turnaround, early growth, or a mature growth business? (Believe it or not, the answer to this question is not always clear to marketing teams who are focused on supporting individual product lines and sales targets quarter to quarter.)

WHAT ARE THE TOP METRICS THAT YOU AND YOUR INVESTORS MOST CARE ABOUT, AND WHY?

They are annual recurring revenue (ARR), monthly recurring revenue, annual contract value (ACV), churn rates, customer LTV, renewal rate, revenue retention, to name a few.

WHAT IS THE INTERNAL DESIRED OUTCOME FOR THE BUSINESS IN THE NEXT TWO TO FIVE YEARS AND IN THE NEXT TWELVE TO EIGHTEEN MONTHS?

Is it to get bought, to go public, or to get another round of funding? Is it to dominate your specific market? Is it to be the best in a category or to try to create a category? Do you have a company purpose or mission? What do you aspire to be?

WHAT IS YOUR COMPETITION DOING THAT WOULD CREATE AN OPPORTUNITY FOR YOU?

Who is ahead of you that you most want to emulate, and why? Who is coming from behind that might threaten your current standing? In what ways can they create chaos for you and you for them? What advantages do they have that you don't? In what ways can you create an advantage for yourself?

WHAT DO YOUR CUSTOMERS MOST NEED AND WANT FROM ANY VENDOR THAT THEY AREN'T GETTING TODAY?

What is your standing with your current customer base? Do they love you, or do they tolerate you? What customers are most loyal, and why is that so? Is there a segment of customers that is more passionate about what you have to offer than others, and why?

SELECT A STRATEGIC PLAYBOOK

As a CEO, what comes next will be easy for you to grok theoretically but must be applied in practical terms for your marketing to work. To de-risk your plans and gain a competitive advantage, you must anchor your marketing plans on your true business situation.

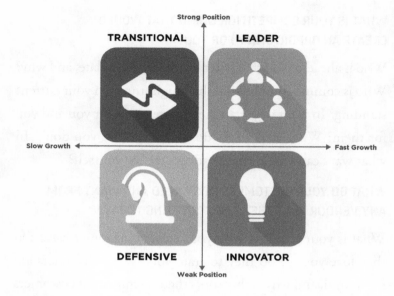

Figure 5.1
Strategic paths.

 TRANSITIONAL: You are a mature or transitional company with a strong competitive position, but the market is slow or on the decline. Often legacy with cheaper or next-gen competitors looking to take customer base. Consider how to diversify or innovate.

 LEADER: You are a visionary leader with a strong competitive position in a defined market that is expanding quickly. You are defining the market and finding ways to integrate functions, expand your base and grow share. Find ways to secure your base and future position.

 DEFENSIVE: You have a weak position and slow growth and may be late stage or distressed. Either make big moves to improve competitiveness (retrench, innovate, and reposition) or reduce costs, divest, or liquefy. Focusing on your core business is critical; consider doubling down on a segment or niche.

 INNOVATOR: You are a startup or early-stage company in a quickly evolving market. You may be an innovator, but you have a weak market position or a limited reputation. Focus on securing brand reputation, delivering product innovation and consistent customer delivery. Gain leverage through partnerships or big moves.

A major disconnect that happens all the time is that many *transitional* or *defensive* companies are financially functioning in the proper quadrants but have set up their GTM and the key metrics as if they are competing like *leaders* or *innovators* based on either their growth aspirations or one or two product lines they have. This disconnect can lead you to create a GTM engine that doesn't match your investment strategy, customer or market perceptions, or the competitive realities you face. This can lead to your marketing team developing a marketing plan that is unrealistic or not addressing the right perceptual challenges and your sales team unable to get the at-bats they need.

Having everyone aligned on your business situation seems obvious, but it is very often overlooked, so this is a simple but critical step in your strategic planning process.

Next, you can explore where you need to focus by identifying specific high-priority items as no-regret moves. Then you can think about the two aspects we covered earlier: (1) planning for a transaction with a financial buyer in some set time frame and (2) assuming you will face financial downward pressure. Adding these dimensions helps you focus on the fundamentals that are most critical instead of doing everything. These foundational playbooks can become the basis for your strategic marketing baseline plan.

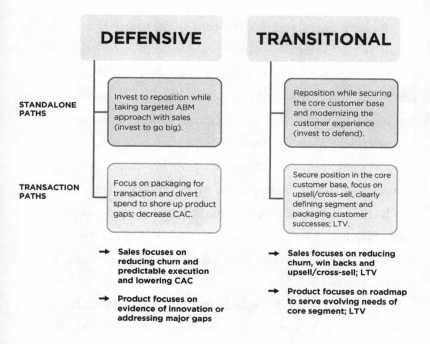

Figure 5.2

Examples of strategic marketing playbooks.

These are meant to demonstrate possible strategic marketing playbooks to consider that will help you focus and build a multiyear plan that best serves both standalone and transactional outcomes. It's critical to start with this type of categorization because it will help your company align behind priorities and not have ornate expectations about your marketing or GTM overall that you have no business considering in the near term.

INNOVATOR

Establish position and thought leadership while activating pipeline with targeted programs and building growth engine for scale (invest to grow).

Build positioning momentum and thought leadership while packaging new wins, tracking conversion trends and establishing GTM traction; ACV. Foundational tech/operations only.

➡ **Sales focuses on predictable win rates, funnel conversion and full productivity, ACV**

➡ **Product focuses on innovation roadmap to capture more share, ACV**

LEADER

Maintain leadership position while feeding/nurturing pipeline and expanding growth engine at scale (invest to lead).

Most likely an acquirer. Expand leadership position and ensure lead to close conversion while looking for ways to consolidate your space.

➡ **Sales focuses on predictable win rates, funnel conversion and productivity gains, shorter sales cycles, ACV, LTV**

➡ **Product focuses on innovation roadmap to outpace competition or consolidate market, ACV, LTV**

When you apply a strategic playbook to your annual planning, it can be useful to guide big investment decisions and weigh pros and cons in the trade-offs. It also helps create united objectives across functions to drive the best outcomes as a standalone business or leading up to a transaction. Of course, businesses can be complex, and many variations of these paths can be created, but it's also useful to know what major boundary conditions are most critical, especially for marketing, which will need to focus its precious resources.

While the four macrobusiness situation categories can be universally applied, it's important to go through the playbook options with all the core functions (product, sales, marketing, services), agree on the biggest priorities. Also agree on the way you wish to lean, towards a transaction or standalone, and assess where grand tactics would diverge down each path. This will be the basis for how you make decisions when times get either frantic or tough. This will be especially helpful for marketing because, contrary to popular belief, they cannot do it all. With a strategic marketing playbook now in place, you can focus on the next step.

Define a Market Segmentation Strategy Based on Customer Needs

Knowing which segments to walk away from is one of the hardest things for companies to do. It's important to carefully consider what customer segments you must win in and why. Defining a market segmentation model the entire company can rally around can be a powerful tool for maintaining focus on how to win over the market segments that matter most. Also, it will be used to determine your *unique* market position, segment-based messaging, and aligned GTM execution. Let's discuss what customer-needs market segmentation is.

Segmentation is the process of dividing a market into different groups of buyers or customers who have different needs and targeting each group with a more personalized customer experience, ideally from inquiry-to-close and support-to-repurchase and evangelize. Customer needs–based market segmentation is a specific type of segmentation that focuses on the customer's needs rather than verticals or firmographics such as size (e.g., SME, commercial, or enterprise). This type of segmentation model is crucial for a company that wants to be truly customer-obsessed.

Often, companies defer to market segmentation based on size because that's typically how the sales coverage and compensation model is defined. For targeting and qualification, this doesn't always work because while these companies may be easily grouped into some attributes (such as number of users that helps define price), it doesn't always account for their tendencies (outsourcing versus in-house or best-in-breed point solutions versus good-enough platforms). Nor does it account for their decision-making or buying process (decentralized versus centralized or tech driven versus line of business driven). You have probably already experienced this because many departments in very large enterprises can act like small businesses in how they solve problems and acquire technology.

There are several benefits to using needs-based segmentation. First, it makes your marketing more impactful because you can more strongly position and differentiate yourself, not just blast out generic messages that get lost in space. Second, by nurturing engaged customers and buyers, it can grow your early funnel and reduce the sales cycle because opportunities are being qualified along the digital journey. Finally, it improves the ROI of marketing investments because it reduces the number of wasted, low-value activities that may cast a wide net but not result in anything. By understanding the needs of your customers, you can create more relevant and impactful marketing messages that resonate with your target audiences and help you stand out from the competition.

GOOD CUSTOMER NEEDS–BASED MARKET SEGMENTATION IS

- derived based on a common set of problems, needs, and beliefs of a certain set of customers and prospects;

- a method to help you prioritize where to focus your energy and resources and, more importantly, help you decide where you are not going to focus; and

- a way to help customers and prospects self-identify as being a good fit for you in a digital journey.

CUSTOMER NEEDS–BASED MARKET SEGMENTATION IS NOT

- buyer personas (these exist under the segmentation model);

- oriented around company size, titles, or industries (though there may be attributes of these elements that help define a segment);

- based on products or sales coverage models (coverage models are ways to reach a segment); or

- a set of use cases, though some use cases may be a good fit for a particular segment.

Picking your battlefield is an important lesson for anyone who wants to succeed in any competitive endeavor. It's essential to pick the right battles or select ones that are strategic opportunities versus picking the biggest battles you have no business winning. To focus on the right segments means considering what resources are available to you and analyzing your competitors' capabilities before deciding where to compete.

Committing to finite customer segments doesn't mean you can't sell to other segments. It just means that you are choosing to invest marketing dollars in segments that give you the highest possibility of success, and the rest of the segments are opportunistic. The thing that is most important to realize is that there may be customer segments that just aren't ideal candidates for what you have to offer.

> **The worst outcome is being so generic that you mean nothing in the market or ending up with a bunch of customers that aren't a great fit for what you are offering.**

When you take the time to consider how you solve a problem for a particular group of customers, you cannot go wrong in your long game or in your short game. There are a thousand books you can read about being a customer-led company, and you may already be customer focused in many ways today. Being customer led doesn't just mean that you listen to your customers and prospects. It's *how* you solve a particular pain point in such a way that your customers can't ever live without you, and it's how you go to market to get your solutions in the hands of people who need them as quickly and efficiently as you can.

You must have a means of listening to your core customer segment that helps you put what you hear—your customers' feedback, desires, and beliefs—into a framework that can help you unify your strategy and operationalize your business. This type of segmentation framework will help you prioritize, make better decisions, set great metrics, and get rid of distractions. Having this discipline helps contextualize customer feedback so you are analyzing it properly, which leads to better and more precise decisions versus making generic, sweeping decisions that aren't helpful in the end. With great segmentation, you can align your product, GTM, and customer success initiatives to meet this unique market segment's needs.

> Your market segmentation model is the foundation of your GTM strategy, yet so few software companies have one. If you aspire or claim to be customer led, you must have one.

You can make strategic decisions with 100 percent certainty about where you need to invest across products, sales, and marketing if you listen closely enough to what 20 percent of your customers are telling you. If you have any kind of established customer base, the sooner you establish the foundation for getting feedback from customers, the higher the probability that you will achieve the outcomes you want.

WAYS TO GET THERE
Bootstrap
There is a way to fast-track the creation of your model using different methods and group processes that will at least give you something to start with. It's not statistically perfect, but based on my experience, you can get it about 80 percent right. You agree on major customer needs criteria or attributes that

make up the segment based on parameters that matter in your market. You then gather some publicly available information on sizing and do an exercise to evaluate attractiveness, competitiveness, and opportunity. Then through practical application, you can refine it over time based on what you learn.

With this approach, there's less science involved, but it provides an organizing principle for how the company makes decisions about creating customer value and delivering the most impact possible across functions. This approach works great but has the following requirements and limitations:

a. The company needs to have decided on the strategic playbook (see figure 5.2).

b. The right participants, who have had *a lot* of customer interaction, need to be in the room.

c. Everyone must agree that done is better than perfect, which can be a challenge for certain company cultures.

d. The right expectations need to be set for how it is used; this would be the codified and common approach everyone agrees to align behind as a business practice.

e. Understanding will be limited to the big brains in the room, so there will always be blind spots to work out later.

Big Data

With the right data, you can use a couple of different methods to create the model. You can use predictive or look-alike data modeling to find and target customers digitally who look like your own customers. Another way is to analyze your own data to create some clusters to evaluate in more detail. A great reason to invest in making sure you have great customer data! This is a decent way to get started, but the following are some major considerations:

a. It requires that you have a meaningful amount of customer data (and therefore customers) already.

b. It may require you hand over that customer data to an outside data party to analyze and match with their big data pools. Some companies may shy away from this because of either the condition of their data or the restrictions they set on data management and privacy.

c. It might mean tapping into some ABM data firms that can help you run some pilot programs to test ideas, but that means you need to have all the operations, processes, and workflow in place to execute on them with sales. This method is used if you already have an a priori segmentation model in mind.

d. If you have good data and a couple of hotshot analysts or a nearby university to grab some graduate students, they can use clustering algorithms and regression analysis on your own data and unlock some great insights.

e. Using data mining and analysis is a mirror, so it can create a model for you to understand and use in activation, but it's based on the customer data you provide, thus, the customer base you already have.

f. The limitation is that because it's a mirror, you may miss important segments entirely.

g. You aren't really listening to customers; you are listening to the data. It's important to follow up with some of your insights and assumptions using customer groups, advisory boards, or mini focus groups that you recruit to fit your segments to get colorful feedback and deeper insights.

Big Guns

You can engage a specialized research firm to do this for you as a custom research project, but it is the more expensive option. Buyer beware, there are very few market research firms that do customer needs–based segmentation well. Many will claim to, but over the years I've learned that they can get the data, but the analysis isn't always that great and ends up being hard to apply. However, there are some great benefits to hiring an outside firm if your company can afford it, such as a model that is more statistically valid if that's a crucial for success. It sometimes helps with change management and company adoption to have an outside consultant come in. You will need a triple-digit budget, though, so be prepared.

Pure methods involve a two-phase approach using both quantitative and qualitative research and analysis. This works well for complex, global companies, but it's not for everyone. If you will be making multimillion-dollar bets and can afford it, by all means, spend the money! But not every company can do this, especially small and growing ones.

YOUR SEGMENTATION MODEL
DEFINES HOW YOU COMPETE

Knowing your core segments defines how you want to compete and sets the context for how to position yourself. With a clear segmentation model, you can educate your buyers, set traps for your competition, decrease your CAC, and increase your ROI on marketing. Also, the product teams can use segment-specific feedback to prioritize their roadmap and not just respond to the latest customer issue. Who doesn't want that?

Start-ups and growth-stage companies tend to have a better idea about what customer segments they are focused on. As a company ages, it is easy to lose touch with who your segments are and how they are evolving if you aren't paying attention, especially if the primary focus is new customer/user acquisition versus customer fit. No matter what age your company is, it's important that market segmentation be a living framework in your planning cycle that evolves with you as your customer needs shift and change.

Segmentation can also be invaluable in a transaction. After a potential buyer looks at everything the bankers and quants will give them, analyze the numbers, and look at churn data, they will seek answers to deeper questions such as:

- What's the market need? How big is the addressable market?

- How many active customers do you have? What are they using, and why?

- What's the potential expansion opportunity? What would they buy? Is it in the roadmap?

- How many are loyal? Why do they leave? Where do they go?

- What drives the most customer value? Can pricing or monetization be optimized?

You may be able to answer all or some of these questions at an anecdotal level, a high level, or a product level, but by implementing marketing segmentation as an overall business discipline, you can answer these questions with much more fidelity and confidence. The real benefit, though, is that because you use such a model, you are engaging with customers on these questions in the first place. This means you will have far more precise data (and great customer examples) to share with a potential buyer than you would otherwise. If you play your cards right, you might even be able to get customer quotes and testimonials more easily, which go a long way in a transaction.

Summary

Setting your strategic playbook and defining a customer needs–based segmentation model is the basis for setting your course to the intended destination. It sets context for conditions you face and how you will compete. As you assess the wind and currents to navigate effectively, understanding your unique customer segment based on your path helps you make focused decisions about product development, marketing strategies, and positioning for the long haul and keeps you from reacting to every squall that comes along that may divert you.

By prioritizing segments, you can divide your journey into stages that help you better manage the course effectively and feel less compelled to take on every customer need all at once. Each segment represents a stage of your marketing strategy, and you can tailor your messaging, use cases, and offers to each segment's unique needs and preferences as it evolves over time. Staging it this way helps you allocate your resources efficiently and focus on the segments with the highest potential for success, given where you are starting from.

By being mindful in how you plot your course, you can achieve both focus and flexibility to navigate successfully and reach your desired destination.

You can get a great foundation for a strategy by (1) deciding on a strategy playbook based on where your company is and what its challenges are, and (2) applying a customer needs–based segmentation model.

➜ To help you choose a path, there are useful frameworks based on proven methods for setting investment priorities that potential buyers in a future transaction will understand.

➜ Having a customer needs–based segmentation model helps act as an organizing principle across functions and should be adopted as a business practice.

➜ Combining these two elements into a strategy will put you in the best position in a transaction for rationalizing priorities and understanding your customers and your market.

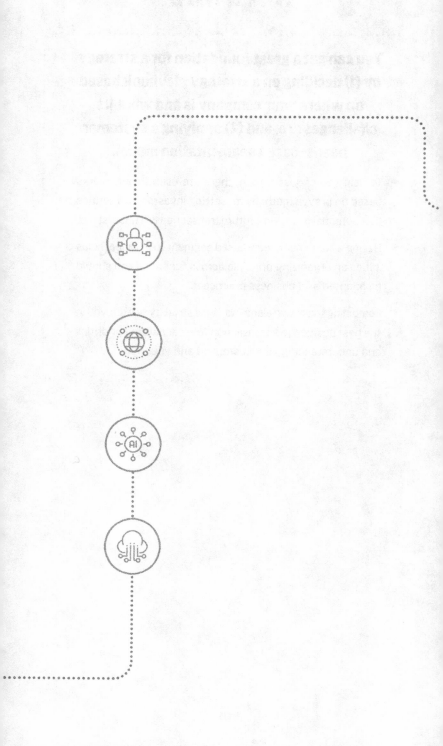

CHAPTER 6

UNITY

NOTHING TESTS UNITY MORE THAN CHAOS.

We were sailing in Greece in August, and between enduring the oppressive heat, wrestling tourists for partial views of ancient and unrecognizable rocks, and dodging the violent moods of the Meltemi, both our nerves and patience were just as fried as our noses. To escape the abuse of the local wind conditions, we found a lonely inlet to share with a luxury yacht already secured and successfully resisting the wind at the beam.

It took us some time to agree on a plan for the two of us to do a Med mooring, which is essentially a three-person job. We dropped the anchor and backed in with full engines in reverse to hold the position once the anchor bit down. We got the two duffel bags out that held the one hundred meters of mooring line, fifty meters each. Then my husband jumped off the back of the boat with the end of the line and swam for shore. My job was to (1) feed the line off the port quarter so it didn't get caught in the propeller (since we were in reverse) as he swam to find a rock to secure it to, and (2) mind the helm at the starboard side to adjust the engines to keep the boat straight. Did I mention it was a three-person job?

Then as it is with sailing, the unexpected happened. First, the wind accelerated at the beam and began to pivot our boat, firmly on the anchor, toward the yacht beside us. I dashed to the helm to make the adjustment, but we were already drifting, so the best I could do was slow the inevitable. As the skipper atop the dazzling teak vessel beside us gave me a scowl only a Viking would appreciate, I scrambled back to check the line. Our boat was drifting away quickly as my husband began scaling the jagged rocks, so he would need a lot more line than the expected first fifty meters. Then I discovered that the opening on the second duffel (holding the second half of the line) was tangled in a knot, and I couldn't release more line that he desperately needed to secure the boat. With the boat's slow but deliberate drift into an insurance claim, the absolute priority in that moment was to get my husband more line and sacrifice the duffel bag.

At shore and helpless, I could read his frustration and confusion as I suddenly vanished into the boat without a word. I grabbed scissors from inside and ran to the back with the boat, freed more line from the bag, and quickly secured it to the cleat just in time for him to lasso the loop over the peak of the boulder he had been clinging to. Crisis averted as I realized we were within just a couple of meters of the yacht beside us, with a tidy line of eight sets of eyes gazing at us in contempt.

So much here went wrong but could have been so much worse, especially if we started shouting at each other over the wind or micromanaging each other. This situation was a great reminder that we took the time to make a plan and shared the same goal. We had different jobs at that moment and had to trust each other to make the right decisions in a rapidly evolving situation. There was no time for discussion or debate; there was only time for execution. I had to free the line, and he had to lasso the rock. Same goal, different objective.

Let's face it, running a software company today is managing chaos on a good day. The unexpected always happens. This is what makes the idea of radical unity so critical.

The following are four fundamentals to radical unity across GTM:

1. Unity of effort with delegated authority

2. Aligned opportunity commit targets

3. Aligned and equitable incentives

4. Unified view of the customer journey

Creating Radical Unity with Delegated Authority

Radical unity means shared mission and effort, but it also allows swift decisions at the point of action. Your entire GTM motion (sales, marketing, customer success/services) needs to have unity of effort, but in some cases, each area of the business has different ways of achieving the goals. For example, marketing's traditional job has been to create markets and demand by nurturing a positive position and reputation for the company, attracting and educating prospects, and helping create customer loyalty. Sales has traditionally been responsible for converting that demand into customers and, in some cases, upselling and expanding existing accounts. The role of customer success is to ensure value, increase loyalty, and in some cases, deliver renewals (depending on your structure). Same goals, different objectives, different experiences, different incentives, different leaders, different teams, different tactics, and different decisions—when these functions align, it can be a powerful combination, but it requires radical unity without unneccessary debates and second-guessing each other.

Radical unity is not just a decent business discipline. For a future buyer in a transaction, what they want to see is that you are demonstrating focus and have full command of your GTM motion. They will want evidence that people are being held accountable and that no space exists for pipeline leakage, so sorting out the marketing, sales, and success alignment is critical. When they form their investment thesis, they want to spend money to see you grow more, not spend time and effort getting the business aligned and set up on a modern GTM engine.

Once radical unity is achieved, it's up to each functional leader to be accountable for execution while also having the decision authority to make tactical changes as the situation evolves, with urgency. This means that each function needs to trust one another to do their part, and each function needs to do their part no matter what.

Remember that you are on a quest to defeat half measures as you sail toward greatness, or a transaction, so I'm sure this advice seems obvious. In practice, however, while decision authority is amply provided to leaders in sales, support, development, and finance, in marketing it's a mixed bag. Do you often second-guess or challenge decision authority when it comes to this function? Is it trust, or is it your perception of competency?

Trying to solve this inconsistency in decision authority by forcing strange reporting structures such as nesting marketing into sales or creating matrixed decision-making is futile. One of the biggest dangers of not giving functional leaders appropriate autonomy is that it can lead to inefficiencies and delays in decision-making, as more people seek broader circles of collaboration and approval for even minor decisions. This can slow down the pace of execution and lead to missed opportunities. Remember, functional leaders are often the most knowledgeable about their specific areas of expertise and are better equipped to make informed decisions, and this is no different in marketing. By not empowering them to make decisions, you may miss out on the benefits of their expertise and risk making uninformed or misguided decisions without the proper context. It can also lead to frustration and disengagement and ultimately affect the overall performance and success of the business.

Now that that's out of the way, let's get to the heart of the matter and explore the following four ways you can get radical unity across your GTM: opportunity commit targets, proper incentives, buyer's journey, and a shared customer experience methodology.

Aligned Opportunity Commit Targets

Most companies do a great job of setting quotas for closed deals and dollars with their sales teams. If there is a shortfall in any given quarter that needs to be made up for in another area, both sales and marketing are asked for ways to help make up for the gap. The problem is that this is like learning how to plug a hole in your boat while it's already sinking! Not the best time for new brainstorming. This should have been well thought out as part of your strategic plan. Furthermore, everything marketing does affects the future, not the now. This makes in-quarter and often next-quarter marketing impossible to have an impact on.

The typical rule of thumb is to go into every quarter with a three to four times pipeline, depending on your sales opportunity-to-close rate. This is the basic method most software companies use to think about whether they can meet their numbers. Depending on a company's data quality and maturity in using that data to look two to four rolling quarters out as a combined marketing and sales team, it's still a reactive way to manage potential shortfalls. Often, there is fidelity on where the sales shortfall is and what reps aren't making their numbers, but it's rare that a CMO and sales leader can sit down and pinpoint what precise levers to turn to secure a particular outcome on any given day because of some of the system and data challenges most companies still have.

On the marketing front, there's usually an exercise that happens in the planning stage where marketing is asked to drive some percentage of revenue—between 15 and 50 percent, depending on the type of software service it is. Those with more complex sales cycles (more decision-makers, bigger deal sizes, etc.) or the earlier the product or service is in the product or market maturity life cycle, the lower the number. The more transactional or commercial the buyer's journey is, the higher the number.

Let's talk about how to get everyone aligned behind all the revenue targets. To do this, I will illustrate an example of a basic subscription model. How you think about this framework will depend on your own business and what teams you expect to drive which revenue streams.

The example I will cover next is for a company looking at revenue targets of $500 million with multiple products and an existing customer base, but a simplified version can be used for a smaller or growth-stage company. The main point is to make sure everyone is aligned with the right targets, and this model gives you a framework for how you may want to think about it.

The core idea is that every team within the GTM motion needs to have an *opportunity commit number* by product or service, including net new, expansion, and renewals.

Annual Targets	YR GOALS			
Revenue Assumptions	$ 500,000,000.00	MKT>BDR	BDR CC	PRODUCT
Installed Base Upsells Prod A	10%	10%	0%	0%
Installed Base Upsells Product B	35%	40%	30%	10%
Installed Base Upsells Product C	35%	40%	20%	10%
Installed Base Upsells Product D	10%	0%	10%	0%
Installed Base Upsells Product E	10%	0%	0%	0%
Net New A	20%	0%	0%	0%
Net New B	30%	30%	20%	0%
Net New C	20%	30%	30%	0%
Net New D	5%	0%	10%	0%
Net New E	5%	0%	0%	0%
Net New CHANNEL	20%	0%	0%	0%
Total		$ 124,000,000	$ 83,500,000	$ 24,500,000
Total Bookings %	200%	24.80%	16.70%	4.90%
Marketing % Target	42%			
Revenue Amounts		MKT>BDR	BDR CC	PRODUCT
Installed Base Upsells Prod A		$ 3,500,000	$ -	$ -
Installed Base Upsells Product B		$ 49,000,000	$ 36,750,000	$ 12,250,000
Installed Base Upsells Product C		$ 49,000,000	$ 24,500,000	$ 12,250,000
Installed Base Upsells Product D		$ -	$ 3,500,000	$ -
Installed Base Upsells Product E		$ -	$ -	$ -
Net New A		$ -	$ -	$ -
Net New B		$ 13,500,000	$ 9,000,000	$ -
Net New C		$ 9,000,000	$ 9,000,000	$ -
Net New D		$ -	$ 750,000	$ -
Net New E		$ -	$ -	$ -
Net New CHANNEL		$ -	$ -	$ -
Number of Deals	ASP	MKT>BDR	BDR CC	PRODUCT
Installed Base Upsells Prod A	$ 200,000	17.5	0.0	0.0
Installed Base Upsells Product B	$ 100,000	490.0	367.5	122.5
Installed Base Upsells Product C	$ 50,000	980.0	490.0	245.0
Installed Base Upsells Product D	$ 20,000	0.0	175.0	0.0
Installed Base Upsells Product E	$ 75,000	0.0	0.0	0.0
Net New A	$ 200,000	0.0	0.0	0.0
Net New B	$ 150,000	90.0	60.0	0.0
Net New C	$ 50,000	180.0	180.0	0.0
Net New D	$ 75,000	0.0	10.0	0.0
Net New E	$ 25,000	0.0	0.0	0.0
Net New CHANNEL	$ 15,000	0.0	0.0	0.0
Total Closed Deals by OPP Source		1757.5	1282.5	367.5

Figure 6.1

Example purposes only: opportunity commit modeling.

This example shows how a multi-product company can take a $500 million top-down revenue target and apply it to both land and expand motions across the various teams. This company has an established installed base and wants to grow net new conservatively. It has multiple use cases and sales teams aligned by sub-segments of the market. It is in a market that requires targeting and human engagement in the sales process (more technical buyers, better qualifica-

OPPORTUNITY COMMITS - Closed Won						TOTAL	
STRAT	ENT	SME	VERT	CSS	PARTNERS	$	500,000,000.00
90%	0%	0%	0%	0%	0%		
0%	20%	0%	0%	0%	0%		
0%	0%	30%	0%	0%	0%	$	350,000,000.00
0%	0%	0%	0%	90%	0%		
0%	0%	0%	100%	0%	0%		
100%	0%	0%	0%	0%	0%		
0%	40%	0%	0%	0%	10%		
0%	0%	40%	0%	0%	0%	$	150,000,000
0%	0%	0%	90%	0%	0%		
0%	0%	0%	0%	100%	0%		
0%	0%	0%	0%	0%	100%		
61,500,000	$ 42,500,000	$ 48,750,000	$ 41,750,000	$ 39,000,000	$ 34,500,000	$	500,000,000
12.30%	8.50%	9.75%	8.35%	7.80%	6.90%		100%

STRAT	ENT	SME	VERT	CSS	PARTNERS	Total Revenue by GTM
31,500,000	$ -	$ -	$ -	$ -	$ -	$ 35,000,000
-	$ 24,500,000	$ -	$ -	$ -	$ -	$ 122,500,000
-	$ -	$ 36,750,000	$ -	$ -	$ -	$ 122,500,000
-	$ -	$ -	$ -	$ 31,500,000	$ -	$ 35,000,000
-	$ -	$ -	$ 35,000,000	$ -	$ -	$ 35,000,000
30,000,000	$ -	$ -	$ -	$ -	$ -	$ 30,000,000
-	$ 18,000,000	$ -	$ -	$ -	$ 4,500,000	$ 45,000,000
-	$ -	$ 12,000,000	$ -	$ -	$ -	$ 30,000,000
-	$ -	$ -	$ 6,750,000	$ -	$ -	$ 7,500,000
-	$ -	$ -	$ -	$ 7,500,000	$ -	$ 7,500,000
-	$ -	$ -	$ -	$ -	$ 30,000,000	$ 30,000,000

STRAT	ENT	SME	VERT	CSS	Referrals	Total Deals by GTM
157.5	0.0	0.0	0.0	0.0	0.0	175
0.0	245.0	0.0	0.0	0.0	0.0	1225
0.0	0.0	735.0	0.0	0.0	0.0	2450
0.0	0.0	0.0	0.0	1575.0	0.0	1750
0.0	0.0	0.0	466.7	0.0	0.0	467
150.0	0.0	0.0	0.0	0.0	0.0	150
0.0	120.0	0.0	0.0	0.0	30.0	300
0.0	0.0	240.0	0.0	0.0	0.0	600
0.0	0.0	0.0	90.0	0.0	0.0	100
0.0	0.0	0.0	0.0	300.0	0.0	300
0.0	0.0	0.0	0.0	0.0	2000.0	2000
307.5	365.0	975.0	556.7	1875.0	2030.0	9517

Figure 6.1 *(continued)*

tion). Again, it is easy to adjust if your company is more commercial or product-led. I kept it simple; you can do one by ARR, ACV, or a blended number. I just kept this one generic revenue target.

If you are leading a start-up or a smaller company, this specific example is overkill, but the concept may be useful for how to think about it as your company grows. The point is, *everyone is responsible for bringing opportunities in.*

Now that you have set targets across the functions, you need to apply your funnel model to determine the right conversion rates. You can apply B2B best practice conversion rates based on the GTM funnel model you decide on. You can use average conversion rates based on B2B SaaS software best practices.

Figure 6.2

Examples of GTM funnels.

It may be that you don't have visibility into conversion rates or have data discrepancies because of lack of consistent telemetry. If this is the case, there are process and system improvements to address, which will be covered more deeply in chapter 9, "Efficiency."

When doing the math on the opportunity modeling, you need to use conversion targets across the funnel. Your funnel might differ whether you are a high-touch model or low-touch/transactional model or you aspire for a product-led funnel (which you may recall from section 1).

The marketing team can use the targets set in the opportunity commit modeling to calculate their marketing targets across the full mix of channels. A traditional planning methodology is the waterfall method (see figure 6.3); however, its effectiveness is only useful if there is operational and data reporting maturity within the company. While this is the most basic, well-understood model used, it has its limitations, but it can get you in the ballpark to determine if you are investing the right amount in activation.

WATERFALL METHOD

FUNNEL ASSUMPTIONS	
Company Annual Revenue Target	$ 500,000,000
Average Selling Price for Marketing Commits (Blended)	$108,000
Marketing Led Percentage of Deals	32%
Sales Opportunity to Close	30%
Sales Qualified Opportunities/In Pipeline (with or without close date)	50%
Conversion from MQL to Sales Accepted Leads/Meetings	60%
Conversion from Response to Marketing Qualified Leads	20%
Average Response Rate	3%

ENGAGEMENTS
5,287,222

VISITORS
158,617

CONTACTS
31,723

MQLs
19,034

SALs
9,517

2,855	Marketing Led Deals
$ 308,350,800	Estimated Contribution
$ 231,263,100	In Year (75%)

BUDGET ASSUMPTIONS	ENGAGEMENT	MQL	
ACTIVATION	5,287,222	31,723	
CPL	$ 15	$ 100	
TOTALS	$ 79,308,333	$3,172,333	ROI %
Total Activation Budget Required	$ 82,480,667		273.8
Marketing Activation Budget Required as a Percentage of Revenue	16%		
Industry Benchmarks Vary Based on Situation and response/conversion rates	10%-30%		

ROI Formula: Subtracting your total investment in marketing from your total revenue, then dividing the number by the total investment. Multiply the resulting number by 100 to get your ROI percentage. The higher the percentage, the better your ROI.

Figure 6.3
The traditional waterfall method.

Marketing may use a method such as this to outline assumptions for conversion rates and cost per activity based on what they have seen historically or on the best practice targets you may have set in the previous illustration. Your marketing team may use a different model and adjust it based on the conversion rates and cost-per-lead targets they are tracking to.

You will notice the number of deals as a percentage was used instead of percentage of revenue because the deals are what marketing can track to from where they are standing as a leading indicator. This is important to understand because the tendency is to track backward up the funnel at the end of a quarter (or end of the year). This never satisfies anyone because (1) few companies of this size are at the point where they can attribute and link every customer touchpoint as they travel through the buyer's journey, so this number is typically underreported, and (2) it's done well after the sales cycle is over, so it's a lagging performance metric not aligned to making more agile decisions much earlier.

You will notice in this model that the total amount contributed will be larger than the amount calculated in the initial opportunity commit calculation. This is because you will have to account for marketing efforts being at least a quarter out, and the sales cycle may get pushed out as marketing funnel is nurtured in that year. It's also useful to account for existing pipeline, as this model assumes blank slate marketing funnel.

Now this is only for the marketing-led contribution. Of course, marketing helps support all pipeline activity. I would argue 100 percent of the deals are marketing supported in some way, shape, or form. The point of it is, you can start to get the marketing team's head wrapped around how they contribute to the bigger efforts and get them more tightly aligned to sales.

Also, I know what you are thinking: "OMG, 16 percent of revenue on marketing?" Yes, it's entirely possible you are underspending, and it is historically the case in B2B software. We will cover marketing investment in later chapters, so don't worry, we'll get there.

> ### ⚠ WARNING ON THE WATERFALL METHOD
>
> As I mentioned, there are limitations to the waterfall method, but it's a good place to start. It is useful in planning to determine if you are in the ballpark to achieve the targets with the budget you have. It doesn't typically work for tracking metrics in real time in year one (because you have no historical data for actual conversion rates). Companies that get this to work for tracking and metrics are those with the most mature systems and data platforms, so it's best to have realistic expectations on how to use it.
>
> Also, this model assumes a very linear customer journey, which isn't how customers engage, as we've discussed. It also assumes you can track attribution, which any CMO will tell you is hard.
>
> The best way to apply the model is to use it to ballpark a budget, track CAC, and track how your GTM teams are collaborating to get deals done. By tracking conversions at each stage, they can identify the operational problems that get in the way of great results.

Now that everyone has their numbers, there is an aspect of change management involved in getting everyone to align with them. Often, the sales team has a hard time with this activity because they are typically used to being given a number, and it's up to them to figure out how to deliver the number. Taking it to the next level and contemplating which products or services they expect to drive may create some resistance. However, it's worth it if only to understand what marketing is accountable for as a partner to them. Also, for companies with multiple products, it helps everyone make sure the targets are right for certain aspects of the business that may need to demonstrate aggressive growth versus just everyone trying to pull their numbers from anywhere.

What you want is all teams working together toward the same targets and people who are highly motivated to deliver results. For example, a big pain point in marketing is that often salespeople aren't required to follow up on marketing-generated leads, even though they want marketing to create more pipeline. I've always found that to be an odd problem. Sales will often accuse marketing of not generating enough leads but then fail to follow up on leads in their workflow. On the other side, marketing is being asked to account for contributions to pipeline, but they aren't tied to any hard numbers.

Attribution seeks to determine what pipeline marketing was responsible for and where that came from and ultimately seeks to define performance metrics across marketing that are granular and measurable. While no single attribution model is universally applicable or accurate for every business, each model has its strengths and limitations, and the choice of the model depends on the business goals, available data, and your own business dynamics. However, knowing what the targets are, no matter what model you use, is the basis for setting marketing targets with teeth.

A couple of brief points on marketing attribution: First, if the data, systems, and processes aren't linked to your funnel model from end to end, you will not have a good idea what pipeline marketing is driving versus sales. Second, the numbers that get reported are often based on how the attribution model is defined, not which part of the marketing mix is working best. It's likely many engagements contributed to a customer win, so the attribution modeling really needs to account for the full journey of the buyer, not the last touch before they converted to a meeting. Finally, companies can spend more money trying to measure and map attribution than they spend driving demand and leads, so don't fall into this analysis trap.

It's better to pick some proxy measures across the customer experience and refine them over time than to over-engineer metrics tracking. My advice is to start with proxy measures that create focus, like trial conversions, for example, then invest in fixing the end-to-end customer experience and addressing operational and data problems versus wasting money trying to track metrics based on a broken operation.

> **Have you ever wondered why marketing doesn't want to take a number?**
>
> **It's not because they are afraid of accountability; it's because typically, there is no agreed-upon set of unified goals or because attribution targets are impossible to track given the conditions of the data, processes, and systems.**

Aligned and Equitable Incentives

Ah … Tahiti. Everyone loves President's Club—everyone in sales. As the customer journey gets more digital and as marketing moves closer to sales, it's important to rethink incentives overall across your GTM. If you have adjusted this already, you are a step ahead, but if you haven't, it's time!

For marketing to be effective, it needs to be more directly tied (and incentivized) to achieving the targets it controls. What's typical today is that bonus structures for marketing leadership are aligned to some portion of company goals and some portion of personal goals. The problem is that the personal goals are much more qualitative in nature, and there are aspects of the company goals that aren't in their direct control. Instead, the bonus structure can be used to reward marketing leaders for meeting trackable conversion targets based on an agreed-upon set of opportunity commitments against some attribution proxy.

I don't feel like I'm going out on a limb here to say that marketing people prefer accountability and would love to participate in incentives for reaching targets that they don't broadly enjoy. This is especially true in the world of SaaS, where users, trials, and conversions are happening more directly online.

The state of your data and engagement-to-close process notwithstanding, you can never achieve nirvana if you don't start by getting commitments across sales and marketing for who is responsible for driving which type of pipeline and engagement in the customer journey. Incentives are the easiest decision to make here. How to track and measure it can come after you define targets and set incentives. It's amazing what process gaps get filled when people are motivated. You know this because you already see what happens when you give salespeople a quota.

With today's modern tools, it's possible to track customer interactions, conversions, and certain attribution metrics by channel even if your engine isn't fully modernized yet. This will help give credit for these interactions to the right teams and incentivize the proper behavior. To solve attribution and incentivize the right behavior, you must nail the customer journey and design metrics to fit the function that supports each engagement. Having a customer-oriented approach to setting targets based on engagement is so much more useful than using conversion metrics alone. This can only be done through a unified view of the customer journey.

Also, there's an opportunity to offer incentives to a broader group of marketing people who directly contribute to sales programs or plays by being able to participate in similar sales performance incentive plan. For instance, if there's a shortfall in the commercial space for a certain product and marketing runs a program to generate demand, there may also be a target for driving immediate in-quarter opportunities. It doesn't necessarily mean increasing the comp structure. With blurring lines, it might just be time to rethink your incentive program across GTM as a whole.

In any sales organization, it's important to make sure that the incentive structure is aligned with the shared pipeline objectives. Otherwise, you run the risk of having a sales team that's more focused on their own personal quotas in the quarter than on other activities that help everyone nurture their future pipeline. Instead, try tying a portion of the sales team's commission to closed or won deals that originated from marketing or adding accelerators if a certain number of marketing opportunities progress, even if it's in future quarters. This ensures that both teams are working together toward the common goal of closing deals, and it also rewards the sales team for their efforts in converting marketing leads.

Unified View of the Customer's Journey

The customer experience is now the most important battle-ground for businesses. Depending on what study you look at (and there are many, so feel free to research it on your own), data shows roughly 70 percent of customers are willing to pay more for a better customer experience. Also, roughly 60 percent of customers say that they would switch brands if they had a poor customer experience. With such high stakes, it's clear that businesses need to invest in creating a great customer experience for these reasons alone.

But what a mess! While you have access to more data than ever before about your customers, somehow having a unified understanding of them remains ironically elusive. Unfortunately, many businesses suffer from poor customer telemetry because of siloed systems in which customer data exists. This means that while you may be able to track individual pieces of data, such as page views or sales numbers, many pieces remain separate from one another instead of being connected into a single comprehensive picture of the customer journey and overall happiness with your brand. It can be difficult to get an accurate assessment of how successful your efforts are and where improvements should be made to create better experiences for customers overall in a way that matters most to them.

Here are some of the biggest challenges in delivering a customer-led business model:

CHALLENGE 1: INTERNAL PROCESS DEFINES CUSTOMER EXPERIENCE

One of the most common challenges faced by businesses when it comes to customer experience is managing consistency across engagement channels. Customers expect a consistent experience, whether they are interacting with your company digitally or in person. The problem typically is that each function might be a business owner's particular set of tactics or systems that automate processes within that experience. For example, marketing might own the demand generation activities for all campaigns and digital programs and the marketing automation that happens to support those programs in the marketing automation system. They may also be responsible for the web experience for the acquisition. So far, so good.

But then purchasing might own the transaction experience (if you sell your software online or need a purchasing engine to set up a free trial, for example). Depending on how your purchasing system works, it could send a confirmation email that was set up by someone from finance. Or sales may own the opportunity-to-close process, where engagement is managed through a sales-managed CRM system and scripts are built by the sales support teams. Then the customer onboarding or support content and pages might be owned through a customer portal or through other means by the customer success or education teams, who may sit in a different group depending on how big your company is.

For companies starting out, it's easy to create a unified end-to-end customer journey to unite the engagements as the systems and processes are being defined and adopted. But for companies that have been around for a while, process, engagement, and systems silos may be tough to break out of if there isn't a deliberate method to map the customer journey from the outside in and figure out the best way to get consistency across all touchpoints.

Mapping the ideal customer journey and what changes need to be made internally is tedious and can be politically charged in some cases where old ways of doing things are challenged. It shouldn't be taken lightly since it can truly be a transformative initiative. However, it creates a huge value driver if done quickly enough to have an impact on customer loyalty, which matters in a transaction as well as in any sustained business.

CHALLENGE 2: NOT TRACKING METRICS PROPERLY

Another challenge faced by businesses when it comes to customer experience is not tracking metrics properly. Without proper tracking metrics such as net promoter score for loyalty and referability, customer satisfaction score for point-in-time interactions, or customer engagement score for product usage or disengagement, it's impossible to get an accurate picture of how well you are delivering on your customers' expectations or areas where improvements may be needed.

To track these metrics accurately, it's important to think of customer metrics as a system of tracking the customer experience across their journey, not as one finite customer measure across the board. One metric may be the proxy you give people bonuses on, but to get a full picture of what is going on and how to drive the right internal behaviors, it takes multiple layers of tracking in most cases and must be looked at holistically.

Now that you've defined your methodology and have been holistic in looking at the outcomes you are trying to drive, it's time to hold people accountable. Not only should you set KPIs, but it's also time to develop action plans for each metric and assign responsibility for achieving the goal, outlining the resources needed, and creating a timeline for implementation. Be sure to involve all departments in this process, as everyone has an impact on customer experience outcomes. This will also help ensure that each team understands its role in contributing toward achieving the desired result.

Finally, it's important to hold executives accountable for driving results. This means setting clear expectations about what needs to be achieved and continually monitoring progress against the action plans and the targets. It also helps to reward employees who exceed expectations or go above and beyond in their efforts to deliver great customer experiences. By rewarding excellent performance, you can encourage others to strive for excellence and drive better results overall.

PROBLEM 3: SILOED CUSTOMER TELEMETRY

Everyone wants a single view of the customer, but it can be hard to achieve and maintain. CRM systems were adopted decades ago to help create a better understanding of customers but are used mostly by sales to close deals. For many software companies, CRM became a functionally owned system to help sales manage their accounts and their in-quarter pipeline. Since nature abhors a void, other systems have popped up to solve other parts of the customer journey and been adopted by customer success and services teams, and marketing uses a trove of martech tools to plug into the CRM, but we all still have a way to go.

Having clear customer telemetry across the end-to-end experience is critical to understanding who they are, how they are interacting with you, what their sentiment is, where they get stuck in the buying process, how long they spend on the different web or product pages, what problems they are having most when using your product, what value they are getting based on usage, and what upsell or cross-sell opportunities might be on the table for you. By tracking this data in a unified way, you can gain insight into how effective you are as a business at serving your customers in a way that will make or break you as a company.

The solution is not only the consolidation of customer telemetry data but also unifying the end-to-end processes and handshakes between functions that create the best user experience, not the best internal reporting. By integrating disparate sources of information into one view so that everyone can access accurate customer telemetry, people are empowered to make better decisions in real time about how to optimize engagements in this fast-paced digital world. Doing so will not only provide more efficient tracking capabilities but also ensure that customers have a positive experience when engaging with your business.

The customer experience is never a straight line, and customers can skip around, which is why it's so important to align across your business to deliver consistency across touchpoints. It provides a method for mapping internal workflow and breaking down silos because it requires the organization to understand what actions need to be taken for a potential customer to progress through the stages as they travel in and out of your universe. Once there is an internal shared definition of the buyer journey, you can start to align the goals of sales, marketing, product, and customer success for each customer segment so that everyone is working toward aligned objectives.

What follows is a basic overview of the different categories of the journey. Mapping it out is certainly more detailed and complex depending on the market segment and the types of buyers and decision-makers that are involved. There are many resources and methods that can help you map this out, and it's highly likely you've already adopted such an approach.

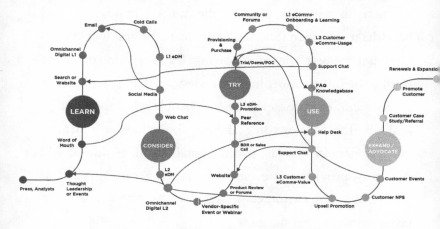

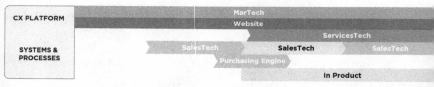

Figure 6.4

Mapping out the complex customer journey provides internal alignment and a better customer experience.

LEARN/CONSIDER

The potential customer seeks to learn more about the problem or need that they have. At this stage, customers aren't ready to buy anything, but they are starting to do research to scope out their problem. Engaging with prospects at this stage is critical because you can help mold the requirements and become a trusted source of information. Your role is to help educate them on your unique point of view about how to look at the problem.

TRY

The goal is to get people to try and get hooked on your products as fast as possible. They are comparing different vendors and options and narrowing down their choices. It's at this stage that they are trying to understand different vendor approaches, the quality of the customer experience, types of features, and cost. Once they have compared different options and decided which one is best for them, it's easier to commit to something that comes in bite-size chunks versus swallowing a whole elephant. Here, software companies need to make it easy for potential customers to prove out a use case in a bounded way. Your role is to make the initial commitment to either use, purchase, or procure your solution easy and effortless.

USE

After the customer has committed to the initial service or free trial, there may be an activation, onboarding, or configuration phase. Arguably, this phase is critical and has become the do-or-die phase for the modern software buyer. This is where your customer success or service teams need to shine. Your role is to make onboarding and using your solution as simple and streamlined as possible.

EXPAND/ADVOCATE

Finally, in the retention stage, you work to keep customers engaged with your product or service after they've made a commitment to buy or use it. It's when the entire GTM team works together to make sure the customer sees the value of the product and is encouraged to expand usage (either with more modules, more users, or broader use cases or product modules). Aside from having happy customers who will buy more from you, happy customers are also powerful advocates for your company in the form of referrals that helps increase brand value, which ultimately impacts your valuation.

UNIFIED CUSTOMER EXPERIENCE MANAGEMENT

To properly engage with customers and prospects, your sales, marketing, and customer success teams need to take a multifaceted approach that touches on all stages of the customer journey but shouldn't be held captive by it either. Orienting around the journey has unifying power and ensures each function understands how they contribute to various customer touchpoints. More importantly, it helps deliver a seamless experience to your customers and prospects.

Customer experience management has become an essential business management methodology as sales, marketing, and success move closer together to deliver a customer-led model. Improving customer experiences can have a wide-ranging impact on growth, customer loyalty, and brand reputation. However, implementing a CX methodology across the functions needs to be a dedicated strategic initiative if it isn't already one.

> Do this right, and you will finally have a fully aligned sales and marketing team, and all the biggest internal debates will end.

RADICAL UNITY IS A NO-FAIL MISSION

If you are in any other quadrant than the leader's quadrant, as discussed in strategic playbooks (figure 5.1), especially in a down market, executing in unity is a no-fail mission.

This industry tends to be open and collaborative in the name of being agile, which can complicate how decisions get made or obscure accountability. Software companies can be a beautiful mess, but you will not get growth and scale by staying this way anymore, especially if a transaction is on the horizon. You have a finite amount of time to get your business in the best possible condition, so you must act with urgency to get all this squared away.

No-fail missions tend to have the following attributes:

1. They have clear objectives, and everyone understands the strategy to get there.

2. They have time sequences that are clear.

3. They have radical unity with delegated authority.

4. There is a higher risk tolerance in execution—people are allowed to make mistakes as long as they recover.

No-fail missions call for no-fail mission leadership that can answer the following questions: What are the specific goals, and how will you achieve them? How many opportunities and deals are needed, from whom, and by when? What tactics are required to achieve those targets, in what order, and at what cost? What risks (in cost, resources, and disruption) are you willing to take to succeed no matter what? Who is in command of the execution, and what decisions are they authorized to make? How will accountability and incentives be aligned to ensure success?

As a CEO, perhaps you have already answered these questions, but here are a few other things to consider when you think about radical unity as your no-fail mission. Surely you are using some of them already.

- Efforts must be harmonized across sales, marketing, product, and support functions, and everyone needs incentives, not just sales. Often, these types of change initiatives fail because people lower in the ranks understand them to be new obligations on top of what they are already doing, not a new way of prioritizing that might change what they are doing. By addressing incentives as you would with sales, people will quickly understand they must be dedicated to the outcomes.

- Every no-fail mission has an empowered strategic commander within each area who is expected to make decisions. Who is yours for marketing, and what accountability and autonomy are you prepared to give them?

- Market the mission and targets internally with great internal communication and change management. Doing this ups the ante on accountability and unity and sets the stage for situations that require swift and potentially polarizing decisions later. If everyone understands it's a no-fail mission, the team executing it will face less internal resistance to change—not to be confused with no resistance to change.

- Dedicate a customer experience transformation lead. There will be system and process changes that need to be made that no one is probably focused on today. Appointing a commander will help you get this going and oversee the strategy needed for technology, streamlined CX processes, unified data flow, insights, and metrics to deliver on the goals.

Especially in a transaction, you will want to be able to show that you drove intentional outcomes against these metrics, not just that you got lucky or were able to execute random acts of heroism. You will want to have evidence that you achieved the targets you set and that it can be done in a repeatable, scalable way. Also, you will need to show transparency in your customer experience and leading indicators of growth that everyone can understand. Finally, you want to have modern technology and workflow in place because financial buyers typically don't want to invest in getting that done. In fact, many of them have already burned on this one. Having modernized operations will make your business more attractive to potential buyers because their investment thesis will be based on investing on more product innovation and market exposure, not on fixing the plumbing.

Summary

During a sailing race, the crew on a sailboat is assigned to specific roles to ensure efficiency and aligned performance. The skipper is responsible for steering the boat and making strategic decisions during the race. The tactician provides guidance based on their analysis of wind patterns, competitors' positions, and racecourse conditions. Trimmers are responsible for adjusting the sails to optimize their shape and trim based on the wind conditions. The pitman controls lines, sheets, sail controls, and running rigging. The grinders operate winches to trim sails or control other lines that require significant physical effort. The navigator focuses on the boat's course and ensures the crew is aware of the race rules and regulations.

Each member plays their role, but they do it through radical unity, which requires coordination, teamwork, and communication. All crew members need to know the desired outcomes, play their positions, and orchestrate maneuvers in harmony.

Here are ways you can improve radical unity in your GTM:

- Set aligned opportunity commit targets so every GTM function understands who is accountable for driving different aspects of the revenue model.
- Armed with opportunity commit targets, marketing can create meaningful targets that the budget can support and has a method for tracking attribution through proxy metrics that help drive ongoing improvements.
- Reimagine incentives across marketing, sales, and customer success to get the outcomes you want holistically.
- Define a holistic customer experience that takes the focus off internal silos so GTM teams can focus on outcomes that drive the most value for your customers.
- By leveraging CX methods, you can massively increase internal alignment, deliver better customer value, and improve your multiples.
- Radical alignment is a no-fail mission, and there are practical ways to ensure success.

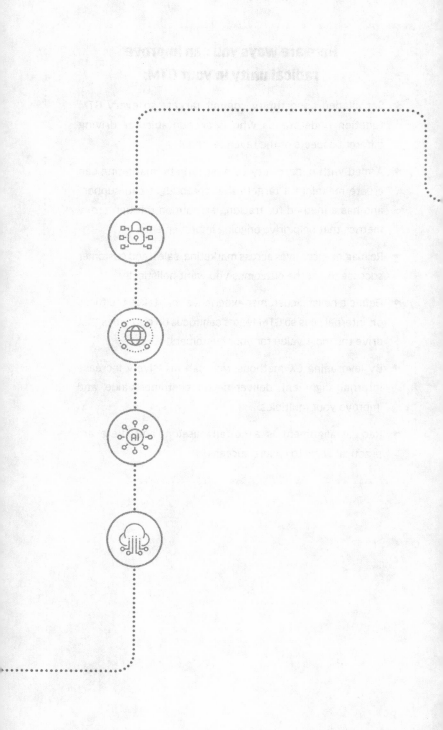

CHAPTER 7

REPUTATION

YOUR STARTING POSITION can determine the race.

Participating in regattas has taken years off my life, but it's just *so much fun*! The start is always two parts adrenaline and one part terror that's weirdly exhilarating and has me constantly shifting between "Woo-hoo!" and "We're all gonna die!" The boats are insanely close together and going way too fast, in my opinion. Fast, mind you, is probably really more like five miles per hour, but speed and distance dysmorphia appear to be side effects of sailing, I've found.

A favorable starting position is crucial to having a strategic advantage because you can get clear wind, avoid congestion, and get better access to desired areas of the course. Having that advantage means you have more options during the race because you are in a position of control and not reacting to the boats ahead of you. Also, it can provide a psychological advantage by boosting the crew's confidence, morale, and determination to win. Having a favorable starting position sets the tone for the entire race, assuming you can keep your wits in order and your lunch down before the starting horn blows.

There is only one tiny downside to winning: the expectations it puts on you to perform in the next race because now you have a reputation to uphold.

Whether you are competing in the Volvo Ocean Race or in a local beer can regatta, getting and holding your starting position is a huge advantage. The same is true for market positioning. Everyone wants a strong market position and knows the pressure of staying on top. I call this section *reputation* because it includes positioning for success, repositioning, and maintaining a positive reputation no matter what race you are in.

To compete successfully, you must set the rules for how you want to compete, capitalize on your strengths in a compelling way, and position yourself advantageously in relation to the other alternatives. Just as important is to consistently deliver on your promises to your customers, building lasting trust in your company that keeps them coming back. By positioning yourself strategically, you have a better chance of creating momentum and building a valuable brand reputation in the market.

Being purposeful about your market position and reputation is critical to creating the Power of Surge. Today, what people say about you becomes your position, regardless of what you say about yourself. This is why simply having product positioning alone isn't enough. How people brand you is based on their entire experience with you, not just the features of your code base, so you need to have a unique, compelling, and holistic value proposition.

> **And remember, you will have a market position whether you are deliberate or not, so it's best to be purposeful about it or risk your competitors creating one for you.**

What Is Positioning?

Simply put, positioning is a little spot you own in people's heads signifying you are interesting and different. For such a simple concept, it is fantastically hard to do. A great positioning strategy communicates where you compete and what you uniquely promise your customers as an end benefit (e.g., Southwest Airlines = efficient, friendly, no-frills air travel).

The key here is clearly communicating what your company stands for to a specific market segment that can be easily understood in seven seconds or less. When Southwest Airlines first came out, they didn't just say they flew airplanes; they positioned themselves as a cheap and easier option for people looking for no-BS regional flights versus the drama and overhead being offered by traditional airlines.

One example of a modern SaaS company with a compelling and unique positioning strategy is Slack. Slack is a messaging and collaboration platform, and when it first launched in 2013, there were a ton of other communication and collaboration platforms already in broad use. Slack decided to focus on being the go-to platform for tech professionals, mostly developers and tech users who wanted to collaborate inside and outside a company. This strategy proved immensely successful, as early users began signing up and evangelizing the product even more. Word of mouth quickly became one of Slack's most powerful tools for growth, allowing them to expand rapidly and build an engaged user base that extends well beyond their initial target market segment. They have now positioned themselves as the go-to platform for workplace communication and have built a loyal user base through their focus on ease of use and customization.

The lesson here is that what Slack offered wasn't necessarily different from alternatives in terms of the benefits it offered. It was focused and targeted on a specific segment of the market, which helped them build a broader appeal over time. Slack could have tried to be all things to all people, but it would have been much more difficult to get traction. By focusing on a beachhead where they could win, they were able to gain a broader appeal over time that would have otherwise been too difficult to achieve out of the gate.

> The critical point is that ideally, you should connect your market segmentation model to your positioning strategy. Positioning isn't just about communicating what you offer; it's about communicating it in a way that is relevant to a particular type of customer or user.

Key elements of a good positioning platform are surprisingly straightforward.

- **POV** (What is your view of the world as it relates to the situation or problem?)

- **CONTEXT** (How do you see the pain point and draw a line around the category you are in or category you are displacing?)

- **PRIMARY AUDIENCE** (Who is your target customer, and what are they seeking to solve?)

- **UNIQUE VALUE** (How do you describe your solution and your unique value proposition that no one else can claim?)

- **CLAIMS** (What is the outcome your customer will experience—your promise that makes up your reputation and what you will be known for?)

- **BENEFITS** (What benefits does the customer have from your claims, and describe how you are different from your competition or the leading competing alternative for achieving that benefit?)

- **REASONS TO BELIEVE** (Why should they believe you, and what proof points do you have to substantiate your claims and benefits?)

POV	Your view of the world as it pertains to the situation/problem		
Context	How you see the **pain point** for your primary audience and the **category** you are in		
Positioning	Who is the **primary audience** you serve and what they are seeking?	What do you deliver that's unique?	Why should the primary audience care; what's the **ultimate benefit**?

Message Pillars

Claims	Claim 1 (substantiates your positioning statement)	Claim 2 (substantiates your positioning statement)	Claim 3 (substantiates your positioning statement)
Benefits	What is the benefit of this claim?	What is the benefit of this claim?	What is the benefit of this claim?
Reasons to Believe	Proof points of claim	Proof points of claim	Proof points of claim

Figure 7.1

An example of a typical positioning framework.

Here's a litmus test for getting it right:

IS IT DIFFERENT FROM WHAT EVERYONE ELSE IS SAYING?

There's a lot of froth in software, so articulating how you are unique is critical.

IS IT RELEVANT TO THE PROSPECT/CUSTOMER PAIN POINT?

You need to connect your solution to why it matters to what customers are experiencing today.

IS IT BELIEVABLE COMING FROM YOU?

You can get aggressive in the creative execution of your positioning, but the nuts and bolts of it need to be grounded in something credible coming from you.

IS IT SUSTAINABLE?

Will this statement last years or just until your competitor comes up with a new feature set?

Many B2B software companies struggle to get this right, so let's explore why.

IS IT UNDERSTOOD IN 7 SECONDS OR LESS?

That's right, in a digital engagement, that's all the time you have. It's how long it takes someone to view your main homepage.

DON'T CONFUSE POSITIONING STRATEGY WITH MESSAGING.

Positioning is being able to articulate the one thing you want to be known for. It's the top of the pyramid for everything you rally your company around and squats on a unique place in someone's head.

Messaging is how you substantiate your positioning in the form of a claim. Many technology companies get wrapped up in how they describe features that they forget the messages are supposed to support your positioning strategy, not articulate everything under the sun.

1.) DON'T BE AFRAID OF SPECIFICITY.

The most common way companies fail to execute to good positioning is by not wanting to be too specific for fear of missing out on a broader set of opportunities. Remember, this is about setting your course so you can win! If you are everything to everyone, you are nothing to no one.

Don't worry. You can expand your focus as you grow, but you must start somewhere to be relevant and either gain a good beachhead or fortify a position in a space you must defend at all costs. The tighter your positioning is, the more uncomfortable it may make portions of your sales team. That's how you know it is good. If sales had it their way, there would be positioning statements for every customer under the sun, but that's called messaging and comes later.

2.) BE SPECIFIC TO THE TARGET AUDIENCE IN THE CONTEXT OF YOUR MARKET SEGMENTATION MODEL.

In the earlier section, we discussed the importance of a customer needs–based market segmentation model. The more precise you can get on thinking about your ideal customer in the context of the market segment you have prioritized, the better your positioning is. This is another way you can be uniquely specific and relevant in the market to a finite and targetable set of people.

3.) THIS IS BROADER THAN PRODUCT POSITIONING; THIS IS COMPANY POSITIONING.

In software, there is a DNA-level desire to focus on describing the product, what it does, and why it's interesting but resist your inner neanderthal. Your company sells a product but is more than the product! You offer an experience, a community, maybe certain add-on services, or best practices for easy onboarding; your people are awesome; or you have a great ecosystem with rockin' APIs. You get the idea. Chances are, in the world of software, there are at least twenty other companies that have a similar product to you, but what makes *you* the vendor to bet on? What do you want your reputation with customers to be? If you are successful, you will offer more than just one product, and you will have multiple product offerings with their own unique value propositions and even unique categories. You can cover all that in your level-two product messaging.

4.) COMMIT ALREADY!

As a marketer, it's heartbreaking to see a great positioning strategy get developed and agreed to only to be constantly tweaked and tuned based on anecdotal feedback here and there to the point where it's no longer recognizable. A company must commit and be disciplined in its use across all channels for a positioning strategy to pay off. The CMO must have the executive leadership team's commitment to that. If you keep evolving your positioning strategy, you are constantly moving the target and altering the ability to gain momentum. If you don't commit to what you stand for, how can you expect to ever stand for anything meaningful to customers?

Choosing a Positioning Strategy

In truth there are a finite number of positioning options in B2B software versus consumer products, which tend to be more emotion based. The positioning strategy option you chose should also align with your strategic marketing playbooks discussed in chapter 5 (refer to figure 5.2). Those playbooks are defensive, transitional, innovator, and leader, and they each offer stand-alone elements as well as transaction elements.

Based on what path you are on, it becomes much more clear which positioning option to pursue since the marketing strategy and positioning must support and align with what you are trying to accomplish. You can also apply the stand-alone versus transaction flavors, which are typically complementary and can be pursued without any material regret.

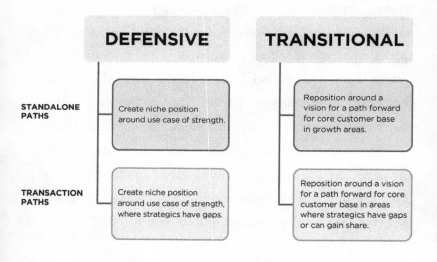

Figure 7.2

Examples of positioning options as a standalone
company or approaching a transaction.

DEFENSIVE: FOCUS ON YOUR NICHE

On this path you want to defend a territory to own the space, but you probably have limited budget and resources to fortify or reposition yourself in the market. Your marketing and sales activities need to be precision targeted and tightly aligned. You must focus on reducing churn and may even need to contract, shedding low-value customers or customers who drain resources because they aren't a good fit. This is where a tight positioning strategy, which clearly says who you are for and who you are not for, is helpful.

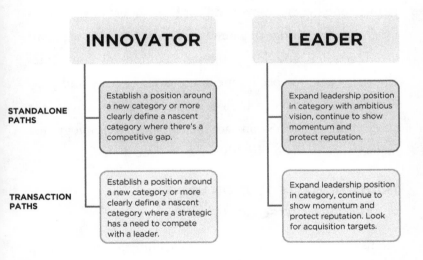

Figure 7.2 *(continued)*

Consider your target market segment and what unique attributes make up that bulk of that segment. Is there a particular use case they care most about or start with? Are they common types of companies (in a particular vertical industry or technical maturity)? Do they face specific and unique challenges because of compliance or regulations? Are they budget constrained, and can you offer the right fit for what they can afford?

If you are considering an eminent transaction, consider who your potential strategics are and what gaps they may have in their portfolio that you can augment. Are they trying to go down market with a simpler solution or upmarket with a full featured offering they can expand on? Does the use case you solve for give them a bridge or gateway into a new market segment?

DocuSign and Dropbox are examples of companies who kept true to specific niche use cases initially and grew into market leaders in their respective segments. Icertis is an example of a SaaS contract management technology that focuses specifically on healthcare as its core niche.

TRANSITIONAL: FOCUS ON YOUR PLATFORM/PORTFOLIO

In this scenario, you may be a legacy incumbent actively trying to protect your customer base. First and foremost, you need to keep and create affinity for the customers you have and not have them taken out from under your nose by someone else. Often, the churn happens due to a combination of product maturity and lack of customer awareness about the breadth of what you do. This can be the unintended consequence of some combination of your marketing team only focusing on net new logos, your sales team being too specialized or siloed, and customer success mostly focused on problems, migrations, and renewals.

Your positioning strategy in this scenario needs to be about painting a broader context for why customers have a path forward with you and how you will make their lives easier over the long run. In truth, very few customers want to switch, but they hate the idea of being locked in, so you need to paint a vision for what the future looks like with you. It may also be the case that you've had to reengineer some legacy business processes or fix some of your system issues of the past to modernize and deliver a more frictionless customer experience, and you're a bit tight on marketing dollars to do as much as you would like. The good news is that marketing to your customer base is much more cost-effective and can be done well with an aligned approach to sales and customer success.

These often manifest as platform positioning strategies where a core base mostly buys one thing, but you have some peripheral products or offerings that deliver additional value. In a platform approach, not only is it about making sure your customers stay and expand over time, but it's also about creating connections and broadening an ecosystem that can deliver more value to customers. This means your efforts are to still land new customers, but you should also be making sure you are expanding your base and your ecosystem strategy to offer more complimentary add-ons that customers can benefit from.

Zoho and HubSpot are examples of companies who position around a platform strategy.

INNOVATOR: FOCUS ON A NEW WAY

In this scenario, you see yourself either as a competitive option to a strong leader, as an up-and-comer in a high-growth space, or delivering a new way to solve a problem. I would generally put most start-ups in this bucket. In this situation you would be doubling down on marketing and sales to gain as much share as possible.

This is the time to go big on defining where you uniquely play and what you uniquely offer that's different from the current leader. This strategy is often used to define nascent categories in more mature categories (if you think in terms of Gartner taxonomy). The other option is to stay in the same category, but perhaps you have a completely new approach to solving the problem. There are thousands of modern B2B software companies popping up in various categories, delivered through various models. Determine where you can uniquely plant your flag, be clear about the space you are competing in, and go for it!

For a transaction, you will also want to determine which strategic partners will want what you have to augment their visions. Look to market leaders who may see you as a threat and want to consolidate.

Twilio, Navan, Miro, and Zoom are examples of companies redefining new or nascent spaces in their respective markets to position themselves against other leading competitors or alternatives.

DISRUPTIVE: FOCUS ON NEW CATEGORY INNOVATOR

Uber, Airbnb, Shopify, and early Amazon are just a few technology-based companies that had such a unique and compelling idea that it created a whole new category. There are many books written about the bliss and rapture of being in this position and creating a compelling new market through breakthrough innovation, but the fundamentals remain largely the same. For these companies, however, there is a bigger burden put on market education, creating a network effect, engaging early adopters and coinnovation, and engaging in provocative thought leadership and PR. All of those things can be addressed in your GTM plan.

If you aren't sure if you are developing a new category, you probably aren't. The one question you need to answer is, "How big and broad of a market are you disrupting?" Uber is big. Airbnb is big. Horse to motorcar was big. Amazon—even the name is big. It's critical to do some soul-searching to determine if you are creating a new category or are part of a rapidly evolving category that industry analysts are already contemplating.

Love it or hate it, the analysts do hold us hostage to their taxonomies, so unless your product is viral, disruptive in how it changes all the rules, or unless you have the money to pull multiple analysts into strategic advisory engagements over a two- to three-year period of time, it's important to consider the pros and cons of creating versus expanding an existing category. It takes a lot of effort, time, and money to define a new category and educate the market if your product doesn't do the heavy lifting for you, so just be aware of that going in. In many cases, it can be more effective to start with a category that is already defined and expand it or further refine it than it is to start from scratch.

> ### ⚠ WARNING ABOUT NEW CATEGORY CREATION
>
> The overwhelming majority of young companies believe they are creating a new category, and that's what they want to position. If creating a new category is supposed to make you different, by virtue of how many companies claim to be doing it, it's not differentiating at all. The focus shouldn't be on the 'new category', it should be on the problem you are solving.

LEADER: FOCUS ON YOUR TECHNOLOGY VISION

In this scenario, you are the market leader but need to work hard to maintain your edge against competitors right behind you and new innovators. In this situation, you would be doubling down on marketing and sales to continue to gain as much share as you can while making swift adjustments to how you scale your marketing efforts and manage growth internally.

It's likely you already have strong positioning in the market, a strong customer orientation, and more mature processes and systems across marketing, sales, and services. This is the time to drive the narrative about where your category is going and push analysts and influencers to expand market requirements in your favor. As the leader, you get to define the vision for the category to keep followers in your wake, so don't be afraid to be bold in your future predictions and how use cases will evolve. You set the standard.

This may also be the time to look at opportunities to augment your strategic vision. Look to small innovators or niche vendors as evidence of where you are headed. It's likely you would be an acquirer, not an acquisition target.

Salesforce, ServiceNow, and Adobe are examples of aggressive market leaders.

Maintaining Your Reputation Takes Effort

Securing a strong market position is important, but it's also important to be sure you're maintaining and growing your reputation in your customer and employee base. You will have a reputation either by accident or on purpose, so it's worth being purposeful. Building a positive preference for your company through brand loyalty is a concept that's been around since the 1990s. Three decades later, we still aspire to create ferocious loyalty in our customers and employees that drives the kind of cult-like following achieved by the Grateful Dead rock band and longtime Apple users. You can only do this by focusing on it from the start.

> Your brand reputation in your customer base becomes an important intangible in your valuation. A future owner of your company wants to know there won't be a mad rush to the exits when a transaction gets announced.

Investors want to know customers and top employees are locked in as tight as possible, either with pricing changes or retention bonuses. But you don't want bitter customers and employees either. Through a solid customer engagement strategy, you can help drive brand affinity and create a reputation you can be proud of in your customer base.

Being constantly top of mind with your customer base, no matter how much of a commodity your offering is, should be a primary business objective. It seems obvious to say that your customers should know what your company is doing, how your company's products and services are evolving, and what your company's intentions are in the marketplace. It's often the case that software companies can be so focused on the transaction or getting a renewal that they forget to communicate to customers *why* they are an exciting vendor to do business with.

Whose job is it today in your organization to keep customers informed at a macro level? Sales reps trying to expand the account? Renewals team trying to get customers to sign the contract? Customer success helping to solve the most urgent problem or bug fix? Is it one person, a team, or a combination that is responsible for communicating and telling them what's going on? Is there a strategy for keeping your company relevant and in the minds of your customers all the time?

Unfortunately, many customers have no insight into the product roadmap or even what is currently in the portfolio beyond what they were originally sold.

Marketing can play a key role here, obviously. But most marketing teams in small to midsize software companies focus on driving net new opportunities, not creating avenues for customer communication and engagement. Dedicating a resource to focus on customer communication, customer references, and customer advisory boards early on is a great place to start.

Once you establish basic communication with your customer base, there are other ways to drive customer share of mind, from how you talk to the market broadly to more specific ways you engage with them.

Yes, the product needs to be awesome (such as Apple) for many people, but it doesn't need to be for everyone (such as the Grateful Dead). The magic is in proper market positioning within key customer segments rather than being everything to everyone. That is a huge trap for small and hypergrowth software companies. This is a problem all marketing people live to solve but very few executive teams can commit to doing— but what if you did? Think of the advantage you would have!

In a rush to acquire new customers and show huge per-centages of year-over-year growth, companies can be quick to primarily focus marketing on new opportunity development and take their eyes off the customers that got them where they are today. Regardless of whether you shored up your market positioning strategy more broadly in the market, you must have one for your installed base no matter what.

> **Have a core set of beliefs about where the market is going, pick a position, and be interesting when you engage with customers.**

Just as the Grateful Dead didn't get to legendary status doing gigs featuring a mix of disco, punk, and reggae, you won't get to legendary status trying to be a wedding singer with your installed base. Not wanting to alienate anyone or not wanting to turn away customers ends up watering down your brand position and disintegrating what you stand for, which, in turn, ends up turning away customers anyway. If you pick a strong point of view and find a segment of the market that shares the same view, they will want to follow what you talk about and tell other like-minded people about you as well. It's just like having friends. You have a shared view of the world, which is probably why you are friends.

In my experience, leaders in all functions at all levels logically understand this concept, but it is extremely difficult to get executives to commit to something with teeth for even just a twelve- to eighteen-month time frame. You must take a position and stick to it, knowing there will be some customers who are turned off by it. Your sales team, by the way, hates this because in their mind, a deal is a deal. However, as a leadership team, it's important to be deliberate about the kind of customers and the type of customer community you want.

What good is it to get a bunch of users that will never upgrade from you? Any investor can see through this. It means that someday you will want to start charging or upgrading them, and they will all be angry because now they have to pay, and then you will be known as being too expensive.

Another thing software companies are starting to get better at is having something close to an interesting personality. Software is such an exciting industry, yet many companies come across as blander than sawdust. If you want to be interesting, do interesting things; there's no magic in it. To be an interesting company, you must have interesting perspectives on the world and engage in new and interesting ways. Challenge your teams to do this with your core customer base, and as a CEO, challenge yourself to push the limits of your comfort zone in how you talk about the unique ways you solve your customers' problems. Go for it!

A Strong Brand Position Creates Space for Customer Forgiveness

Fundamentally, you want to attract customers who share the same philosophies or points of view as you do. If you attract customers who are a perfect fit for what you have to offer, that's where the magic happens. When you first start out, you are more open to selling to anyone who wants to buy, but the unintended consequence is that you end up with a bunch of customers who might not be a great fit for you, and that can be a drain on support and development resources.

In B2B tech, customers must buy into a certain philosophy, whether it's outsourcing their business applications, moving their infrastructure to a cloud platform, or consolidating into a single pane of glass. The philosophies that customers bring to the equation might have organizational consequences on their end, which can dictate whether or not they are a good match for you. If your brand and your positioning nail this, you get a golden ticket. If you attract customers who believe what you believe, they are more likely to forgive feature gaps, bugs, etc. because they trust that you are taking them where they need to go.

The grandfather of this strategy was SAP, but it's worked for many companies ever since. In its heyday, it was widely know that SAP's products were difficult to use and not (at all) the cheapest option. Whole ecosystems were built around SAP to help customers be successful. But the thing was, customers believed and trusted that SAP would take them where they needed to go, and they bet their careers on it. To SAP's base, they were considered the leader when it came to providing industry vision for cosmic integration of all core business processes into one monolithic system—a philosophy that was desirable to a certain segment of the market, but it's certainly not for everyone.

SAP was incredibly good at building deep customer relationships with these customers, which was a major differentiator at the time. As the company continued to evolve its products, customers were along for the ride because they invested in the initial promise of where SAP would take them. They had trust in the brand, believed in the vision, and were forgiving when there were gaps in the feature sets.

There's a lesson in this, even though the nature of B2B software has changed and customers can subscribe and unsubscribe in a moment. If you can create a brand position to attract like-minded customers who believe what you believe and take care of them like family, you will create a cult-like following and be afforded more leeway for product shortfalls or gaps in your portfolio.

Brand Reputation Is an Executive Priority

Having a discussion about the opportunity to improve strategy positioning and brand reputation as a means for value creation is an incredibly difficult concept to get across in an executive leadership team meeting, even by the most prepared and brilliant CMO. It's like trying to make a case for climate change to a bunch of people fighting a fire when all eyes are on the latest customer win back or the net new logo shortfall.

Sadly, these topics tend to be either too controversial or exotic to try to discuss when everyone's focus is on pipeline conversion. It can be an incredibly unpopular topic to broach when there are sales shortfalls or customer problems, but it must be discussed somewhere.

> Make space to explore ways to build out your brand position and improve your reputation because the market will form an opinion of you whether you work on it or not!

In today's climate, false narratives are inevitable. If you don't take proactive measures to have a good reputation, your competitor will do it for you. Your competition is setting traps and creating doubt in every conversation because, well, they are doing their own sales and marketing. The antidote to this is to make sure you are communicating what you are getting right and why customers love you. The best defense against being out marketed and losing opportunities or not even getting considered is to do your own good marketing. It's pretty simple.

Summary

Just as only one or two boats can start a race in a great leading position, not many software companies can get their positioning right out of the gate. However, it's not hard to do, it's just hard to commit to. If you can get this right, you will get clean air and perform well in the markets you compete in. Doing this successfully can take courage and a lot of willpower to stay the course, and competitive moves can create doubt leading you to question if you are on the right course. However, having a great starting position and sticking with it are often what define a good outcome because it is harder to establish a market position if you keep changing it during the race.

Having a great brand reputation isn't hard—it just takes discipline.

➔ A solid positioning strategy is critical to differentiating your company in the market in seven seconds or less.

➔ Use the strategic playbooks to determine your best positioning options that match your business goals.

➔ Focus on how you are uniquely different as a company and why customers can't live without you; then deliver on it.

➔ There's a critical relationship between executing your positioning strategy and creating brand value, which starts with your customers and employees.

➔ Great positioning to the right, like-minded customer segment can help you create a cult-like following that gives you leeway on product shortfalls.

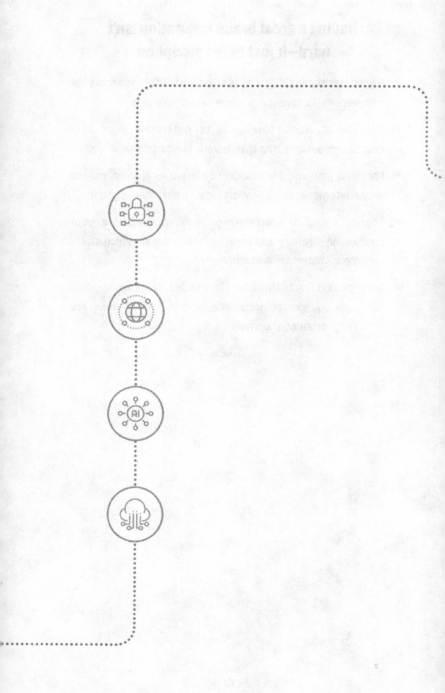

CHAPTER 8

GAINS

IT'S NOT TOP SPEED THAT matters; it's average speed that counts.

When we first started out sailing, we figured what was important on a boat was being self-sufficient and having all our stuff aboard. So we packed the boat with literally three tons of bric-a-brac, which I regretted later because it dragged down our average speeds.

There's this magical moment on a sailboat when everyone suddenly and simultaneously tackles their phone cameras to take a picture of the boat speedometer as it hits top speed. Cool for bragging rights, but top speeds are not what's impressive; average speeds are. Unfortunately, the more stuff you have, the more weight you have, which means you can't sail in light winds and can't get higher average speeds. You have a lighter boat with less stuff, you go faster in less wind, and you get higher average speeds. So do I need a waffle maker, or do

I want to pick up an extra knot or two on a longer passage to be able to avoid a storm?

Since the planet is 70 percent water, average boat speed matters in a circumnavigation, and one can achieve this by combining many small adjustments to make a bigger impact. Gains come from proper seamanship in finding the right wind angles, using the right sail plan, and making the tiniest adjustments to the sails that allow us to pick up a knot here and a knot there that add up to something significant. It's not easy to make these tiny gains, and keeping stuff off the boat takes discipline. But by putting in the right average miles every day, you can cut an ocean passage by up to two to three days. This is a great outcome!

Achieving the Power of Surge means taking small advantages from anywhere you can get them and not just looking for growth or large cuts in one area to save you. Company visions should be ambitious, but when goals are set too high or gains are seen as coming from a maniacal focus on sales execution alone, you may miss achieving gains from hidden corners of your company that are otherwise just sitting idle. More than before, investors reward those companies that focus on profitability, as you well know by now. This means looking holistically at your business to consider ways to drive the right results.

You can unlock hidden value by accumulating gains in new ways. By expecting and collecting small victories in many places, you might create new streams of profit and value that may surprise you. Also, by rewarding small wins in many places, your people will build both confidence and a deeper desire to win.

Evidence of Growth Potential

You have a monumental opportunity to show evidence of how you grew value for your company using small wins that you can begin collecting today. It starts with thinking of marketing as a force multiplier in your business, not just a cost center, and using it to your advantage.

Let's start with the end in mind.

You are going through the exit process, and potential buyers are looking at all the valuation information the quants provided. You believe deeply that the company is worth more but have no way to quantify it. For the purposes of this book, I will focus on the aspects leading up to the due diligence process that are relevant to where marketing has an impact in areas you control.

Any serious buyers would conduct some due diligence surveys to the industry or customer base to collect their own data and find out what customers say about you. Outsourced research teams execute most of these paid exercises, and (generally speaking) they are less than pure in their methodologies as they relate to your unique business. The methods aren't terrible; they are just set up to be highly repeatable and fast, which gives decent general information but can be biased in many ways and lack nuances of what is really going on in your business. If your market is broad and you serve many segments, the research they conduct may not be able to capture the strides you have made.

This means that in the transaction process, you may face data that someone else conducted outside your control using a method with which you may not fully agree. It works for the potential buyer because they use this data to get insight, but they also use the research to make judgments on the value of the business and pressure test their strategic hypothesis about what they intend to do with the business once it's theirs. So how will you measure the progress you have made?

You will need a body of evidence that includes the respondents' understanding of your core positioning, rating your customer experience, and measuring the gains you have as evidence to show that the company is going in the right direction. So for the transaction, you may need to come armed with your own research, including a baseline study and follow-up pre- and postefforts with your customer base. If you are a turnaround or a company in transition, you must prove that a change is underway or provide evidence that you tapped into a unique position in the market that is valuable. There are many methods to do this, but make sure you have the baseline done many months before the transaction with a bounded sample size so you have the data.

What you know, which may not come out in the research, is how hard you worked to create customer appeal, loyalty, and awareness in the niche areas you care about and build meaningful customer and ecosystem relationships. The kind of research I just described is a look in the rearview mirror and doesn't always address the reality and potential that you know are there, which will matter a lot, especially if you have your heart set on a strategic buyer or a growth-oriented PE firm. Very rarely does transaction research focus on momentum and growth potential; it often focuses on what's wrong.

Beyond strides in brand positioning and reputation, here are some areas you can find hidden value from marketing and provide metrics of progress during the transaction.

Marketing as a Value Driver

Now let's talk about what you can do to set yourself up for a more productive conversation once you are at the transaction table and armed with data and research that show the best version of your company and the successes you have collected along the way. To lead the narrative here, you need to have favorable data in research you control that highlights and quantifies the value drivers that may or may not exist on a financial spreadsheet. You will have many business metrics to refer to. But in this section, I want to highlight some areas where marketing can uniquely contribute. They are as follows:

- Growth measured by ACV

- Customer loyalty and expansion measured by LTV

- New marketing-led revenue streams measured by additional ARR

- Lowering costs measured by decreasing CAC

As you know, judgments on your value will be made based on how you stand up against whatever method the potential buyers are using (e.g., the rule of 40 or the algorithm of the day).

MARKETING VALUE DRIVER 1: DEMONSTRATING ACV GROWTH

When new potential investors look at a company, they want to get in on the initial growth surge. If the growth had already happened, it wouldn't be such a great investment. However, at the transaction table, everyone wants to look at growth in absolute terms based on what happened in the immediate past, even though there is a broad understanding of the investment-to-return time lag of anywhere between eighteen months and four years.

The tendency is to show the increase in sales and marketing investments (as one line item in P&L) and what that investment indicates in the previous six to twelve months. The flaw is that typically, up to this point, the company has increased sales coverage but kept marketing flat because sales is much more immediate in terms of driving tactical outcomes. Therefore, the data will suggest an increase in the cost of sales and only anecdotal evidence of better conversion since new reps are still ramping up to full productivity. The theme will be that the reps are only limited by more at-bats, but there will be no data to support what level of growth the company can expect if that were to magically happen. Then various sales leaders will be brought in to talk about what they need to get the growth everyone is looking for. They will say things such as more marketing events, more leads, more contacts, and better messaging. So while the investments were focused on sales, the dependency for sales execution to prove growth comes full circle back to marketing where it's presumed there's been a fair investment.

Then marketing comes to the table and talks about what they were able to do with flat investment. They might show a decent ROI but can't show an impact on growth because the budget envelope barely covers bare metal marketing (website, search terms, core product content, sales enablement, basic PR, etc.). The growth story from marketing breaks down because there likely was a lack of investment to create closed-loop reporting to show the direct correlation from modern digital marketing spend to deals closed. Then a bunch of discussion ensues about system and process challenges across sales and marketing that everyone is working on to improve but in earnest is no one's full-time focus.

This circular conversation doesn't help your business case for growth. When potential investors see marketing as an expense and not as a growth driver, there is no way for you to show evidence of growth potential.

> You can engineer marketing to prove out your growth potential based on the business strategy you choose.

Marketing can play a huge role in supporting your growth narrative leading up to an exit if you are deliberate in your decisions twelve to eighteen months before your planned exit.

What I'm about to tell you is so simple that you will dismiss it immediately. So instead, I welcome you to keep an open mind and ask yourself whether you tried it.

A year before you plan to shop your company around, sit down with your sales and marketing team and agree on the following:

1. What product or service in your portfolio is the most innovative and has the most greenfield potential from a net new ACV standpoint?

2. What is the lead-to-close conversion calculation to show a meaningful growth in a twelve-month period of time?

3. For that offering, what is the ideal target market segment where you can win, and what specific target accounts would be best suited?

4. How would marketing and sales execute together to penetrate this segment?

5. How would you lock customers in for three years to reduce churn?

6. How would you use initial wins as an expansion opportunity later?

7. What needs to be put in place to track conversion across sales and marketing based on what systems/processes you have in place today?

8. Who will drive the initiative, and how will all the teams across sales and marketing be incentivized to make it successful?

9. What will it cost to be successful across marketing and sales as a focused initiative, with marketing carrying a higher percent contribution on net new opportunities?

Sounds like a sales play, right? Or maybe a marketing campaign you tried before? Think again. Maybe you did numbers 1 and 4 and maybe to some degree dabbled in the rest—but what if you did all nine things?

At a minimum, you want to show a pocket of success in a high-growth area to prove growth potential. Because of budget and resource constraints, and even maybe because of your legacy customer base, you can't do this across your entire business, but you can do it as a pilot hypergrowth program or a change initiative to prove it can be done internally and to showcase it as a growth proof point for the transaction later. By being aggressive in your marketing contribution to opportunities, you won't take many sales resources away from supporting the rest of the business, and you will allow the opportunities to develop so they are ready for sales to execute in time to show results at a transaction.

MARKETING VALUE DRIVER 2: INCREASING LTV THROUGH CUSTOMER LOYALTY AND EXPANSION

The lever here comes down to customer expansion and churn. In its most crude form, it's how you manage renewals. If you take a more strategic view, it's how you deliver customer success and value. So what does marketing have to do with any of this?

Your customer engagement strategy is unique to your business model. If you sell a SaaS software service to small or midsize companies, it's very much a product-led motion where customers initiate the engagement, but marketing supports the triggers. If your company primarily services developers, it revolves more around a marketplace model with tools, and the community is the main form of engagement. If your company offers early market technology or supports complex business processes, it centers around a more high-touch, consultative customer engagement model.

Although the models vary, the following are two major ways marketing can help drive customer engagement and expansion:

1. Initial try and use experience

2. Customer success and expansion experience

Engaging through the product/service experience begins when someone first hears about your company and goes to your website. So let's start there.

Often, the software product, the website, and the customer support portal are built in separate silos. Perhaps at some point, there are similar elements applied to the website that may or may not be included in the product or in the portal environments. I don't just mean the right versions of logos and colors here. I mean the taxonomy and language used to describe the products, services, or feature sets; how a prospect or customer moves from one system to the other; how they log in, see information, receive emails about topics across all platforms, etc.

For born-SaaS companies that are small and growing, this is less of an issue. For larger companies that have been around for a while and maybe grew through acquisition, there can be a lot of disconnected artifacts and language that need to be cleaned up. Managing the customer experience can induce cultural treachery if change isn't managed properly. Whose job is it? It's everyone's job, which means it's no one's job. This continues to be a contentious topic in many growing and evolving companies and really needs executive interference to get it right.

There's a strong case to be made for having marketing spearhead this effort. In larger companies, it's already happening with the evolution of large enterprise CMOs also being called customer experience officers or digital experience officers. But smaller companies can think this way too. What marketing does well generally is map the engagement steps to determine what content should be served and when and how it should look for maximum impact and click-through. It doesn't mean they need to decide the specifics, but they have a strong ability to look at the big picture and clean up engagement gaps in messaging, design, and the overall experience. It's what they do. The web team can help with the data they learned and track regularly on user behavior digitally and what terms to use when.

There are also a ton of great AI tools that marketing teams are familiar with that can help inform better decisions at every touchpoint related to customer propensity to buy, customer health, cross-sell/upsell, and preventative churn that are not included in tools used to track support tickets and lead forms.

Marketing can also help build community and expand programs in the online experience. They will do this because it will be easier, cheaper, and quicker and will get better results than database marketing and paid search as a means of reaching existing customers. By working with customer success, marketing programs can be specifically targeted to accounts that are three to six months before their renewal date and help cultivate loyalty by showcasing an ROI. They can also be set up to target accounts that have logged a certain number of support tickets on a particular topic to deliver more education or tutorials to augment the AI tools and create a deeper experience. The opportunities are endless if the whole customer experience is connected as a large, organic digital system in online communities.

Getting back to what potential buyers for your company want to see—they want to see that the customer is well cared for and has no silly reason to leave, such as engagement friction, gaps in the experience that create engagement leakage, or customer frustration because they can't get the right information or the right person to respond. Study after study on this topic reveals that people will stick with a subpar product if the customer experience is delightful. They also want to see ways you can more quickly secure and expand your accounts, what kind of headroom there is for growth beyond price increases, and what else makes you sticky beyond strong-arm changes to contract terms.

Aside from rebuilding or integrating everything, you can pick a particular area of the business to get right first. It might not always be the customer segment most at risk. Perhaps it's setting it up for the hypergrowth segment of your market so you can show the business case for better LTV.

MARKETING VALUE DRIVER 3: CREATING NEW REVENUE STREAMS

Marketing can help develop better pricing models and service packages (consulting or retainer based) as your company either matures as a cloud business or pivots to one. In highly consultative or ever-changing managed services, the options are endless. One of the biggest innovations in B2B software for small or midsize companies is accessing content through subscriptions and memberships for best practice resources, datasets, or insights. Content can be monetized. This is a completely untapped area for most companies and a place where marketing can uniquely help, if given the opportunity.

Every software company solves a basic set of customer needs, no matter what the use case is in its simplest terms (e.g., workflow efficiency or automation, integration or consolidation of capabilities or functions into a single console, and transparency or reporting of metrics, operations, or intelligence to power better decisions and allow seamless connections to broader ecosystems). That's pretty much what software does, and we think of it as an enabler or tool. So one could argue that your company's software will functionally do the same things that another company's software does once they write the code for it.

A real opportunity to differentiate is the ability to deliver meaningful content, intelligence, and best practices that are hard for anyone else to replicate; this always comes back to your people, your methods, and your unique experience. As the world goes digital and companies deliver and manage everything in the cloud, you can basically build and deliver content-rich working and learning environments where your customers can get things done and where your company uniquely delivers value that is sticky—something every investor wants to hear. If we shift our mindset from tools to content and experience, our ability to drive value looks very different. There are huge opportunities to package and monetize data and content into subscriptions, access, or augmented programs such as rich learning or certification.

If done right, there could even be revenue generated to also fund marketing, turning marketing into a profit center as a self-sustaining unit. I experienced this model firsthand, and I predict that if companies start pivoting their marketing organizations to be content-based business units with a P&L, it will not only drive a unique competitive advantage but also stop the endless conversations about marketing budgets and resources that nauseate everyone involved. It's worth considering the opportunity for an always-on content delivery model with different ways of monetizing the content and community aspects.

Monetizing in the digital verse/metaverse (or whatever we are calling it these days) may also be an area mature enough to seriously consider. The future will offer a more immersive way to interact with a company's digital entity and comes at a time when people are more open to such an experience with the virtual working environment. New marketing methods, content delivery, education, and community opportunities are waiting to be discovered. This isn't at all a new concept, but it does break traditionally held ideas and paradigms about marketing's role in this new era.

MARKETING VALUE DRIVER 4: IMPROVING EBITDA

Often, when executives of software companies this size think of improving EBITDA, they strictly look at lowering expenses. When setting or cutting budgets, leadership goes function by function and cuts where it can. This siloed approach to finding better EBITDA with respect to GTM is fundamentally flawed.

Marketing has a core responsibility to help reduce churn, which I discussed at length previously, and lower the overall CAC. Unfortunately, this is a conversation that is rarely explored when it comes time to make reductions or optimize across the full GTM process. What leaders discuss are solely the metrics around marketing-led closed deals and ROI at that point in time, not on a historical funnel or customer LTV basis. It's important to be precise when trying to achieve EBITDA favorability as it relates to marketing.

Lowering CAC is straightforward. It's about increasing the number of quality opportunities and decreasing friction and touchpoints in the sales process. This can be done, as discussed in the chapter on unity, by mapping the customer experience which makes funding decisions much easier. We will dive into this later when we talk about marketing invest-ments in chapter ten. Here are some ways marketing can help you lower CAC so you aren't looking at cutting expenses in a vacuum. This will be most helpful in understanding areas *not to cut* when this boils down to a functional budget exercise.

What to keep when times are tough:

1.) POSITIONING

Better positioning and messaging help your company stand out in the market and attract buyers who think like you. Great positioning is half the battle and is massively underutilized as a strategic weapon. Spending time creating, executing, and committing to a solid positioning strategy is hard, but it is the cornerstone to attracting the right buyers and lowering CAC.

2.) ACCOUNT-BASED MARKETING

This is precision targeting by partnering with sales on account-based methods to focus on the accounts that matter. This approach is valuable because marketing, in coordina-tion with sales, develops and executes ABM strategies so you can precisely target program dollars. If this is done, you get a better CAC. If this isn't done, your sales team will spend time doing it anyway, which makes them less productive and increases CAC, even though you may have cut the marketing budget somewhere else.

3.) PROSPECT AND CUSTOMER NURTURING

If the sales team must start fresh every quarter to build a new pipeline, this is the slowest, most inefficient way to lower CAC. Your marketing program should include processes and methods for nurturing leads and existing customer accounts for future quarters and address leads marked closed because they weren't yet ready. This would be for opportunities that were opened and engaged with your company but ended up wandering away somewhere or getting lost. A dedicated, effective, and automated nurturing program helps give sales warmer leads and more of them throughout the course of years, not quarters.

4.) ENGAGING, AUTOMATED, DIGITAL CUSTOMER EXPERIENCE

We talked a lot before about how important the experience is for creating expansion, growth, and loyalty, but it's also critical for nurturing. However, to be good at it, it requires a martech infrastructure to support it all, which requires a digital strategy, a tech roadmap, and some kind of investment. Many small and growing companies do their best to *keep the lights on* when it comes to marketing, starting with their website. They do the bare bones and try to add more bones when money comes their way, but this doesn't scale. In this stage, when you need to show lower CAC, shorter sales cycles, and growth potential, a hindrance is the piecemeal, cobbled-together, barely working martech infrastructure that hinders its own ability to automate and accelerate growth.

What to cut if you absolutely must:

1.) INDUSTRY EVENTS AND TRADE SHOWS

Salespeople love events because they're tangible, and they can shake hands and kiss babies. But these events have by far the worst ROI in the entire marketing budget and do a number on the CAC when rolled up and factored into the calculation. ABM or company-hosted VIP events should be the preferred methods, with strong customer community programs and events specific to your user base.

2.) TRADITIONAL PR

Paid and unpaid media are a whole different thing than they were even a few years ago. This is particularly true when it comes to smaller software companies in noisy markets. The media doesn't cover technology and tools; controversy, IPOs, and acquisitions get coverage, and that's about it. Sadly, no one even cares about facts anymore, so relying on reporters has diminishing returns. Stop wasting money on empty press releases and retainers with PR firms. Hire an amazing social media marketing person and invest in content and influencers. Be committed to great content, immersive techniques, executive thought leadership (with voices of their own and something interesting to say!), and a few key channels to syndicate or amplify.

3.) INDUSTRY ANALYSTS

There are one or two analyst firms in the world that matter, but until your company is larger, you can't afford to pay their crazy fees that get you a fully effective analyst program. For some companies that are highly technical, there are those magic quadrants that make sense, but you can't do them all well, so pick wisely. With SaaS specifically, the closer you get to a marketing-led volume model (versus a direct, sales-led model that tends to be highly technical), the more broader influencers will matter rather than analysts.

Bare Metal Marketing

As you approach a transaction, there are ways to dial down marketing costs to a bare metal state, but these should be reserved for when a transaction is imminent. This isn't the most fun part of the process, but it always happens, so it's worth covering. As you enter transaction negotiations, you can dial down costs, and this is typically done three to six months before a transaction. I will also preface this by adding that most of this can't be done unless you have implemented a customer-led GTM engine and streamlined business processes across marketing and sales to begin with. If you have done that, there are ways to outsource many aspects of your marketing program and dial internal costs down.

Let's assume you are wall to wall on a modern CX platform, integrating your digital, marketing, and sales processes, and have a modern web platform that's not a hairball of despair.

With any major platform such as this, you have access to an ecosystem of certified marketing vendors who can take on aspects of execution. Here are some examples of things that can be outsourced, but generally speaking, it would be anything that would be considered marketing-services oriented:

- Campaign development and marketing automation
- Asset development and templates
- Content development, SEO, and social media
- Web maintenance and optimization
- Digital marketing, paid search, and syndication
- Communications and media services

Marketing functions to keep in-house leading into a transaction include the following:

- A CMO to participate in the process and provide support during a transition up to day one
- Product or solution marketing, anything where product knowledge and contextual IP is critical
- Communications for handling the transaction and employee communications
- Digital demand generation, to explain how the engine works and manage the workflow in flight
- Partner marketing people who are closest to the relationships across the ecosystem

- Customer community people who are closest to the user community or customer communication

Summary

Finding small gains is a meticulous pursuit. Sail trim, rigging tensions, weight distribution, and steering techniques are all carefully examined and refined. Whether it's leveraging wind shifts, perfecting sail shape, or making subtle adjustments by hand-steering, these enhancements accumulate over time and make a significant difference.

Going into a transaction, investors look for a strong management team, an innovative product roadmap, and a dependable growth trajectory. Sometimes, however, not all these things exist in perfect combination, and they will rely on their own contracted and rushed due diligence research that may not show the full picture of what they know your company is worth. This is why it's so critical for you to be able to show gains as evidence that you have increased your overall boat speed and are not simply showing a snapshot taken at peak speed.

With the help of marketing and proper planning, you can show promise of growth and demonstrate small wins in the recent past that help project the future. Marketing can help in many ways to demonstrate that hidden growth exists by helping to expand the market size, accelerate customer acquisition, improve customer retention rates, decrease the CAC, and prove the company can be scalable as a digital-first business. With the help of marketing, you can achieve many small gains that can give an investor confidence that the business can yield long-term success.

Gains can be made in many places across the business, and here are ways marketing can help:

➜ There is an untapped opportunity to garner value leading up to a transaction by using marketing to improve key performance targets.

➜ Marketing can improve ACV by focusing on specific areas where demonstrated growth is required versus taking a shotgun approach.

➜ Marketing can improve customer retention and LTV by focusing on customer marketing, communication, and expansion activities.

➜ There are ways marketing can help create new revenue streams that may also be used to fund more marketing.

➜ Marketing can improve EBITDA and lower CAC in highly focused ways versus taking a broad approach to cost savings.

➜ There are options to establish bare metal marketing, outsourcing in areas just prior to a transaction, but there are functions fundamental to a successful transaction to keep in-house.

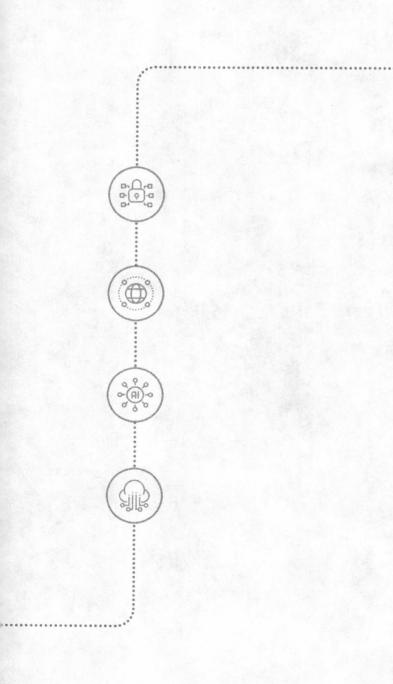

CHAPTER 9

EFFICIENCY

BARNACLES.

If you have ever walked a marina, you can see these crustaceans hell-bent on impartially clinging to the belly of any vessel within reach. Boat owners go to great lengths and expense to avoid barnacle accumulation, including acquiring expensive copper hull treatments, attaching elaborate hull liners, or hiring divers to tickle the boat's underbelly with a hard brush while dodging fuel leaks, meat loaf compost, and brain-eating amoeba. These little buggers can significantly reduce the speed and efficiency of sailing vessels by hugging the hulls of ships with all their tiny might, creating a thick layer of shell crust that is estimated to increase a boat's weight and drag by up to 60 percent! Barnacles are small matter but are no small matter.

Barnacles are microscopic beasts that you don't see coming. Little by little they invite their friends and build up over time to muck up the system, creating unnecessary drag and friction. Every year sailors lift their vessels out of the water and blow these menacing creatures to oblivion with 3,000 PSIs of pressure. This job can take days or weeks depending on how long the hull was neglected, leaving blasted remains to toast in the summer sun to generate that spectacular boatyard aroma that is forever burned into our earliest evolved memories from back before we walked on land.

Does your GTM have a barnacle problem?

An effective GTM engine requires you to have a clean foundation to execute from and an understanding of where to gain efficiencies or remove friction. You need to know what is causing delays across sales, marketing, and customer success workflows, where your data has gaps, what meaningful telemetry is missing, and why. You can accumulate gunk in the system without even realizing it until you reach a point where nothing works right. By then it can be very disruptive and expensive to fix, so it's better to be intentional and consider ways to design for efficiency in the first place.

Go-To-Market with Speed, Agility, and Impact

Almost everything is in place. You have the right marketing strategy that aligns with your business strategy. You've determined your market segments and have aligned your GTM functions teams for success. You've determined the right positioning approach and have committed to being disciplined about executing it. Now it's a small matter of making sure you have the right foundation for efficient execution so you can get a remarkable outcome—and make every dollar act like $3 as you scale.

If you participate early and effectively in a customer's buying process, you can set the agenda for decision-making and set competitive traps. If you follow up on a customer engagement first, you can get in the decision cycle early or be the first to a demo. If you participate in the right conversation at the right moment, you can force the right budget decisions.

Speed and efficiency are essential to taking advantage of opportunities as they arise. It's no longer about getting to market; it's about getting to the right person at the right time with the right message through the right methods that matter. Precision targeting, agile execution, and meaningful engagement are the new definitions of success today, and this can only be done if you have a clean foundation for success and great talent to support your modern model.

> You will spend less money on marketing if you have the right foundation put in place to support efficiency and velocity at scale.

It's time to do in marketing what you have already done in other areas of your business. You would never just tell your dev teams to build whatever they want without a prioritized roadmap, an aligned development approach, and tools to do their job. You would never tell your sales teams to just go sell whatever they want without providing them with proper enablement, an operating rhythm to monitor forecasts and activities, and systems for success. Yet when it comes to marketing, executives struggle to understand why it's important to spend time and effort to create a solid foundation for success.

Remember, marketing exists to build meaningful customer engagements and relationships through compelling, always-on experiences that measurably increase the value of the business. To do this, you need a solid customer experience platform powered by great talent.

Let's talk about the technology stack first.

THE EVOLUTION OF CUSTOMER
EXPERIENCE PLATFORM

We are in the fourth wave of modernization when it comes to managing the customer experience. Once upon a time, there were the software behemoths who built CRM functionality into their ERP systems or created stand-alone CRM on-premise systems that were hard to use and super expensive.

In the second wave, cloud-based CRM promised a better customer experience as the main benefit. Over the years, depending on how a company grew, changed hands, or changed leadership, because software companies are full of people that (you know) like building software, some of the internal databases and core financial systems were custom built and required custom integrations into the CRM and other systems to work right. Little by little these systems became Frankensteined to within an inch of their lives and are now their own complex systems that are expensive and hard to use.

In the third wave, to solve the system and data silo problems, many companies took on data lake initiatives to try to extract insights from the existing databases, systems, and other unstructured sources to make sense of it all, but they proved to be too expensive to manage or failed as monolithic initiatives. Those without data lake initiatives took to creating internal armies of data scientists either in SalesOps or offshore to figure out the true state of our businesses or help fix an internal reporting problem any given function has on any given day. From this, reports were developed that were never easy to replicate and were usually counter to the data someone else had when you were using them to make your point in an important internal budgeting meeting.

Data management platforms offered their own method for solving the data problem and their own level of complexity. One of the main problems with data management platforms is that they were designed mainly to provide anonymous profiles, so it is more difficult to store and work with known data.

About that same time, customer data platforms (CDPs) arose to basically act like data middleware to map and connect interaction data across the omnichannel experience as martech tools began to evolve with verve and become more and more fragmented. Marketers liked them because they were bidirectional and could be used with other platforms without replacing existing ones such as CRM. The main limitation of customer data platforms is that they're based on the same systems and workflow in the first place. Same CRM Frankenstein, same data problems, same broken processes, same silos.

The problem with many of the fixes and workarounds is that they are all after the fact. The back-end reporting delivers trailing indications, not real-time indications, of customer opportunities or problems. Furthermore, the core customer experience hasn't improved because while sales can now create better forecasts, marketing can better prove attribution, and support can better manage help tickets, the underlying process friction for the customer remains unchanged.

THE FOURTH WAVE

Now we are in the fourth wave of technological evolution, and the story is getting juicy. Martech, sales tech, and customer tech have gone off the hook, going from five thousand to over ten thousand vendor tools in the last five years. Larger, established CRM SaaS vendors are now mature and have continued to acquire feature sets. Meanwhile, new disrupters came from the ground up and have natively added features as they have emerged as the next generation of leaders when it comes to creating a platform for engaging and managing the digital customer relationship. Many gained early traction by gaining smaller businesses as customers through freemium models or just because they were just so dang cheap! As these companies have grown, they are truly offering enterprise-class solutions, and companies are starting to notice.

Next-generation solutions offer a bounded set of configured tools that basically anyone can use and configure, so you don't need an internal team of system admins or experts to get what you need done, unlike their predecessors, who created systems with fully featured toolsets that you could develop and use any way you want. What these newer vendors realize is that less is more, and everyone has been burned by system customization and just wants proven best practices out of the box. What they deliver is end-to-end—across marketing, sales, and customer support—one platform, one data model, and one reporting engine that's easy to use, quick to implement, and cheap relative to the multimillion-dollar-a-year contracts others charge for their CRM that no one wants to use.

Here's Where this Story Takes a Turn

Many executives at start-ups or high-growth companies come from companies that were in an earlier wave. They get to a new company and decide to simply adopt a CRM system that existed in the past, not yet understanding where the future is headed on the CX technology and AI front. It's critical to take the time to understand modern capabilities and how they can create a seamless, omnichannel customer experience spanning your marketing, sales, and customer success functions. What you absolutely don't want to do is use old tools and paradigms and expect different outcomes.

> **Remember, as a software company, your customer experience platform is just as important as the software you sell.**

Technology is vital for creating a seamless customer experience and must be considered a strategic priority for any modern software business. In today's hypercompetitive environment, companies that define a customer experience first and then design their systems, workflow, processes, and people to match it will move faster and beat competitors who are stuck in the past.

If you can take a fresh fourth-wave approach, you will benefit in several ways. First, you will be able to collect data at each touchpoint in the customer journey that can be used to not only delight the customer in real-time but also predict and improve future interactions. Second, because there is a shared understanding of the customer data with shared reporting and operations, everyone is truly on the same page and can spend more time debating what should be done and less time debating the data or where it came from. Finally, using unified methods, you can create seamless, personalized experiences for customers that meet their needs at every stage of their journey and look like they're coming from one company.

Whether you are a small and growing company with not much yet put in place or a larger organization with a bunch of legacy, the first thing you will need to consider is what your ideal roadmap should be across your customer life cycle in an ideal future state. Rather than reinventing the wheel, there is a common set of requirements that a company starts to need over time. For simplicity, I've outlined that in the table on the next page, but it's not exhaustive.

PRODUCT	MARKETING	SALES	SERVICES	PARTNER
Customer Data for User Onboarding	Prospect/Customer Database	Prospect/Customer Database, Entitlements, Renewal Information	Customer Entitlements Records in Database	Partner Database
Product Engagement Feedback Capture & Routing	Contact Management & Enrichment	Contact and Lead Management, Contact Enrichment, Conversation Capture & Routing	Contact Management, Conversation Capture & Routing, VOIP, Email, Chat	Contact Enrichment
Upsell Automations	Marketing Automation, Campaigns & Funnels (Built in Best Practices)	Sales Automation: Prospecting, Opportunity Mgmt., Forecasting, Pipeline, Activity Management (Built in Best Practices)	Services Automation & Helpdesk; Account/Contact History, tickets	Partner Program Automation
--	DAM for Assets & Templates	DAM for Templates/Scripts/Playbooks	DAM for Templates/Scripts/Playbooks	DAM for Assets & Templates
In-App Support & Guides	CMS for Marketing & Web Content	CMS for Content in Sales Cycle	CMS for Knowledgebase	CMS for Partner Content
--	Web Build, Landing Pages (self-serve) & Web Analytics	--	--	Landing Pages (Partner Specific)
--	Omnichannel Tracking; Ads. Social, etc.	--	--	--
--	SEO	--	--	SEO
In App A/B Testing	A/B Testing, Lead & Predictive Scoring	Predictive Scoring based on Activities & Interactions	Predictive Scoring	A/B Testing & Engagement Scoring
In App User Analytics	Analytics, Reporting & Attribution	Integrated Reporting, Analytics, Insights, Attribution	Customer Insights & Research (CSAT, cNPS, etc.)	Analytics, Reporting & Attributions
Video Server (linked to App Tutorials)	Video Server, Conversion & Analytics	Video Server (Sales-specific content)	Video Server (Support-specific)	Video Server (partner-specific), Conversion & Analytics
Customer Account Portal	Customer Portal (GEN)	Customer Account Portal	Customer Service Portal	Partner Portal & Programs (Incentives, Assets, etc.)
In App Chat	WebChat	LiveChat	Chatbot & LiveChat	LiveChat in Portal
Workflow & Task Management	Workflow & Task Management	Workflow & Task Management	Workflow & Task Management	Workflow & Task Management
Dev Tools	Design Tools	--	--	--
Webinar Platform	Webinar/Events Platform	--	Webinar/Events Platform	Webinar/Events Platform
--	--	Meeting Scheduling	Meeting Scheduling	--
Payment Platform (In App Purchases)	Payment Platform (Paid Events)	Payment Platform (Trials, Signups & Renewals)	Payment Platform (Add on Services, Upsells)	Payment Platform (Paid Activities)
--	--	Proposals & Quoting Tool	--	Proposals, Agreements & Quoting Tools

Figure 9.1

Example of Unified CX Requirements

This chart is an example of the core customer experience requirements that a growth or mid-stage software company will need across functions as it matures. You can see in this basic example that across the organization, there are some related needs that can be solved in silos but would benefit if considered holistically. As a company grows quickly, many tools will be adopted in silos because in the past, they were provided by separate tools or vendors in different paradigms or contexts. It's entirely possible that each functional area will buy separate tools to solve their needs, and you can end up with a hot mess of third-party services and contracts that aren't fully optimized. It's better to have a tech strategy that helps you grow into the roadmap you will need over time.

You can now have a much more holistic stack that is also much cheaper, configurable, and simpler than the complex, integrated, heavily customized systems of the past that needed heavy implementation support and specialized administration and management.

Because of this, it's important to think about where you are in your systems and process journey and ask yourself the following questions:

- If you are a start-up or an early stage company and haven't yet committed long term to certain systems, is now the time to lead with a CX strategy and a CX tech roadmap to support it?

- If you are a mid-stage company or in hypergrowth mode, are the functional tech silos aligned to a CX model currently, or are they holding you back from fully aligning functions end to end?

- If you are a legacy or mature company that has over-customized systems because of acquisitions or custom-developed add-ons over the years, is it time to take on a digital transformation to modernize?

- If you think it's time to implement a CX model and the technology roadmap to support it, is it worth looking at next-generation systems and technologies to support you beyond what you are familiar with today?

If you answered yes to any of these questions, there are options for you. I won't endorse any tools in this book, but I will admit that I have my favorites. Without going into too much detail, here's what you can accomplish if you are looking to adopt a CX model and the CX tech stack to go along with it.

For start-ups or early stage companies, you get to start fresh because you don't have much already! Right now, you may either be using free tools or a mix of free tools plus a major CRM system that's getting expensive, so you will want to rapidly determine if you are on the right path and create a roadmap to support where you want to go for a full-stack approach. At your scale you can do everything you need with probably about six core tools that would take you roughly three to six months to put in place.

For midstage or legacy midsize companies looking to optimize and gain full leverage across their businesses, it's a whole new ball game for you! Your processes and operations aren't scalable, and you may be using a mix of free tools or point products for different use cases. It's entirely possible you have more than you think already; the typical midsize company can use up to fifty tools! But you don't need to. *SIMPLIFY!*

You likely have legacy marketing automation and CRM systems that are somewhat integrated but are constantly being customized. You may be nearing the end of your contract and want to consider something that is (1) simple to migrate and easier to use, (2) is cheaper than what you already have, and (3) helps you make a rapid pivot to a unified CX model to help you scale or sell your company.

You may have built manual processes around it and hired internal system administrators and data analytics people to help you create custom reports and keep the whole thing running. All in all, you might be spending way too much money on the systems and all the internal costs and resources to support them by a team of people whose jobs depend on them telling you how complex it is to maintain. In many cases, it can be worth doing a full modernization depending on the state of your systems. In truth, you can accomplish everything you need with under a dozen core tools, and it could take you six to nine months to fully migrate if you wanted a fresh start on a modern engine.

The benefits of such a modernization would be that you would have full customer telemetry, unified SLAs, and workflow across your organization, which translate into a better customer experience for a lot less money than you might imagine, particularly if you are migrating from legacy systems and already spending millions today.

Another benefit is that many of the out-of-the-box configurations on these tools include best practices for SaaS or cloud-based companies, so you don't need to reinvent the wheel if process and workflow aren't your strengths. More companies want their operations and processes to be simplified, with more configured best practices versus custom, and while it's great that there are more tools to use, more does not mean better!

YOUR MODERN MARKETING TEAM

Having the right marketing talent is as essential as it is hard to find. It may seem like a daunting task to find and retain top-notch marketing professionals, but it's well worth the investment and time to get the right people in. There are some core capabilities required for B2B software companies, which we will cover next. There will be nuances, of course, if you have a unique business model, are more focused on developer communities, or have a heavier e-commerce aspect of your business, but the recommendations should provide good guidance for the marketing capabilities to consider. If you are a small business or a midsize organization, the functional requirements are roughly the same. In smaller organizations, often, one person wears many hats, and as a business grows, or over time, the functions get more specialized with a dedicated focus on each vocation.

Also, there is little difference in capabilities when looking at the strategic path options, but there is a difference in the girth and the emphasis of the functions. The difference would be the number of resources and funding you would put behind certain initiatives, not whether you would have them at all. For example, if you are adopting a transitional playbook, you would put more effort into customer engagement initiatives because your primary focus is protecting your base. If you are using an innovator playbook, your focus is to take share as fast as possible so you may focus most of your attention on demand activation and thought leadership programs.

Generally, regarding level of experience, I've seen the most success when you hire up versus exclusively hiring junior, specialized talent across the board because you get more out of more seasoned people. Smaller companies struggle with this concept because they would much rather hire more developers than marketing people. The problem is that precisely when you are small and growing, you need the highest quality, highest volume of work done in the shortest amount of time. When you hire an experienced generalist marketer for your team, you're hiring what you would otherwise get from two specialists in some cases. I'm a big fan of hiring high-potentials, but they need strategy and coaching, so you still need a couple of senior people to get the most out of your entire team.

As an early stage company, if you had to hire more senior talent and combine roles, the priority would be to hire a great strategist who can work with you on the strategy, positioning, segmentation, and solution messaging work and who can focus on building out the demand activation first. The next more senior priority would be in thought leadership and communications, especially if you are executing on innovator or leader playbooks. If you are gearing up for a transaction, this function becomes especially important, as it will handle internal and external rumors and do a lot of the heavy lifting through internal communications for change management.

For a midsize or legacy company, it's time to bring in a seasoned marketing leader or CMO. Beyond that, you should hire up for a solution marketing expert and demand activation role. The rest of the roles can be more junior people with mentorship from this core team.

While it's true that different business models may have nuances for talent needs, these are examples that tend to fit a large percentage of organizations generally speaking. There's always bespoke talent requirements, but I would say this formula is right for about 80 percent of B2B software businesses.

START-UP AND EARLY STAGE SAMPLE CAPABILITIES

Below outlines the differences on how each function would scale as the requirements mature. The capabilities for larger companies are similar, but there would be more of a dedicated focus as the business requirements grew. Note: These are functional capabilities, not necessarily individual people and are for example purposes, generically across software models.

CMO/Strategist sets the strategy and leads a unified effort

This is typically your most senior marketing leader, as at this point you may not have a formal CMO, head of marketing, or a fractional CMO. This person works directly with the CEO or executive team to build the overarching strategic path, market segmentation model, positioning strategy, and thought-leader narrative. They set the framework for the overall program and a plan for success.

Demand activation drives digital and in-person opportunities

This function is the workhorse of your marketing team, as they define and execute an always-on stream of engaging and relevant campaigns and drive traffic to your website and trials. This function executes digital, content, assets, events, and ABM and may also manage the business development representative (BDR)/sales development representative (SDR) if needed (which at this point might be either a junior or outsourced resource) to qualify opportunities.

Digital experience ensures digital cohesion across the customer journey

This function oversees the digital customer experience across the web channel, including content, engagement, trial conversion, and customer support. They may also manage the portals and online communities technically speaking. Content and messaging is a team effort at this point. This can be outsourced initially but should be brought in-house at some point.

Solution marketing delivers enablement, consideration, and onboarding content

This function creates messaging for the full solutions and use cases, creates sales or partner enablement and solution messaging, and may also lead pricing, packaging, and promotion initiatives. They may also develop the onboarding experience and content for a digital-first experience in conjunction with product management. Often, in start-ups and smaller companies, the product manager covers this. As the requirements on the product management side grow, it becomes harder for one person to do both roles. With a dedicated resource in marketing, they can also help the sales team initially with business development.

Thought leadership, communications, and social help build and maintain a positive brand reputation

Initially covered by the CMO, this is the function that would expand to either a dedicated role or set of agency resources responsible for your media and analyst relationships. They also may manage the blog and speaker placement and may drive organic social media topics. This can initially be an outside resource, but as the company grows, there should be a resource in-house that may be supported by an agency or a contractor.

Customer and community engagement fosters loyalty and helps customers effectively use products and services

This function is focused on customer/user engagement and may also support the partners and customer success teams on broader programs. This is particularly important in freemium models or in developing a user base and set of customer advocates.

Operations and analytics help you track metrics, trends, and ROI

This function finds ways to optimize programs, interprets prospect/customer data, and tracks program effectiveness and ROI. Initially, this may be handled by demand activation or digital experience function, but as the business grows, you will need a data strategy, marketing automation, and deeper analytics capabilities. If you choose a single tech platform, you may not need this role for a while.

MIDSTAGE AND GROWTH SAMPLE CAPABILITIES

While the roles are the similar, there are differences in the talent experience and quantity in midstage and growth organizations.

CMO/Strategist sets the strategy and leads a unified effort

At this point you would typically consider bringing in a CMO. This person should be a generalist with an emphasis in digital demand creation preferably because you are in the mode where you need to build a scalable engine. This person works directly with the CEO or executive team to develop a vision for scale, optimize resources, and pull in outside help.

Demand activation drives digital and in-person opportunities

By now you may have hired a dedicated in-house person executing digital, content, assets, events, and ABM, and they may also be running your website with the help of outside agencies or contractors. It's likely this function would max out first, so adding dedicated resource to focus on other areas (such as website and content) would be ideal.

Digital experience ensures digital cohesion across the customer journey

Similar to start-ups and early-stage companies, this function oversees the digital customer experience across the web channel, including content, engagement, trial conversion, and customer support. They may also manage the portals and online communities technically speaking. Content and messaging is a team effort. This would form the basis of your tech stack, and this team would evolve the digital capabilities and have a vision for the customer experience, information architecture, and a broader CX technology roadmap.

Solution marketing delivers enablement, consideration, and onboarding content

This function creates messaging for the full solutions and use cases, creates sales or partner enablement and solution messaging, and may also lead pricing, packaging, and promotion initiatives. They may also develop the onboarding experience and content for a digital-first experience in conjunction with product management. At this point there are dedicated in-house resources in marketing. They can also help the sales team with technical marketing/demos, trial development, deeper expansion content, and product review security.

Thought leadership, communications, and social help build and maintain a positive brand reputation

This is the function or agency responsible for your media and analyst relationships. They also may manage the blog and speaker placement and may drive organic social media topics. This can initially be an outside resource, but as the company grows, there should be a resource in-house that may be supported by an agency or a contractor. As the team gets bigger, there should be a dedicated focus on social media and influencer programs when appropriate.

Customer and community engagement fosters loyalty and helps customers effectively use products and services

This function is focused on customer/user engagement and may also support the partners and customer success teams on broader programs. This is particularly important in freemium models or in developing a broad user base but also nurtures sales references and case studies. This team may oversee higher touch customer or user advisory groups, loyalty programs, or broader participation in online communities.

Operations and analytics help you track metrics, trends, and ROI

Like early-stage companies, this function finds ways to optimize programs, interprets prospect/customer data, and tracks program effectiveness and ROI. Initially, this may be handled by demand activation or digital experience function, but as the business grows, you will need a data strategy, marketing automation, and deeper analytics capabilities. If you choose a single tech platform, you may require a smaller team with outside support.

Summary

Barnacles are what we get if we are careless about keeping our business in order, don't design an engine purposefully up front, or avoid proper attention to talent, workflow, and systems over time. Everything might look good on top, but below the waterline, things can grow crusty and stop working right. Just as no boat can function with a layer of barnacles, no business can function with a slow accumulation of buildup as the result of poor planning on the foundation or misalignment of the talent required to run a modern execution engine.

The best way to think about it is that you can invest in a solid foundation now for less, or you can run inefficiently now and also spend a lot more money and time later fixing it. You will pay either way.

The difference between getting acceptable marketing and getting remarkable marketing is a matter of investing the time to think through a purposeful approach to what your CX platform needs to be, what workflow maximizes efficiency, and how to best take advantage of new technologies and talent capabilities that help you scale. With the right team, the right processes, and the right tools, it's easier than ever to optimize your marketing expenses and ensure maximum ROI. Investing in the right foundation not only sets you up for success once these strategies are implemented but can also ultimately lead to decreased costs across your teams and lower overall spending on marketing as you mature.

With a little planning on the foundation, you will have the speed and agility of a company three or four times your size with legacy technology and fixed methods.

Here are some suggestions to get more efficiency from your marketing investment:

→ To create efficiency and scale, you need the right foundation made up of modern processes, a modern tech stack, and the right functions and talent.

→ Having the right modern tech stack that supports best practice execution helps you better measure success and ROI; it also helps focus your business on the end-to-end customer experience. It's cheaper and easier than you might think.

→ Investing in the right marketing functions and talent is key, especially as the software industry continues to explode and you compete more aggressively for the best people.

→ It's great to have a mix of junior and experienced talent, but there are key positions where you should hire up to get more value, impact, and return from your full-time equivalent investments.

→ Marketing functions are similar across business size but might have different emphasis or resource requirements in some areas based on the strategic path you are on or the level of dedicated focus needed in certain areas to support the business requirements.

SMOOTH SAILING

WHEN I FIRST CONSIDERED A circumnavigation it sounded bonkers, and immediately, my mind began to speculate the awful things that could go wrong. All I could envision was clinging with white knuckles as waves tried to devour me from every side. (There's a reason the earliest maps of the ocean included tiny drawings of sea monsters and angry gods.)

Little by little I began to appreciate that ocean travel not only provides many opportunities for survival, but it also provides incredible opportunities to see and do things I may not have had an imagination big enough for! I realized that once you learn what to do and how to do it, smooth, successful execution always depends on having the proper resources, good leadership, and a solid risk management plan.

When it came to funding and resourcing this enterprise, we had no idea what it would take to tackle a circumnavigation. We researched what others were spending, and it was all over the map: new or old boat, big or little boat, working from the boat or not working, sailing part time versus full time, marinas or anchorages, taste in food or drink, DIY or professional maintenance, levels of insurance, levels of draw from investments if any, use of fuel versus waiting for wind, cruising over a longer period versus not making any stops, and it went on. We concluded that we had to prioritize investments that matched success criteria most critical and unique to our personal sailing plan, which might be different for someone else seeking the same outcome.

Next, we needed to decide if we had the right leadership to even entertain this fantasy. Now my choice of husband came with a bonus prize because he already had decades of sailing experience. While we were both confident in his sailing ability, it took more time for me to come up the learning curve to take on voyaging and gain skills to handle a situation if he fell ill or worse. I quickly realized that good seamanship could take many lifetimes to learn, and there's no such thing as me *catching up* to him because as my learning progressed over the years, his did too. I needed to come to terms with having my own opinions on things but ultimately trusting his judgment in the end because he will always just know a little more than me about certain things.

Finally, we talked to a lot of people who had taken on this kind of sailing to learn what mistakes they made, what advice they had, and what they would do differently. There's a lot to be learned from those who made mistakes before and learned the hard way. We took all those learnings and figured out ways to reduce the risk to our little endeavor.

At some point I realized that embarking on this kind of journey can have striking similarities with how to approach business. Even though each individual boat may have the same overarching goal to go around the world, how one approaches the journey will define success or failure from the start. Allocating the resources specific to your unique situation, ensuring you have the right leadership and crew dynamic, and applying a learning mindset all provide subtle nuances that will define the outcome despite the navigational course being the same. You would want to begin a trip with the proper gear, provisions, and insurance to ensure you had every opportunity for success. You would also want to start the mission with a skilled navigator who knows the ropes and can guide you through treacherous conditions. You would also want to start the journey with a wide range of advice and perspective from others about how to adapt and make decisions along the way and what dead reckonings could take you unwittingly off course.

In this final section, I will be providing ways for you to think about your marketing investment and advice for finding and keeping a great CMO. Also, I'll cover some major pitfalls to avoid and advice from some of the B2B software industry's most respected marketing leaders. Before we get to these important concepts, let's do a quick review.

The following illustration covers the key requirements of modern marketing that we have covered up to this point. The

SURGE principles are the strategic enablers that define a great marketing strategy and are supported by executives top down. Unified execution is possible with key functions in place across marketing that are all working in harmony with tight operations and workflow. In the center is the modern CX tech stack that acts as the engine for today's digital-first customer experience. The foundation is based on five operating priorities that make modern marketing successful.

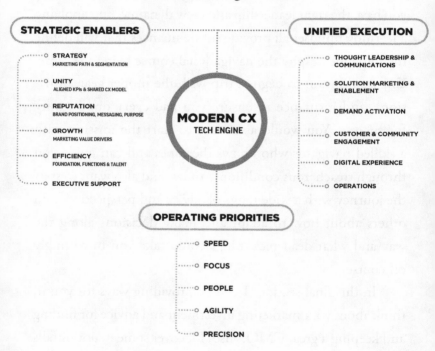

STRATEGIC ENABLERS

- O STRATEGY
  MARKETING PATH & SEGMENTATION
- O UNITY
  ALIGNED KPIs & SHARED CX MODEL
- O REPUTATION
  BRAND POSITIONING, MESSAGING, PURPOSE
- O GROWTH
  MARKETING VALUE DRIVERS
- O EFFICIENCY
  FOUNDATION, FUNCTIONS & TALENT
- O EXECUTIVE SUPPORT

MODERN CX
TECH ENGINE

UNIFIED EXECUTION

- O THOUGHT LEADERSHIP & COMMUNICATIONS
- O SOLUTION MARKETING & ENABLEMENT
- O DEMAND ACTIVATION
- O CUSTOMER & COMMUNITY ENGAGEMENT
- O DIGITAL EXPERIENCE
- O OPERATIONS

OPERATING PRIORITIES

- O SPEED
- O FOCUS
- O PEOPLE
- O AGILITY
- O PRECISION

Modern marketing methodology for success.

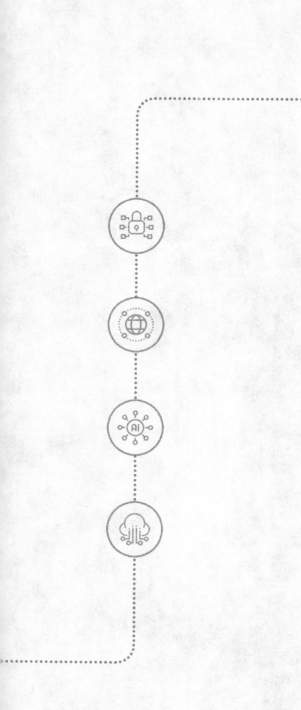

CHAPTER 10

THE MARKETING INVESTMENT

YOUR MARKETING INVESTMENT is the main sail that powers your entire program. It is critical to the success of your endeavor, as it provides steering control for where you want to go, helps maintain stability and balance across the marketing mix, and allows for course corrections as conditions change. Its role in a successfully executed marketing program cannot be overstated.

What's the Right Investment?

The truth is, there are more ways than ever to spend money on marketing and an infinite number of ideas on how to spend it. There's no magic number; it's uniquely based on your starting point, your strategy, your in-house capabilities, your technology stack, and your time window. There's also an old saying in marketing, "You can get it good, fast, or cheap but only two of these things at a time." This remains true today.

Reframing the *marketing budget conversation* as a *foundational business investment conversation* helps set the stage for properly discussing priorities and trade-offs across the business instead of thinking of the spend in a functional silo. Modern marketing includes a lot of technology, data, and process to get right, so it really must be considered more like an R&D investment to generate meaningful value.

Often, CFOs try to determine the magic number that should be spent on marketing. To find it, they scour the books of other competitors (mostly public companies, which you may not be) to determine the appropriate percentage to spend on marketing. Sometimes, the amount is difficult to determine, as it is rolled up into one *sales and marketing line item* as a percentage of revenue, so it's not always clear what the relative allocation is, which, from experience, differs from one company to the next. One company may be in a hypergrowth stage and have overhired in sales, with a much less mature marketing program. Another company may include things in that bucket that other companies account for elsewhere, such as marketing technology, IT outsourcing, and subscriptions.

Further, when breaking down the allocation between sales and marketing, companies account for programs differently in many cases. For example, one company may consider field marketing events as sales expenses or roll up BDRs in sales operations, while others account for that as a marketing allocation. A public company who is an established market leader with mature products and an active channel needs to spend money very differently than one who is a smaller, PE-owned innovator who doesn't yet have market demand. A company that has a hybrid offering and legacy renewals process invests differently than a pure SaaS vendor with a productive product-led growth (PLG) motion. One company might count partner market development funds in their sales budget, not their marketing budget or their website as part of their technology/product budget, not their marketing budget and so on and so on. I can tell you with confidence that no two B2B companies categorize their marketing the same way, so it's futile to try to run a competitive spend benchmark with any degree of confidence in the insights.

So how much should a B2B software company allocate to marketing? One analyst source will tell you somewhere between 5 to 10 percent of revenue should be spent on marketing, while another one will tell you it's more like 50 percent if you are pure SaaS transacting online trials, for example. Generalizations such as this can be misleading because it really depends on many factors that are unique to the business situation, market standing, condition of operations, and maturity of the GTM as a whole.

For growth companies, the investment may need to be higher because there will be a surge of effort to build a digital-first foundation to rapidly acquire new customers at scale. Companies in a growth stage need to invest more heavily as a percent of revenue than they would as a start-up or as a mature leader. As a business grows, those percentages might start shrinking so that more money can be spent on other projects, such as product development or expanding into new markets with a sales-led motion. For more mature companies in more mature markets where growth is low, there is more pressure on expenses and more of a need to expand within the base versus acquire net new.

Figure 10.1 can be useful in determining your general situation and how to think about investment and mix overall. I've seen many cases where companies will be acting like leaders or making a major pure SaaS play with their product and sales functions, but their marketing is still in a basic state, operating more like start-ups. For all the elements to work properly, the business needs to align across functions to achieve unified success.

Figure 10.1
Marketing evolution on investment and mix.

Marketing Mix: MATURE

- All previous capabilities
- Sophisticated Segmentation & Data Targeting
- Brand Sponsorships & Paid Placements
- Thought Leadership / Authorship
- Demand Centers in Region
- Mature Ecosystem Program
- Value Engineering

Marketing Mix: MID-TIER/GROWTH

- All previous capabilities
- Positioning Platform & Brand Foundation
- Segmentation & Targeted Contact Acquisition
- CX Aligned GTM Motions & PLG Elements
- Full Funnel Operations x Sales & Marketing
- Customer Programs & Community Building
- Localized Field Marketing & Precision ABM
- Always On Engine & Nurture
- Social/DevRel Engagement

Marketing Mix: BASIC

- Comms, AR/PR, Social Broadcast
- F2F Events/Industry Tradeshows
- Product/Tech Content & Sales Enablement
- Light Field Marketing
- Push Marketing - eDM
- Customer References
- Brand Templates & Artifacts
- Siloed CRM & MAP

To go from one stage to the next, you need to master the requirements in each stage, then add capabilities on top

Established Leader
Sales Expansion, Marketing Led Net New,
Channel. 20/50/30

10% Early Market, 3-5% Mature Market
>$500m+, Global Scale

Challenger or Pivot to Cloud
Sales, Marketing, Partner. 33/33/35

12-15% for establishing new market due
to surge Domestic + Targeted Regions

Startup or Niche
Sales Led Motion.
Marketing Supported. 80/20

7-8% of revenue for established/mature niche
market; 10-12% for new market or pure
cloud model Domestic or Global Pilots

251

Ultimately, the percentage you allocate for marketing will depend on your business realities and the size and goals of your company. But one thing's for sure: you need to invest in marketing if you want your business to grow at market growth rate.

> Stop looking at what your competitors spend on marketing as a percentage of revenue when determining what you should spend on marketing.
>
> Instead, determine the costs of what needs to be done in the customer journey based on your strategic plan and priorities.

The traditional way of looking at marketing investment was once confined to the elements covered in the first column of figure 10.2. It's a start, but it should be looked at holistically across the entire customer journey to determine what needs to be done in each stage to get the results you want. If you look at what engagements need to happen across the entire customer journey, investment areas can be much easier to prioritize based on where the biggest gaps exist. For example, ask yourself what engagements create the biggest pipeline or deal flow or where you need to automate to bring CAC down. Where do customers expect you to have self-serve digital engagements versus live engagements, and where can you speed trial conversions and onboarding?

CUSTOMER JOURNEY

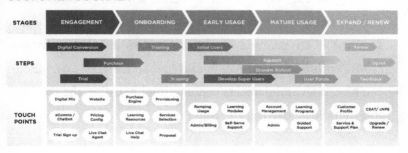

Figure 10.2

Determine investment priorities based on friction in the customer journey.

If you align the customer journey across marketing, sales, customer support/success, and technology, it will become crystal clear where you need to prioritize investments. Align customer touchpoints first, then overlay the conversion rates across your funnel; determine what should be high touch, low touch, or product-led; and then determine where you can reduce friction across the customer life cycle.

The investment calculus depends heavily on your conversion rates at every step. It's critical to understand what these rates are so you have the proper expectations when your sales and marketing teams are setting targets and investment envelopes. Many companies simply tell themselves they need a three or four times pipeline because that matches their close rate in sales, but there are so many other conversion rates to consider. To assist, I've summarized the B2B SaaS conversion rate expectations for each engagement stage using two different types of motions as examples.

Figure 10.3 is a full roll-up across a macro GTM funnel and types of conversion rates for illustrative purposes only. The first is an example of a more traditional B2B software model with both high-touch and low-touch motions, where you have sales and partners driving roughly half of the revenue and marketing driving the other half.

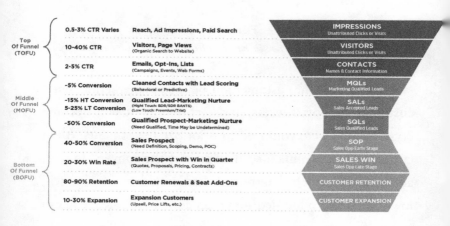

Figure 10.3

Traditional full funnel and example conversion rates based on best practices.

Figure 10.4 illustrates more of a digital-first model, where the motions are primarily marketing and product-led.

Figure 10.4

Example of digital-first model conversion rates based on best practices.

Note that for these examples, I've included all the possible engagement layers, but the best advice is to try to skip as many steps as you can to get as many people as possible to try or demo your product as your primary call to action. Your product trial or a self-serve demo is the primary place you want people to go, so don't make it hard for them to get there.

Back to conversion rates. The funnel you adopt will determine the conversion rates you need to consider and the math that ensues during the planning process when marketing sets targets. It will also depend on where you want to snap the chalk and what marketing is ultimately accountable for. Do you want to measure marketing based on how many marketing-qualified leads they gave to sales, how many sales opportunities they created, or how much pipeline they created, or do you want to measure them based on how many trials were downloaded or converted? Are they measured on retention, renewals, or expansion too, or is that a different team? The way to drive accountability is by being clear on how their success is measured.

Investment Goes with Decision Authority

Decision authority is having the responsibility and obligation to make a decision and the duty to answer for its success or failure. It's never helpful to put accountability for an outcome in one place and the decision authority somewhere else. If you have an expectation that marketing should deliver on something, they should also be able to make decisions on workflow, process, technology, and resources within the investment envelope to get the job done.

This works in B2B technology when it comes to product development. If you want products built, you give your head of products a goal, an envelope, and a timeline. You have an expectation that they will make the people, process, and technology decisions to get it done. You have given them the investment and the decision authority to deliver on your expectations. The same should also apply to marketing. They should be given targets, an investment envelope, and a timeline, as well as the decision authority on the people, processes, and technology to achieve the targets. Earlier, we discussed how modern marketing is drifting into what was traditionally sales territory, so it may be time to look at roles, accountability, and decision authority across your GTM.

If you still have reservations about handing over decision authority to your CMO, it might be time to reflect on why that is. This tends to be a big problem in companies that have evolved over time with legacy business processes and technology that's more fixed and rigid or where functions are aligned to traditional silos instead of being aligned to your prospect or customer journey. In these organizations, breaking out of a fixed mindset is a bigger hurdle than actually solving the problem to create a better customer experience or speed time to revenue.

The investment should exist in the same place where you will direct the glory for success or the blame if the targets aren't met. Yes, it's a team sport, but too many times I see expectations for the result put on marketing without decision authority (and sometimes without the full investment and resource authority) to go along with it. This can undermine the results everyone wants because it just takes too long to get simple changes made to remove customer friction or improve conversions.

> **If you expect marketing to deliver a specific set of outcomes, be prepared to give them the money, resources, and decision authority to get it done.**

Here's an example scenario to illustrate the point: A B2B platform company is trying to accelerate growth by pivoting to a digital-first, product-led model. The goal is to speed trial conversion and customer onboarding, but different functions own different parts of the customer journey. The finance team owns the procurement and billing systems, so they make decisions on the customer billing workflow. So when the prospect enters their credit card information for the trial, it triggers an email sent to the customer with a receipt. Marketing wants to change the workflow so the customer is immediately presented with a set of onboarding steps in a pop-up versus being just sent a receipt. They believe that by doing this, it would speed trial conversion and onboarding, which they have targets for.

Depending on the back-end systems, this change might require a decision across marketing, IT, products, and finance, who may have other priorities. Going around on this could take weeks or months, and I've seen it happen. Everyone would agree that it's a good thing to do in principle, but it may not be a priority for everyone. Agreeing on the right approach is probably done after a bunch of meetings among logical people, but because the systems and workflow that support that digital engagement are across different functions, no one knows who should make the call to change the process. Sadly, weeks can be spent figuring this simple thing out, which can be a huge waste of time.

In this example, by not looking across the entire journey, and by having different people responsible for different digital touchpoints, so much time can be wasted that will ultimately undermine your results. By being clear about who has decision authority for customer experience in the *try, buy, and use* stages of the journey, faster decisions can get made by people who have skin in the game on achieving the targets at each phase.

To a CEO, this can sound like a tedious example, but tiny little problems such as this clog up the system and create barnacles that slow progress.

When deciding what investment and authority to give to the CMO, ask yourself these questions:

- Do you want to hold marketing accountable for leads, opportunities, sales pipeline, trials, or users?

- If you want them to be accountable for revenue for a given channel, they need to be accountable for the workflow (i.e., inquiry to close) for that channel. Are you prepared to give them that decision authority and the investment to execute against it?

- What percentage of revenue do you expect to be marketing led versus sales led? The modern motion is a digital-first endeavor, so consider this carefully.

- Depending on your model, you may want to provide an acquisition experience or process transactions on your website for either trials, trial conversions, or full pricing agreements. Are you willing to make the CMO accountable for a web-led direct revenue target?

- Do you want to hold marketing accountable for retention and renewals in a digital-first model? Consider the execution being digital versus high-touch sales and support.

- Who is responsible for customer expansion, particularly in a digital-first motion, if the outreach is based on personalized but automated funnels?

- Who is responsible for renewals, particularly in a digital-first customer success model?

Where Does the Marketing Money Go?

If we spend $1 in marketing, how much revenue will that deliver? This is the vending machine question that is no longer relevant in the digital-first customer journey. There are things that cost big money, things that cost little money, and things that just need to get done by a set of hands. Not every dollar in marketing is valued the same way, nor does it do the same thing. The results you get come from a combination of integrated activities working together, not from $1 in and $1 out. By combining activities, you can speed conversions across the customer journey, which results in more pipeline, shorter sales cycles, and a lower cost.

> A better question is, where can we invest to most immediately improve conversions across the customer journey?

Marketing is a complex digital system. It's an investment in creating momentum and deal flow for today and quarters to come. Investments need to be made in surge activities, digital transformation or evolution, and brand positioning as well as in driving traffic and leads, reminding customers of your value, and communicating clearly and with impact, which takes many different tactics that either cost money or cost time.

At the highest level, spend falls into three basic categories: above the line, below the line, and always on.

ABOVE-THE-LINE (ATL) activities are made up of investments that are above and beyond the normal run rate. The term *above the line* originated in traditional accounting, where advertising costs were recorded above a line in the financial statement. Such activities might include anything to establish thought leadership, brand awareness, or broader positioning or reputation (or repositioning) initiatives, such as major campaigns, events, branded digital activities, surges in big social media programs, big product launches, or analyst relations strategy sessions to get support for developing a new category, for example. ATL activities in marketing are sometimes purely for awareness but may also include activities that acquire contacts to help augment your database. The goal is market positioning and contact acquisition.

ATL activities include personnel time and effort focused on reputation and vendor consideration that can't always be tied directly to the in-quarter pipeline. These efforts are tracked and optimized regularly, but it takes measuring over the course of sometimes years to gauge their effectiveness in achieving the goals. ATL initiatives can include one-off spikes for transformational activities such as a technology migration, a major web redesign, or a roll-out of a new brand identity. Because of their scope, ATL activities typically involve a budget allocation bubble to get started. Some of the costs can roll into the regular run rate or stop after they are completed. An example of a program that may roll into the run rate is when an analyst engagement to define a category turns into a new annual contract with that analyst.

BELOW-THE-LINE (BTL) expenditure tends to be allocations focused heavily on achieving lead and conversion targets through specialized activities, regular targeted programs, or specific plays. B2B marketing tactics in this category usually include integrated campaigns with a variety of activities that work together to generate the intended outcome, such as targeted ABM programs in a given region or industry. They may include digital, communications, sponsorships, specific industry trade shows or events, partner initiatives, and product promotions.

These activities focus on targeted engagement and interaction with a particular audience, aiming to generate leads, drive conversions, and build customer relationships. As customers interact with a brand on multiple channels, they expect a consistent user experience at each touchpoint, so many B2B software marketers now dedicate more of their investment to activities that ensure the customer journey is smooth and information flows between channels without disruption. BTL activities usually have a more flexible and tailored budget, as they can be scaled up or down depending on the specific campaign objectives, target market, and budget available.

ALWAYS-ON marketing involves a continuous dial tone of activities that establish a consistent and ongoing presence in the market. Simply put, these are things a company needs to do to compete at all. This includes having a website as an acquisition and expansion channel, SEO and basic paid search, rapid/crisis response, core media/analyst relations, solution marketing, content marketing, and sales enablement. It also includes customer communication, email automation, content syndication, retargeting, major events or market moments you just can't miss, and more.

Rather than large campaigns or discrete projects, these efforts make up the foundation that defines you as being open for business and are relentlessly pursued throughout the year. B2B always-on marketing focuses on delivering an enduring message that builds loyalty and interest among existing customers while also gaining visibility with prospective buyers. Ultimately, these types of methods give companies a better chance to reach their goals by being ever present and delivering a continuous hum of momentum and engagement over time.

There is a dangerous assumption that only the BTL demand creation activities matter; ATL activities are those things marketing might want to do but aren't critical, and always-on activities aren't well understood in terms of the general bandwidth it takes to just do the basics. As we covered in earlier chapters, using all methods together delivers more impact faster and improves conversion rates in the mid to late funnel. This happens because you are increasing your odds of generating higher-quality leads for current quarter targets while at the same time creating more prospects to nurture for future pipeline two to three quarters out. Ultimately, this powerful combination enables businesses to reach a broader audience and capture customers at various stages of the decision-making process, pushing them closer to conversion and delivering higher marketing ROI throughout the year.

Whether an activity is classified ATL, BTL, or always on, all activities have wide-ranging applications and are designed (and put in the plan by your marketing team) to work together as a whole, not as discrete activities. As a complex system, given the vast and ever-evolving digital landscape that prospects and customers navigate, it's important to have a comprehensive appreciation of the wide array of channels available to digitally surround customers online with the most effective message at the most critical time. The success of modern marketing depends heavily on using tactics that are complementary to, and build off of, one another.

Surges and Cuts

If you are an incumbent legacy brand trying to reposition yourself as something new in the market or you want to change decades of old perceptions about your company, you must do ATL marketing activities to make a dent in any reasonable time frame. This means you need to plan for a surge in investment. ATL marketing can't be done by taking existing funds from always-on activities and simply moving them. It doesn't work that way, and the value of the money doesn't match what you need to spend. Conversely, when financial pressures threaten marketing investments, executives tend to be tempted to cut specific channels and methods arbitrarily. Instead, it's more effective to determine more precisely how investments can be dialed back or paused for a certain period of time without creating a compounded problem later. Perhaps a content migration can be delayed, or attendance at an industry-specific event can be pushed back a year. Remember that marketing must commit to things sometimes months or years in advance, so deep, unexpected cuts can result in diminishing returns or poor ROI on activities where there are sunk costs.

Align Investment to Priorities to Track ROI

The following is a summary view of the four playbooks, the marketing priorities, general investment envelopes, and how to track ROI based on the four example scenarios. This is a general guideline only; there are many variations, but this offers a good place to start (see figure 10.5).

It is critical to look at the investment in the context of the business situation and what you ultimately need to accomplish versus just looking at what tactics people want or what the financial plan allows for alone. Using this approach to frame the marketing plan is helpful because it sets realistic expectations for what should be done with the money that exists. Measuring marketing ROI is hotly debated, and there are many ways to do it, but the answer is simple if you align it to the strategic playbook.

Again, deciding what percent of revenue to spend on marketing can be all over the map, which makes it even more important to set priorities and crisp objectives that can be measured.

TRANSITIONAL

Marketing Priorities:

- Reposition in the core customer base. To provide a path forward, consider a platform positioning strategy
- Focus on upsell/cross-sell, clearly defining segment and packaging customer successes

Marketing Budget: ~10% of revenue

In slow growth position but must invest to secure base

Key ROI Metrics: Marketing-led conversions in customer expansions or cross-sell trial conversions as a result of marketing outreach to installed base

LEADER

Marketing Priorities:

- Expand position by leaning into vision of where the industry is going
- Ensure lead to close conversion and optimize execution
- Maintain leadership position while feeding/nurturing pipeline and expanding growth engine at scale

Marketing Budget: ~10-15% of revenue

In high growth position but managing costs are more of an issue

Key ROI Metrics: A positive CLV-to-CAC ratio given how mature these companies typically are, share of voice

DEFENSIVE
Marketing Priorities:

- Reposition in a bounded segment or use case where you can win
- Focus on targeted ABM and winbacks with sales
- Focus on packaging for transaction and divert spend to shore up product gaps
- Modernize CX model, optimize processes and systems in a low-cost way for critical solutions

Marketing Budget: ~5-10% of revenue
In slow growth position but must find ways to optimize CX overall

Key ROI Metrics: ABM or marketing-led trial conversions, digital engagement rate for installed base

INNOVATOR
Marketing Priorities:

- Position in new category or more firmly define a growing category and drive thought leadership in an area where the leader has a gap
- Activate pipeline with targeted programs and build an engine for scale
- Invest in CX model and unified processes and CX tech engine to fuel growth and scale

Marketing Budget: ~25% of revenue (if revenue exsists)
In high growth position must be aggressive, time to invest in right CX tech engine to scale quickly

Key ROI Metrics: Trial conversions, digital share of voice (or unique web visits by proxy)

The Investment Is Not the Plan

When companies go through the annual budget planning process, what comes out is a budget, but this is not the marketing plan. In many cases the CFO or CEO provides marketing their budget number and says, "Here's your plan," without much interest in *the actual plan*. It is really important to understand the strategy and core components of the marketing plan in detail because investments and resources allocated at the beginning of the year don't typically align with assumptions and beliefs about what is achievable in that time frame. Sometimes they do, but it's not typical, so understanding the plan in detail is highly beneficial during the planning phase.

A marketing plan is a set of commitments, just as important as your product roadmap or sales modeling. It includes strategies and tactics you will use to achieve measurable business goals and details of the success dependencies that you uniquely can help with. Additionally, it provides key performance metrics needed to track success as well as potential actions required if there are any disappointments in meeting goals. A well-crafted marketing plan can help you understand how your marketing team intends to drive business value in each quarter and throughout the year and the expected return. Crafting an effective marketing plan requires careful thought and analysis, which is why it stands apart from simply allocating funds.

Also, a marketing strategy can be discussed while the investment envelope is being finalized. Your marketing team can give you a strawman strategy and plan as the company budget planning is underway and then commit to the targets once the final dollars are committed. The strategy should be largely the same, but final budget numbers would determine the reach and activation calculations based on the mix of ATL, BTL, and always-on activities. Whether you have a small investment or a large investment, you still need a directional strategy that everyone agrees on.

As a B2B software CEO, you know the importance of having a good strategic foundation and the right people in place to make sure your business succeeds. How do you determine if you have a good GTM strategy that will ensure that you are engaging and converting customers effectively and efficiently? Read on for the essential components that every B2B software CEO needs to address in their marketing plan. Don't worry if you can't answer these questions; they are great areas of collaboration that you and your CMO can work on together.

Top questions to ask yourself to prepare for marketing planning and investment conversations

Here are the top twenty questions you can be prepared for when collaborating with your marketing team on a plan (assuming it's the first time you are doing it). The nature of the questions is to help your team understand where you are coming from, how you see the role of marketing, and what your expectations and pressures are. It's often the case that teams dive into weeds on execution and actually never fully understand the big picture, how a CEO sees the state of marketing, and how it fits into the larger context.

1. What are the biggest issues or concerns of the board or the major investors, and what are the board's expectations of marketing, if any?

2. What does success for the business look like?

3. What are the three strategic goals for the company over the next twelve to eighteen months and what is the strategic playbook? (Remember, growth is not a strategy; it's an outcome.)

4. What are your expectations for marketing, and what does good marketing look like in your opinion?

5. How would you describe what it means to have effective marketing KPIs?

6. What are the biggest market perception challenges that hinder us from achieving our revenue targets?

7. What do you want the company to be known for?

8. What is the revenue breakdown across net new and expansion?

9. What percentage of revenue do you expect marketing to lead, in what areas, and why? Describe the motions.

10. How do you think about the different prospect and customer segments (verticals, needs, use cases, categories, etc.), and how would you prioritize them?

11. Who are the target audience priorities, and why?

12. How would you describe the customer journey today, and how would you like it to be in the future?

13. Who in your company contributes what in each area of the customer journey?

14. How do you determine marketing investment? What percentage of revenue do you think is appropriate, and why?

15. How do you think about measuring marketing ROI?

16. What do you see as the strengths or weaknesses in the current marketing strategy or structure, and where would you rate it in terms of maturity?

17. What are the marketing channels you have a bias for, and why? What have you seen work and not work in your past?

18. What current processes, systems, or data gaps are the most concerning across marketing, sales, products, and customer success?

19. How do you think about aligning goals across sales, marketing, product, and customer success?

20. What decision authority will marketing be given to achieve its goals?

Summary

What makes a successful sailing voyage is never just one thing. It's a combination of conditions and how you respond to those conditions that matter in the end. Having great sails is critical, but sails alone don't make your boat go faster if your boat is beat-up. Your hull must be clean, your crew must be alert and rested, wind conditions need to be favorable, and sailing downwind is always preferred. Just as there is no perfect amount to spend on preparing your boat, there is no perfect amount you should spend on marketing because there are so many factors to consider based on your current baseline situation.

Over the years I've concluded that there is no miracle calculus. I've seen companies that spend too little and spend too much for the return they're getting. Most CMOs will agree that there is a baseline spend just to be open for business, and there are certainly a myriad of ways to spend money. However, if you think of marketing as an investment in helping your customers achieve their goals, either better or faster, investment priorities across the customer journey become immediately obvious.

Also, depending on your stage, there are certain foundational elements of your marketing program you will spend money on no matter what; your digital CX stack and your always-on activities are examples. The question is, do you want to spend a little over time to create consistent execution and market momentum, or do you want to spend a whole bunch later all at once to make up for lost time or to clean up legacy problems? Marketing is not the place to be penny-wise and pound-foolish.

Whether you have a zillion dollars or only one, you still need a marketing plan that's mapped to your customer journey and aligned with your business strategy.

Here are some things to keep in mind when it comes to your marketing investment:

→ When you consider your investment levels, don't simply rely on percentage of revenue or what your competitors spend because it can be misleading. Determine what needs to get done across the entire customer experience and prioritize by impact.

→ Put the money and the decision authority where you will direct the blame or glory.

→ Marketing is a complex system, so not every dollar does the same thing or can be measured in the same way.

→ As a CEO, there are ways you can collaborate with your marketing team to ensure that you're getting the return you want to see from your marketing dollars.

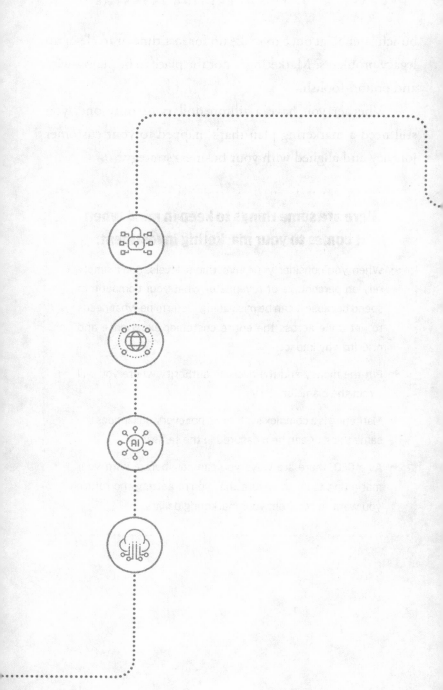

CHAPTER 11

FINDING AND KEEPING A STELLAR CMO

A GREAT SKIPPER will make or break any voyage. The three major attributes of a great skipper are technical expertise, sound decision-making, and leadership. You would expect them to be proficient in boat handling, sail trimming, navigating, and understanding weather patterns to maneuver the vessel effectively, optimize performance, and navigate challenging situations. You would also expect them to have great situational awareness and judgment so they could make informed and timely decisions related to weather conditions, navigation challenges, and crew safety. Above everything else, leadership is perhaps the most important thing. A great skipper must be able to inspire the crew, delegate appropriately, foster a positive team dynamic, and communicate clearly and calmly in any situation.

In the end it's not the boat that determines the outcome of your voyage; it's whether you have the right skipper to handle the boat you have on the voyage you choose. We talked a lot in the beginning of this book about the reasons why you may be struggling in marketing, and certainly, finding and keeping a great CMO is one of them.

Why CMOs Leave

In addition to my own experiences, I've researched this topic exhaustively in B2B technology with the goal to understand the dynamics and disconnects that drive CMO tenure. There are many articles out there, but I went deeper and captured my own quantitative data from about ninety B2B tech CMOs about why they leave.

The top five reasons CMOs leave are as follows:

1. Misaligned expectations about what marketing can deliver within the investment envelope

2. Interest to pursue better opportunity because of compensation/upside

3. Not aligned with CEO/founder

4. Transactional nature of the industry causes change (M&A, PE buyouts, etc.)

5. Lack of authority to make decisions/changes necessary to achieve goals

These are the items most directly tied to CMO success:

1. Alignment across the business around company positioning and market segmentation (strategy)

2. Authority to make decisions or take actions on areas they are accountable for (decision authority)

3. Alignment with sales on the entire GTM plan across sales and marketing (unity)

The following are the biggest pain points:

1. Systems and processes across the business to track marketing impact

2. Sales accountability and/or execution on the marketing leads

3. Marketing having a seat at the table

The top two biggest issues (above all else) contributing to low job satisfaction are as follows:

1. Low satisfaction that executive/stakeholder expectations are aligned with what marketing can deliver

2. Low satisfaction with sales being held accountable to the same standards and scrutiny as marketing

As you can see, some of the main themes here—misaligned expectations, lack of unity and accountability, and lack of decision authority—are what's causing friction from the CMO's side. It's worth noting that dissatisfaction with investment levels was nowhere near the top of the list. Funding is not the issue!

A large point of contention overall is the math. In development, it's about getting the code right. In sales, it's about getting the forecast and bookings right. In finance, it's about getting the P&L right. From the outside, marketing can look like it is part math, part technology, part hocus pocus, and what can appear to be a lot of chaos without measurable ROI. Attributing exact revenue to marketing activity isn't cut-and-dried and doesn't come easily.

Marketing used to be 80 percent marketing as a craft and 20 percent technology and operations. Now great marketing is 40 percent technology, 40 percent operations, and 20 percent marketing as a craft. This is true because marketing has become inherently digital, and customer engagement in B2B technology has moved from high touch to low or no touch as software services, buyer expectations, and the speed of business have evolved to take place almost exclusively online. Getting that combination right is the secret to connecting data and engagements to quantify true ROI in today's digital-first customer journey. However, it can't be done in a silo. It must execute in unity across sales, marketing, and support to be effective and measurable. We've covered this a lot already, but I wanted to reinforce its connection to CMO dissatisfaction.

We also have the time horizon problem. Having different expectations about how long it takes from idea to impact can create competing objectives across functions, divergent assumptions around where investment needs to go, and confusing conversations about what work is being done and the decisions and investments being made. Marketing is a future-focused function. It's important to remember that marketing looks beyond each quarter, and tactics that are being worked on today primarily impact future pipeline and deals (unless you have more of a consumer software buying motion). Too often, marketing contorts itself to fit into a quarterly forecasting model that it fundamentally isn't designed for. If your sales cycle is longer than ninety days, marketing will have a difficult time helping you close in-quarter deals for opportunities not already in the pipeline.

Then we have the trust problem. It's no secret how CEOs feel about CMO performance. There are many articles written that cover CMO shortfalls: not having a commercial understanding of the business, not being great at communicating to the board, lacking confidence or inspirational leadership, or not being trusted by their peers. It seems that a very small percentage of CEOs think their CMOs are best in class, which is heartbreaking but really begs the question, "Why?"

No CMO wants to be without the support and trust of their CEO. This gap in trust at the top is a major contributor to short CMO tenure. You may have gone through a couple CMOs of your own recently, or maybe you have found a great CMO you want to keep. It's important to know that trust plays a huge role in job satisfaction, and without it, CMOs will be tempted by better offers from companies with better products, better brands, and bigger budgets, but no CMO wants to leave a great boss where mutual trust exists.

It's well-known that trust correlates to a perception of performance, but do better trust and communication result in better performance, or is performance a condition of trust? Is it an issue of trust, a gap in communication, or a gap in competency? Is it treachery, a bad hire, or an unexpected elevation of a junior-level CMO that you expect to perform at the same level as the enterprise-class CMO at your last company? Only you can answer these questions.

CMOs certainly have a brand problem, but it's an incredible opportunity because you can help fix it. Just as you would take an active role in developing your chief product officer, you can do the same with your current CMO or a high-potential CMO so they can become the leader you need them to be.

Because of the sheer number of CMOs and CEOs in software, it can't be that everyone is incompetent and untrustworthy. If you can hire the right CMO for the right job, focus on creating a great dynamic based on communication and transparency, and offer good executive guidance and support, you will have an advantage while all your competitors wallow in their disfunction and begrudgery. Your relationship with your CMO can be a game-changer for your business if you want it to be.

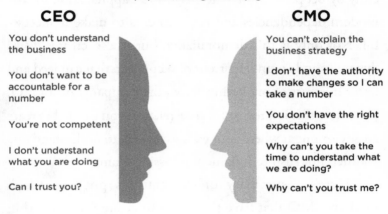

THE GAP OF GRIEF

What people are thinking but not saying

CEO

You don't understand the business

You don't want to be accountable for a number

You're not competent

I don't understand what you are doing

Can I trust you?

CMO

You can't explain the business strategy

I don't have the authority to make changes so I can take a number

You don't have the right expectations

Why can't you take the time to understand what we are doing?

Why can't you trust me?

TRUST & COMMUNICATION

Figure 11.1
The CEO/CMO gap of grief.

Being a CMO in this industry is one of the most complex, least well understood, and most underappreciated jobs in the C-suite. It's something everyone else thinks they know how to do, but it takes years to fully master and is changing all the time. I want to be clear that I don't think CMOs are victims, but I see it as my duty in this book to provoke a different perspective by putting on the table what many are thinking about but may not be talking about. I'm doing this for the sole purpose of helping you understand what you can do to get the strategic marketing you want.

CMOs are told all the time what they need to do differently by people who may not have a full appreciation for the modern dependencies and requirements to make it successful. Not only is this demoralizing, but it also creates weird dynamics and an undercurrent of skepticism that can feed and fester mistrust of marketing across the company. As a CEO, you know this is a recipe for disaster, and you can help create an environment where your executives seek to understand one another, not rush to judgment or assign blame.

Here's a summary of expectations put on today's modern CMO that have the power to create friction within the organization:

- They need to be able to understand the ins and outs of P&Ls and know enough about the magic of finance to be able to ask the right question of the CFO at precisely the right time when money gets moved around unexpectedly, but before it vanishes. Sometimes, they need to understand the inner workings of PE financing and how that impacts expenses.

- They need to be able to speak in sales language and explain how they directly impact the pipeline for things that aren't always directly attributable. They need to be able to convince sales as to why it's a good idea to follow up on leads they are given using personal influence because there may not be internal SLAs or processes that tie the funnel together.

- They need to be able to understand, communicate, and influence engineers and developers in a language they understand, often resorting to deep technical analogies to get their points across. They need to be credible, but not threatening, when asking technical questions, and they need to understand all the nuanced industry trends that are both directly and indirectly related to every product and feature the company either has or is thinking about.

- They need to be able to be their own CIO to manage dozens of outside SaaS services and be able to keep their IT teams adequately informed but not overreacting on issues of integration, privacy, and security.

- They need to be energetic, inspiring, optimistic, and strategic and also be able to cite every current conversion rate, click rate, opportunity count, and attribution percentage for the dozens or hundreds of campaigns and tactics running at any given time.

- They need to be able to be creative and know what good creative execution is and why it works to logical, non-creatives in a way that resonates and gains buy-in.

- They need to be sure all executions and programs offend no one but still stand out in the market globally.

- They need to be epic communicators at big customer events, and they need to be able to create and manage everyone else's keynote content and delivery in addition to their own.

- They need to manage an investment envelope that is highly unpredictable and goes to sometimes hundreds of third parties, vendors, and contractors with whom they also need to build trusted relationships with. They need to manage a network of contracts that are all interdependent.

- They need to manage crises and expectations from every other function at all levels in the organization that have strong opinions about what marketing should be doing without unintentionally offending anyone that might be giving input but has no actual experience ever doing marketing as a vocation.

- Sometimes, they need to do all this resorting to making assumptions about what the business strategy is without any direction.

Can you name any other function with this range of expectations on potential sources of friction besides a CEO? When you are thinking that maybe your current CMO can't cut it, I invite you to reconsider the full picture.

Remarkable marketing allows customers to overlook missing features more easily, helps make the sales team sound amazing so they don't have to work so hard to qualify opportunities, shortens the sales cycle, and creates beachheads to expand existing accounts. Collaborating with your CMO to understand the art of managing perceptions is critical to building trust and appreciation for the full power of marketing. With an understanding of internal expectations and potential sources of friction, you can help support a better internal dynamic and get much better results.

Attributes of a Great CMO

Remember, by the time you decide to hire a new CMO, or your company's first CMO, you are probably already behind where you need to be. The symptoms of not having a CMO manifest a lot later than the root issues take hold, often by twelve to eighteen months. So make this decision earlier than you are comfortable doing and hire up for more talent than you think you need.

As we've discussed, the role of the CMO has evolved over the years, and it will continue to change as new technologies and trends emerge. Beyond just marketing skills and executive leadership, here are some of the key attributes you should be looking for in a CMO:

BUSINESS ACUMEN

A CMO must have a solid financial understanding of how the business works to ensure that marketing efforts stay connected and on track toward broader organizational objectives and constraints. They must understand fundamentals such as balance sheets, investment strategy, and risk management since a critical relationship is that with the CFO. If you have an internal high-potential that doesn't yet demonstrate this, commit to coaching them up on this front.

CUSTOMER-OBSESSED

A CMO must be able to lead and manage the customer experience across various touchpoints and channels. This will require a deep understanding of the customer journey and a data-driven approach to deliver tailored experiences that anticipate customer needs and exceed their expectations. They must have a passionate bias for the customer and prospect experience end to end.

COLLABORATIVE

A CMO must be able to not only partner with other functions, such as product development, sales, customer success/support, and finance, but they must also demand it and drive necessary changes to create unity for achieving the business goals overall. This will require a strong understanding of the business and a deep understanding of the CEO's challenges and pressures. They can help you create and nurture unity across your executive team as a strategic function if you enlist their help.

STRATEGIC

A CMO must be able to think strategically and anticipate opportunities for growth and improvement. They must be able to help develop effective business strategies that align with the organization's overall goals and objectives with a bias to customer and market needs, perceptions, and expectations.

They must have a demonstrated ability to create a market segmentation model and prioritize segments with sales.

DATA DRIVEN

A CMO must possess competence for leveraging data and analytics to make informed decisions about campaign strategies, audience targeting, and overall marketing ROI. They will need to be skilled in data analysis and interpretation to create marketing programs that are based on customer insights and feedback.

TECHNOLOGY AND INNOVATION

A CMO must be able to drive marketing innovation using both foundational systems (CX, CRM, martech, etc.) and emerging technologies such as AI. They will need to stay up to date with emerging trends and technologies to ensure that the organization stays ahead of the competition. Marketing should be the most forward-leaning technology function in your organization with the freedom experiment.

BRAND STEWARDSHIP

A CMO must be able to demonstrate authentic thought leadership and evangelism to the markets you serve. They should be a strong spokesperson externally, and internally, they must be able to drive enthusiasm and inspire the workforce to align with the company's values, vision, and strategy.

I invite you to clearly define what you are hiring for, what you want the CMO to do, how you can help give the CMO the right authority to make the changes necessary to do what you want them to do, and finally, how you can help nurture a relationship based on communication and trust.

Hiring a First-Time CMO

So you start to interview potential CMO candidates, and somewhere in the process, you may say to yourself, "Seriously, why are these people so expensive?" Instead, you may opt to hire a first-time CMO, rationalizing that the individual can grow into the job. Plenty of great talent is sitting on the sidelines, waiting and wanting to step into a first-time CMO job, and this is a great plan. The capabilities are out there, but there is an investment on your part to make sure this person can be successful. You might want to save money initially, but you must also commit to mentoring them if you want to achieve the Power of Surge outlined in this book.

When it's someone's first CMO gig, they truly believe your company can do more to optimize within your current investment (not to mention they really want the job). CMOs are generally eternal optimists; it's our superpower. We sincerely want to save the day, and so we focus on what's possible, assuming we have the support to do the job. New CMOs believe they can come in, make optimizations to prove value and build trust, and by delivering the right results, will be able to exceed your expectations.

But the reality is, for a new CMO, it's their first time doing it. This means the burden is on you to make it work. They will need coaching and guidance in the first year. If you are not willing to do this or invest in their development, you should hire a more experienced CMO. There is a reason you pay for experience.

If you are owned by PE firm and are hiring a CMO who is working in a PE environment for the first time, take the time to explain how it works. Without proper context, a new CMO may see the economic reality (with the debt and the downward pressure it puts on investments and how executives make decisions), and it can be very confusing based on what they may be used to. They just need to understand the model.

Hire Talent to Match Your Strategy

The talent pool is diverse, and there are a few types of talent, but I'll boil it down to generalists and specialists and which situations match those capabilities.

GENERALISTS

The ideal candidates have experience as a generalist across all aspects of marketing and have transformation experience. They understand the strategic planning components required to segment and target the right buyers. They have an operational understanding of how the marketing engine needs to work. They understand the products and nuances to be able to collaborate and debate with the product team on what's most important to talk about, and they have the capability to partner with sales to drive accountability across the GTM strategy. They will be able to do all this plus understand the full marketing stack and all the necessary tactics. These people don't grow on trees, and many are reluctant to work for PE companies.

Broad generalists tend to (but not always) come from various functional areas but have broader emphasis on the product marketing, digital marketing components, demand generation, branding, and operations.

After generalists, there are specialists who tend to come in two flavors: product marketing and digital or functional marketing.

PRODUCT MARKETING SPECIALISTS

These candidates have more of a product marketing bias as specialists but have perhaps dabbled in other areas. These candidates may have deeper technology or market knowledge and be very competent in more valuable sales conversations. There is a strong tendency to hire product marketing talent that specializes in product content and enablement because that can be a big pain point for sales or because it's a skill that a majority of technology-focused executives value most. Because broader marketing can be foreign to some executives, the internal interview team (CEO, head of products, head of sales) will naturally have a bias toward the product marketing person because it is relatable and fulfills a very visible pain point. Please know this bias exists when you interview candidates because even though it's familiar, it may not be your biggest need.

DIGITAL OR FUNCTIONAL SPECIALISTS

Companies tend to hire people who fill a particular gap they need at that time. If a CEO has a desire to create more user engagement and wants to create a user conference and community, they may have a bias toward someone with deep user event or community experience. Or if the CEO thinks the digital program is going fine because a lot of emails are going out but wants more press coverage, they might prefer someone with a communications background. When the foundational operations aren't working, nothing can be measured, and they really need an operational specialist.

Either way you go, make sure the candidate you hire has resources to support the other areas. Either hire a generalist CMO who can hire (or partner) with a strong product marketing lead or hire a product marketing person as the CMO, knowing there may be gaps, so be prepared to also add a very strong digital leader with bigger operational skills that they can partner with. In either case, hire more than you think you need.

What is most critical is choosing a CMO that best fits the strategy you will be pursuing. Refer to figure 11.2 below.

Figure 11.2

CMO fit for your strategy.

TRANSITIONAL

CMO Fit: A more seasoned, experienced generalist, who understands brand transformation & change management. Can manage complexity and ambiguity well with deep CX and modern tech experience. Has the patience to untangle detailed process challenges and is excellent positioning strategy.

LEADER

CMO Fit: A more seasoned, experienced generalist. Expert at brand and thought leadership, personal presence and communication skills. Inspirational leader with demonstrated success unifying sales efforts.

DEFENSIVE

CMO Fit: A more seasoned generalist or a specialist in ABM who has the grit of an Iditarod musher. Good financial awareness and is comfortable with complexity and ambiguity. Must be proactive in getting help to clarify priorities and manage change but must also have nerves of steel with the ability to say no.

INNOVATOR

CMO Fit: A more seasoned specialist may be best here. Understands solution and product marketing with a growth mindset. Has had some experience across omnichannel and understands the principles of building for scale. Must understand or hire for deep CX and modern tech experience.

Keeping Your CMO

CEOs in the B2B software industry know just how important it is to have an exceptional CMO. Finding a great CMO can feel like hunting for a purple unicorn, so once you have one, it's important to hang on to them. You'll want to get serious about creating an environment where they can thrive (decent compensation notwithstanding). That means giving them the strategic context to build a solid plan, access to the right technology tools and data sources, an investment with some room to maneuver, and most importantly, autonomy to take risks and experiment.

These are all good people at this level, so it's worth it to make sure that you have the foundation you need to retain them for as long as possible. Take the time to ensure you and your CMO are on the same page and have the right expectations for success. CMOs leave because they lose the belief that they can be successful in delivering against expectations given the realities of the situation: time horizon, technology or process gaps, cultural resistance to change, and so on.

Here are some ideas that will help you keep a great CMO:

CREATE A COMMON LANGUAGE WITH YOUR CMO

Use the SURGE principles outlined in this book to create a common understanding and context for collaborating with your CMO as they deliver strategic marketing aligned to the outcomes you strive for. If you use this book as a foundation for understanding what modern marketing is and how to apply it together with your CMO, you will be miles ahead of your competition, and your CMO will love their job! No, this book will not solve everything, but it will absolutely start the right conversations, which benefits everyone.

BE OPEN TO NEW IDEAS

A good CMO should be constantly on the lookout for innovative ways to engage and compel customers to act. The nature of a new idea is that no one else is yet doing it, which can be uncomfortable but could result in a great outcome. Progressive organizations are open to experimentation and managed risk-taking by marketing. These can come in many forms, such as introducing innovative thought leadership or brand efforts, pushing for quality over quantity in marketing efforts, or making data-driven decisions in areas that none of the competition is thinking about.

If a CEO allows a CMO space to drive more creative solutions that could deliver growth or value, then it's a win-win situation with benefits all the way around. Showing your CMO that you're willing to take risks can be a great way to keep them motivated and engaged with your company's mission. At the end of the day, the CMO wants to deliver their best work.

RESPECT THEIR EXPERTISE AND DIVERSE PERSPECTIVES

CMOs are experts in their field, much in the same way as your CFO or head of products. A good CMO will bring a lot of knowledge and experience to your team, so it's essential that they are set up to contribute at the same level. A great CMO will have spent their entire career obsessing about things other functions may not fully appreciate.

A CMO also brings balance to a business that can be saturated with technobabble and praise for features, which is a valuable perspective. The CMO must ensure that the technology ideas don't get lost in the noise of the competition or layers within an organization stuck in groupthink. Diversity in thinking and breadth in perspective are powerful tools in business today. Not only does this provide your team with a more enriching collaboration experience, but it also sparks creativity and agility when presented with difficult business challenges.

APPRECIATION

Competition is fierce for the best minds in marketing, but the little things go a long way. Make sure your CMO and your entire marketing team feel valued for what they do and appreciated for the role they play. Realize that marketing now does a lot of heavy lifting in the modernized funnel that may be largely invisible to other parts of the organization. Nothing is more disheartening to marketing than being on an all-hands call at the close of a quarter hearing the CEO acknowledge individual sales reps when many on the marketing team have spent months neglecting their families to help achieve that outcome too. A simple thank you goes a long way.

Summary

Everyone knows the story of the famous Portuguese sailor and explorer Ferdinand Magellan, who was renowned for leading the first circumnavigation of the globe. Sponsored by King Charles I, the Spanish monarch at the time, the aim was to find a westward route to the Spice Islands, which would benefit the crown in completely new ways. Magellan's achievement in circumnavigating the globe brought huge advancements in geographical knowledge and navigation. As a bonus, he demonstrated that the earth is indeed round. Magellan is celebrated as a skilled navigator who changed ocean exploration forever.

Now imagine how this story would have gone if the king had said, "Yes, go do that, but I'm not sure you can get it done, and I don't think you need boats. Good luck." It sounds ridiculous, right?

As the CEO, you are the king, and you make the calls, but the reason you hire a great CMO is to take you where you want to go based on the knowledge and situational experience they have. Assuming you have hired the right CMO for the job at hand, they will need you to be open about your expectations and new ideas, have great two-way communication, and share your vision for success. But they will also need decision authority and your support to drive unity of effort and accountability. By collaborating effectively with your CMO based on a foundation of trust, not only will you succeed in completing your journey, but you might also profoundly change the course of history in the markets you serve!

The following are things to consider when it comes to finding and keeping a great CMO:

→ Industry-wide, there is a large disconnect between CMOs and CEOs today in B2B software that is getting in the way of great execution, but if *you* can fix this gap, you will be ahead of your competition and can use this to your advantage.

→ Consider what business situation you are in when you hire a CMO because different situations and business models call for different capabilities.

→ Determine whether you need a generalist who may have broader experience or a specialist, where you may need added talent to fill out capabilities.

→ When hiring a first-time CMO, consider the role you will need to play to make sure this person is successful.

→ There are ways to make sure you can keep a great CMO, and they are all within your control today.

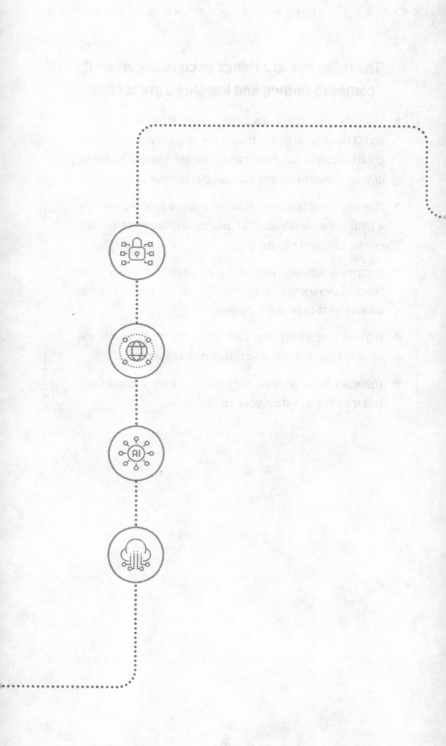

CHAPTER 12

STAYING ON COURSE

BEFORE GPS, MANY sailors determined their position through a method called *dead reckoning*, which involved plotting a series of positions on a chart based on the initial known position and continually updating the positions as the vessel moved, more or less in a line. Unfortunately, this approach proved marvelously imprecise. Because it doesn't account for wind, current, and variations in speed, errors can accumulate over time, leading to gross inaccuracies that could either get you generally where you wanted to go or take you to an entirely different continent.

Some decisions can be a little like this. You set out with the right ideas, but little by little they can take you off course over time. You might not even see the undercurrents while they are happening, so you don't realize how wildly off course you veered until you reach a destination and look backward.

Setting up your marketing program and CMO for success includes three critical organizational decisions you will make. On the surface they seem inconsequential, but you should consider them carefully. All three of the following areas are hotly debated and perilous, which is why I owe it to you to bring them up:

1. Deciding a PLG model replaces marketing

2. Hiring a chief revenue officer (CRO) to lead marketing thinking it replaces a CMO

3. BDRs/SDRs reporting lines

Remember, gentle reader, this applies to small to midsize B2B software companies, not large, sophisticated multinational organizations. We will explore pitfalls and considerations for each of these decisions next.

Product-Led Growth (PLG)

Let's be honest, the B2B software industry has always been product-led. The main idea that has existed for decades in tech is if you build great tech, it will sell itself, or *if you build it, they will come*. As software solutions moved to the cloud, the solutions themselves started to decouple into services, components, or workflows that were delivered in use cases versus through monolithic adoption. As the industry matured and the number of software companies exploded, everything got more competitive. The user experience became more important, particularly as next-generation buyers and users demanded it.

With the evolution of digital, customer engagements went virtual, requiring new tools, data, and automation to attract, acquire, and retain customers across the customer life cycle. Business software vendors aspired to deliver consumer-like attributes akin to Facebook. More competition, consumer-like expectations, and ease of use all became requirements as the cloud/SaaS economics meant costs to acquire and service customers simply had to come out of the equation.

Let's look at the following ways PLG strategies in B2B software are supposed to be distinct from traditional models:

1.) FOCUS ON THE PRODUCT

In traditional B2B software, the focus is often on sales efforts to generate opportunities and acquire customers. In PLG, a product that is intuitive, user-friendly, and provides value to users from the moment they start using it, doesn't need as much explanation, complicated demos, or resource-heavy proof of concepts. By prioritizing the product experience, freemium, easy trial offers, and simple onboarding, PLG aims to drive user adoption and engagement, leading to organic growth and expansion.

Requirement: Make better products that are easier to use.

2.) SELF-SERVE AND USER ONBOARDING

PLG emphasizes a self-serve model, where users can discover, sign up for, and start using the product without requiring direct sales involvement. User onboarding becomes crucial in PLG, focusing on providing a seamless and intuitive experience to help users quickly understand and derive value from the product. This approach reduces the friction in the adoption process and empowers users to explore and evaluate the product at their own pace.

Requirement: Digitize the customer experience.

3.) VIRALITY AND NETWORK EFFECTS

PLG leverages the inherent virality of the product to drive growth. By providing a product that encourages sharing and collaboration or invites other users to join, PLG seeks to create network effects, where the value of the product increases as more users join the platform. This viral loop can fuel rapid organic growth and expand the user base.

Requirement: Create a great ecosystem and customer community because no software exists on an island.

4.) DATA-DRIVEN ITERATION

PLG relies heavily on data and analytics to gain insights into user behavior, usage patterns, and conversion metrics. This data-driven approach enables continuous iteration and improvement of the product, optimizes the user experience, and drives increased user engagement and conversion rates.

Requirement: Modernize your customer experience platform to inform decisions.

5.) CUSTOMER-OBSESSED APPROACH

PLG prioritizes understanding customer needs, pain points, and feedback throughout the product development and marketing process. By actively listening to customer insights and incorporating them into the product roadmap, PLG aims

to deliver a solution that aligns closely with customer requirements, leading to increased customer satisfaction, retention,
and expansion.

Requirement: *Adopt a customer-centric operating model that increases stickiness.*

6.) LAND-AND-EXPAND MODEL

PLG often employs a land-and-expand approach, where the
initial product adoption serves as a foothold within an organization. As users find value in the product, it can spread to
other teams and departments, leading to organic growth and
increased adoption throughout the organization.

Requirement: *Deliver more value to your customers.*

The benefits are glorious! Think of it, a product that doesn't
need to spend money on marketing, sales, or customer support
aside from anomalies and escalations. With PLG, companies
can now achieve sustainable, scalable business growth and
maintain lower customer acquisition and services costs with
only developers! Find me a fainting couch, I'm swooning!

All of these things are requirements for competing effectively as a B2B software company today—period. While PLG
is intended to be a revolutionary business strategy in which
the product itself drives user acquisition, expansion, conversion, and retention, the fact of the matter is, as a B2B software
vendor, these are expected of you to *varying degrees* depending
on how gnarly and expensive the problem is that you solve.

> I believe it should be every B2B software company's ambition to adopt a PLG model as it relates to delivering value, ease of use, and swift adoption, which requires every company to be customer-obsessed ultimately.

Furthermore, it's not that you no longer need to do sales and marketing; it just means your sales and marketing looks very different than it used to. What your GTM now needs to look like is very much what I've already outlined in this book and depends on where you are in your stage of evolution and business maturity.

PLG Dead Reckonings

For B2B software companies who are making the pivot to becoming a PLG company, it's a journey. In practice, shifting to a PLG model overnight is difficult for many of the same reasons it's always been hard to deliver great software that sells itself. It takes time to rebuild old code, manage customer migrations, and go through a successful digital transformation and cultural resistance to changes in process, workflows, and functions.

If a fully functioning new product with a working free trial did miraculously spring from creation overnight, there would be legacy workflow and business systems supporting an old customer experience that might be kludgy at best, built on top of old systems with process and legacy data problems. Complicating the adventure even further are those pesky M&As, where entire software feature sets must now integrate with whatever sales motion or digital customer journey exists that day.

As more product development teams are being asked to broaden their thinking, they have started taking ownership of the end-to-end customer journey, but the result is mixed. In an attempt to drive product management closer to customers, some CEOs have even merged the function with product marketing or taken product marketing out altogether. The benefit is that it has forced product teams to have an outside customer-facing view of how their users experience and interact with the product. The downside is that some product teams have started creating what they believe are new functions to augment their development teams' learning on the fly rather than simply collaborating with experts in sales, marketing, and support that already exist or previously existed and understand the model. This is especially true for young teams that don't fully appreciate the richness that can be delivered through clear lines of responsibility and the strategic role that good product marketing can play when used properly.

Here's a possible scenario. A company wants their product teams to be more customer focused—so far, so good. They disband the product marketing teams altogether and tell the product management teams it is their job to deliver the product in a PLG model. Then they move the marketing team under the CRO in sales (which I'll get to shortly) and tell the marketing team to focus on demand generation.

A couple of years go by, and here's what happens.

The product teams continue to focus on product development and delivery. The sales team hires more sales-enablement people to build more enablement and messaging for every customer scenario under the sun because there are no priorities set for what to focus on. The marketing team hires more demand generation people to support all the campaign plays the sales teams individually want by territory, and because there is no prioritization on the sales plays and no leverage across the campaigns, the individual teams are duplicating activities and targeting the same customers. The customer support team hires more customer education people to create onboarding journeys for every situation to support every sales requirement.

Responsibility for pricing goes to the finance team, whose focus on pricing changes because of bandwidth versus better packaging or dynamic pricing methodologies. The website ends up with too many random pages with no coherent narrative, and the brand suffers in the market because no one was focused on the overarching customer value proposition, and customers no longer understand what you do. CAC goes through the roof because the cost to fill all these gaps was much greater than just keeping the product marketing team and creating deeper collaboration between the two teams in the first place. Right intention, wrong outcome.

It's important to note that this is not a dramatization; it's a situation I've seen many times.

> Product management is a distinct role. Product marketing is a distinct role. They are not the same and require different skill sets.

PLG in a Start-Up

If you are a start-up, you can start fresh, but start-ups have their own challenges. Let's take the example of a start-up delivering a cloud-based offering. They start with a minimum viable product and a development team. Because a young company is still learning and still small, many people are doing many things to make the magic happen, so workflow and the customer life cycle can initially be (let's say) beautifully messy.

Developers are also trying to build a website experience and integrate the trial offer into some purchasing engine. Someone else might be trying to create some onboarding materials or tutorials just before jumping on the phone or posting a YouTube video of a demo they just did. The start-up has a core product and is trying to get it off the ground without yet having a full business model around it to support all the promises of what PLG intends to deliver. Pretty soon the whole dev team is focused on building from scratch a bespoke digital customer experience around it (because they are developers and like building stuff and don't realize what already exists off the shelf). Now you have product people inventing modern marketing and business operations learning on the job rather than focusing on delivering the actual product you are selling.

Finally, there's the tricky bit about getting the word out about your software with thousands of companies in the B2B tech space all shouting at once for a customer's attention.

Taking an old PLG example to underscore my earlier point that it's been around a while, Napster solved a real problem and went viral in a space where you could hear a pin drop. In today's crowded and noisy software market, very rarely is a product so good that it doesn't need some marketing and sales support in the beginning for it to get traction. Yes, there are some but not many.

PLG should be the aspiration of any modern software company. For software that addresses complex problems at high price points, multiproduct companies, more mature companies with legacy processes and systems, or start-ups that haven't fully figured it out yet, it's an evolution, not a revolution. With the digitization of the customer experience, marketers have become more technical and do this stuff for a living. Developers don't need to do this themselves. A huge advantage for you would be to think about how to break functional silos that might exist among sales, marketing, and product teams so they can work together to create the ideal digitized customer experience that makes the product really shine.

CRO Dead Reckonings

Over the last decade or so, many software CEOs have concluded that because marketing has existed as a sales support activity, as it goes more digital, they should hire a CRO and put marketing under this person or fold marketing under the current sales leader. For some, it has worked; for many, the results have been underwhelming at best.

Many CEOs have a natural bias to hire a career salesperson for a CRO position. This is where the role naturally evolved from decades ago as we made the slow turn to cloud in the first place. It seems like a logical decision at the outset. These evolved-from-sales CROs have their own bias on sales execution in any given quarter. Their DNA is all about quarter-to-quarter results, and their focus, their tendency, is at the bottom of the funnel. The world revolves mostly around a three-month period.

The exception, of course, is when a company hires a president who runs all aspects of GTM, say for a larger company, with many business units potentially, or a company over $1B. The mistake is to assume this model also works for a small business, which I will tell you on behalf of me personally and every CMO in software I've spoken to about it, it does not work, and I'm going to explain why.

The role of the CRO started evolving when there was a recognition in technology firms that there needed to be someone to complement a CEO/founder. There was a recognition that in addition to providing product vision, if a company had someone responsible for driving revenue, it would create the best formula for success.

Many sales leaders naturally evolved into these roles, which provided a great career path to become a CEO. In larger companies, this works well because the CEO has many more hats to wear and places to be. It allows the CEO to focus on investors and outside stakeholders and the overall vision or tech roadmap. They can also spend more time with customers, the board, analysts, the press, and so on, thus leaving to someone else the day-to-day operations driving revenue. The scope typically included sales, marketing, support, and services. Sometimes this is also called the chief customer officer.

Smaller organizations started to adopt this model folding of marketing under this function as a progressive way to attract sales talent into the organization. The idea was that by broadening the scope of the role, they could attract and recruit higher-caliber sales talent; otherwise, getting great sales leaders is generally a challenge in software. These sales leaders would have a great sales record, but perhaps they would have less experience in a broader, more operational role in the organization. The logic goes that by folding marketing and other roles under the CRO, the CRO could provide marketing leadership that would negate the need to additionally hire a CMO that may come at a larger price tag or open the options for hiring more *workers* and having fewer *leaders*. This is often the thinking in smaller or early growth companies.

That is a great plan in theory, but it's not paid off for early or midstage companies.

Rather, because the pressure is predictably to deliver revenue at that moment, the CRO can't help but focus solely on hitting quarterly targets. The CRO is in the position where they own both the number and the decisions about how best to use head count to achieve the number across all functions (sales, marketing, support, and services). The math is simple: if they hire more heads and give them more quota, they will make the number, and sales and marketing investment is a one-line item on a P&L statement. In a CRO's mind, sales and marketing is one investment, including anything that immediately contains sales enablement, sales development, and sales tools.

New CROs now responsible for marketing aren't career marketers, nor are they typically experts on the holistic customer experience. They certainly may understand it and be very keen to be responsible for it, but at the end of the day, they're accountable for the number for that quarter. They typically are not measured on anything related to bringing in more leads at the top of the funnel. They're accountable for the deals they close this quarter.

The truth is, they may appreciate marketing all day long, but the way they're measured isn't aligned with what marketing does.

> **Sales exists to find opportunities and close deals.**
> **Marketing exists to create demand and generate pipeline.**
> **They have the same goal but different objectives.**

Meanwhile, any experienced B2B software CMO wants to report directly to the CEO for two reasons: (1) every CMO wants to play a strategic role at a company in creating categories and markets and building world-class brands, and (2) they want to be responsible for what they are measured on, not what is outside of their control.

When a marketing leader is reporting to sales, what gets deprioritized are marketing activities such as securing market positioning, creating thought leadership, changing broader market perceptions, driving consideration and preference, acquiring new contacts to nurture in future quarters or future year pipeline, improving corporate or broader internal communication (beyond sales), and creating larger initiatives for modernizing the tech engine across the functions to achieve scale. These are activities you can't afford to lose. Putting marketing under a CRO means making a choice to fundamentally focus marketing on very short-term results that have unintended consequences.

Any decision you make will have consequences that you may or may not be able to foresee except in hindsight. I have witnessed the following five very predictable outcomes from decisions to use a CRO to also lead marketing:

1.) FOCUS ON THE SHORT TERM

If all the sales and marketing focus is on closing in-quarter opportunities, the opportunity development cycle starts new *every single quarter*. It's all just a forecasting exercise for that quarter, so everything is oriented to the short term.

- Aside from deals that get pushed out, every quarter, the marketing team primarily focuses on three things: hot-or-not activities, sales enablement, and deal support.

- The focus is all on the bottom of the funnel. If prospects are not going to buy this quarter, the prospect gets displaced out of the system because generally, sales reps want a clean forecast, and the opportunity doesn't get developed for future quarters.

- Sales enablement content is heavily weighted to the bottom end of the funnel, and there are very few cycles spent on content and activity to develop next quarter's deals.

- Product marketing turns into deal support. Pulling in product marketing to do the sales pitch can become a bad habit and doesn't scale obviously. It also means they are spending less time helping create content for digital engagements that can happen at scale.

2.) INABILITY TO GET PREDICTABLE DEAL FLOW

If everyone aligns on closing in-quarter deals, the customer experience is very transactional, and there is less effort focused on developing future pipeline that is dependable.

- The BDR teams focus on supporting specific reps doing specific activities that run the risk of not having repeatable pipeline development activities nor consistency in lead follow-up for future quarters. This is especially true if the BDR team is small, new, and operationally less mature.

- Marketing efforts are spent nurturing contacts that already exist, so you are just going back into the same well repeatedly to invite the same people to whatever sales activity is being planned.

- With sales and marketing both focused on the same set of contacts or cold calling, statistically, there won't be enough pipeline each quarter to hit the growth targets since every quarter starts brand new without warm pipeline.

- If you are depending on a more buyer-led sales cycle, it means you would still not have spent enough to drive demand to get the deal flow you want to your website or inbound. If your buying cycle is one to two months, this may be okay for a while, but at some point, you will hit a wall because your growth expectation won't match the deal flow you will need to produce each quarter. If your sales cycle is six to nine months, you will feel this problem more acutely.

3.) MARKET CONFUSION AND THE COMPETITION POSITIONING YOU

Another consequence is the lack of focus on market positioning at the brand level. It's natural in the sales process for reps to have the freedom to formulate the narrative that works uniquely for them in selling the specific product or service in a deal, but having air cover is critical.

- Sales reps take it upon themselves to create the company narrative, so there's a lack of cohesion in messaging and market understanding of what you do, how you are special, and why customers love you. Sales reps have to spend a lot of time educating prospects on a one-to-one basis to get to the qualification stage. It doesn't scale.

- Without a larger company narrative, competitors can say what they want about you. This gives your competition control over your company narrative, regardless of the words on your website. I've seen this happen to the point where competitors create false narratives and major competitive sweeps of certain customer segments.

4.) INABILITY TO EXPAND EXISTING CUSTOMERS

When sales focuses mostly on new deals and ACV, they often leave the customer LTV or share of wallet to the customer success or support teams. In this case, marketing is focused on ACV versus supporting retention and expansion, making customers highly vulnerable to competitive takeouts.

- With sales and marketing solely focused on acquisition, the care and feeding of the customer are in the hands of people whose KPIs are aligned to support, and who may also be seeing head count reductions as companies try to lower cost to serve in a more modern, digital-first model.

- With the customer success team focused on making sure customers are supported, using the product, and renewing the product, they can only help with expansion on a one-to-one basis, which also does not scale.

- The customer success teams don't have enough bandwidth to find new needs within the existing account based on a one-to-one basis to grow or expand accounts.

5.) CUSTOMER CHURN

With companies who have a larger or legacy installed base, without a warm pipeline coming in and the pressure to beat last quarter's numbers, the sales team becomes very transactional, even with renewals.

- The support teams are then focused on solving support tickets and reducing churn, but there is no one talking to the customer about why it might make sense to buy additional modules or different solutions for adjacent use cases or, not making sure customers are migrating to newer versions.

- More agile competitors swoop in and say whatever they want and steal the customers out from under you because they didn't even know you had what they just bought from someone else!

- The transactional nature of both the sales and the support engagements leaves a huge vacuum for expansion in accounts that may have a broader need to buy more from you, but there is no holistic account plan or awareness on the customer's part that you can help them.

- It may be the case that the sales teams have communicated what your offerings are, but remember, it takes ten to twenty-five times for someone to hear something to remember it these days, so explaining it once doesn't qualify as it being done.

- Depending on your solution, you may have multiple decision-makers and different people moving around in the customer account. It could be five to twenty decision-makers, but because the sales or customer success person is the only one dealing with one part of the organization (the person or group they sold the initial product to), they don't know what else is going on within that account. It may be your competitor is in there selling them everything they have and working hard to displace you eventually in the corner you are standing in.

6.) INABILITY TO RECRUIT REMARKABLE MARKETING TALENT

The same challenges in recruiting for great execs across all functions also exist in marketing.

- Every CMO wants to work for the CEO. From a growth standpoint, working for anyone other than the CEO (or the president in a large company) is believed to be career limiting. It's just how it is.

- Having the CMO report to the CRO will mean that you will not get the best candidates to choose from.

- CMO candidates will need to satisfy themselves that the CRO is truly an awesome leader, a mentor, and a supporter of marketing and that they can appropriately represent and advocate on marketing's behalf. If you refer to the beginning of this section about the focus of sales, you will understand why CMOs come in with a bias, so this one will be hard to overcome.

All of these consequences are unintentional because, of course, you would want a marketing program to address awareness, interest, and consideration in existing quarters and future quarters. Putting these crucial considerations under a CRO for your size company may inadvertently change the focus on marketing away from activities you probably also care about. I've seen many companies come full circle on their CRO decision. They all ended up realizing that they must go back, hire a CMO, and pull marketing back out separately, and then they spent another year to build back the marketing presence that was lost during that time.

The key takeaway here is, reconsider the scope of the CRO if you currently have one, along with your underlying intentions. If you expect to hire a CRO and fold marketing in because you don't also want to pay for a CMO, be aware of the pitfalls ahead. Truly stellar CROs are hard to find and tend to go to larger multinational companies, so recruiting will be tough.

IT'S TIME TO THINK DIFFERENTLY ABOUT THE CRO

If you believe you must combine sales and marketing as one because your software business model is collapsing the functions and the customer experience is more digital, it may be time to think differently across the board. If you are looking for a CRO, you may want to consider hiring a great CMO for the role instead of a career enterprise salesperson. This is true particularly if you are embracing one of the more progressive commercial software models such as pure SaaS, MSP, marketplace, or freemium with more techsumer buyers and shorter sales cycles.

In today's digital-first software business models, marketing and sales are a digital and operational motion in a closed loop, which is what marketing has been doing for a while now. When it comes to operations, marketing lives or dies on closed-loop reporting. I would argue it's easier to teach a high-caliber CMO how to do forecasts and hold sales teams accountable for closing deals than it is to teach a sales leader how to navigate the ocean of digital transformation and tools that it's taken CMOs years to harness.

SDR/BDRs Dead Reckonings

This last one is straightforward, so I'll be brief. What I mean by SDRs or BDRs are the people who follow up on marketing leads to qualify them, do outbound cold calling to find leads, or do both and set up sales meetings. They are called different things in different companies.

There's much debate on whether this role goes in marketing or in sales in today's B2B software model. I've seen it done both ways, and I feel strongly that it works better reporting to marketing than to sales for the following reasons.

First, if you put them there, marketing has accountability for sales qualified opportunities, and you can give them a pipeline target. The BDR function naturally acts as a connective tissue across sales and marketing that drives full accountability for the marketing generated leads, the outbound lead generation, opportunity nurturing, and sales qualified opportunity conversion.

Second, they can be responsible for creating the new sales opportunity in the system, and this solves the marketing attribution problem that plagues everyone. Since the opportunities from a sales stage perspective begin with the BDR, the BDR is typically working in the natural marketing workflow and lead management tools, so it makes sense for them to do this, which means you can now track marketing ROI.

Third, BDRs will have higher job satisfaction, and there will be lower attrition. When BDR teams live in the sales organization, they are the lowest on the totem pole and have a tendency not to get the support and resources they need to get their jobs done or have a career path. This isn't always the case, but it varies wildly in the B2B software space for sure. In marketing, sales opportunity conversion from marketing leads is where attribution is defined, so they will be treated like rock stars. Also, the CMO can work with your head of sales to give them a clear path into an account rep role. There is no reason this can't be done in partnership with the sales teams if they live in marketing. Marketing is not on Mars!

Fourth, marketing will stop complaining that sales doesn't follow up on leads, and sales will stop complaining that marketing didn't give them qualified leads. With the BDR team, they can follow up and qualify their own leads. It's been my experience watching various episodes of the same show play out and the same patterns arise that BDRs deliver better leads to sales when they report under marketing.

Finally, the key factor for a successful BDR program is having proper incentives. I've not seen programs work well that were base salary only; there should be a variable component, and this is often the rationale for why they get put under sales, because they have quotas, comp structures, kickers, and bonuses. This alone is not a reason to decide organizationally where they can be most effective. Yes, they must have comp structures like sales, but this should not be the primary rational for putting them in sales.

The biggest upside to having BDRs in marketing is with the right process, tools, and CX model in place, you can now give marketing a number. Even better, you can give portions of the marketing team incentives to drive aligned behavior and reward efforts where marketing is doing more heavy lifting in a SaaS-based model like in demand activation for leads and websites (if trial conversions are core to your success).

Summary

Over the years weather routing evolved because we got better instrumentation to allow us to make smarter decisions about when to leave on a sea voyage and when to wait it out for a better weather window. There is no longer a need for using dead reckonings as a method because we have better data, better electronics aboard, and better tools to help us get where we want to go—with the least amount of drama. Because weather is a complex system, nothing is perfect, but you can rule out a fair amount of error by logically looking at the weather models and trends to make sound choices.

Just as in sailing, dead reckonings seem directionally right but can take you way off course over time if you aren't careful. However, you don't need to rely on outdated methods when you have better methods and logic for getting the outcomes you want. You can stay on track by avoiding some of these pitfalls or at least go into these organizational decisions with your eyes wide open.

Keep an eye on these critical decisions to be sure they don't become dead reckonings for you:

→ The PLG model is what every modern software company should aspire to, to some degree, but it's an evolution, not a revolution, for most.

→ Consider the modern marketing and sales requirements of a PLG model, not that it will replace having marketing and sales functions altogether.

→ If you chose a CRO model for your business and intend to have marketing fold under sales, be aware of the risks and potential unintended consequences over time.

→ If you are considering a CRO, especially if your business model is moving more toward a commercial software model such as SaaS, marketplace, or freemium, you may want to consider recruiting a career CMO who can take on sales versus the other way around.

→ Having your BDR/SDR team report to marketing has many benefits, one of which is the ability to give marketing a quota.

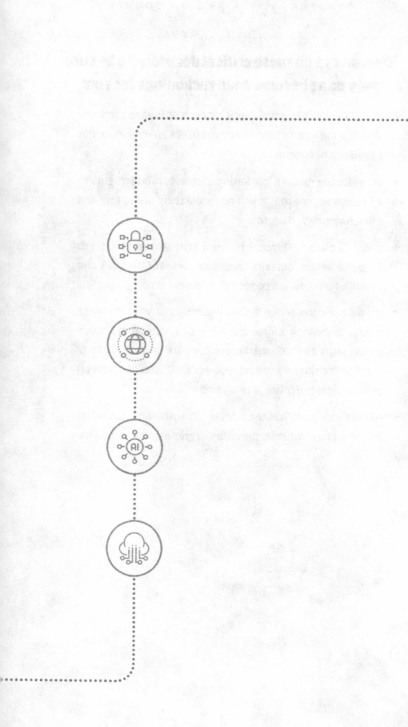

CHAPTER 13

ADVICE

THE MOST COMFORTING thing about talking to other sailors is the personal validation you get that you aren't crazy. Only they can appreciate the strange obsessions, dilemmas, and fears that dangle around in your head at night. Plus, they give great advice.

Counsel among sailors is always brimming with a peculiar type of wisdom on the most obscure topics. I've learned more at sailing meetups than anywhere else, and it is honestly shocking how many hours you can spend collecting enigmatic ideas for solving problems you never imagined you would have—until the second you do. Unsolicited advice is always useful, especially when you are taking on an exotic venture into challenging waters.

Leading through change, through growth, or into a transaction as a CEO can be as thrilling and exhilarating as it is exhausting and daunting, so advice never hurts. There is certainly a lot of work to do as you enter the transaction process itself, but I will leave all that to the bankers, accountants, and attorneys. But before all that, there's a lot to be learned by other CMOs in the industry about what needs to be done to be transaction ready.

To pressure test many of the suggestions in this book, I asked other CMOs what advice they would give to CEOs about using marketing as a value drive. In this chapter I will share broader advice from the previously mentioned survey of ninety B2B software CMOs and specific advice from a few marketing thought leaders that I respect.

Here are the top five points of advice for how to use marketing leading up to a transaction:

1.) COMPETITIVE STRATEGY AND POSITIONING

Focus on having a clear strategy and competitive positioning for influencer, customer, and prospect audiences. Clear positioning can help you differentiate from your competitors and communicate your unique value proposition to your target audiences with impact. You should be precise about markets you do and don't play in and what you are trying to achieve as a business and develop a clear messaging strategy that highlights your competitive advantages and communicates why you are the best choice for potential buyers. Having an understandable and coherent mission, a strong strategy, and a clear market position going into a deal helps build trust that you are valuable.

2.) CUSTOMER EXPERIENCE

CMOs recommend focusing on the customer experience and ensuring that it is seamless across all touchpoints. By engaging with customers and incentivizing loyalty, you can build long-term relationships with customers, increase customer LTV, and improve customer expansion. This can help demonstrate to potential buyers or investors that you have a strong and loyal customer base, that churn is not a major factor, and that there is a valuable customer base that is secure, which can also increase the perceived value of the company.

3.) NEW MARKETING REVENUE STREAMS

There are creative ways to leverage marketing to deliver new revenue streams in nonproduct areas. For example, you can develop and sell educational courses or consulting services that leverage your expertise in a particular area or monetize content of value to your customer base or partner community. This can help increase your overall value, which can be attractive to potential buyers or investors.

4.) SALES AND MARKETING ALIGNMENT

Sales and marketing alignment is critical for achieving KPIs and driving business success. To demonstrate this alignment, you should develop shared metrics that align with the customer journey, (outlined in detail earlier). By tracking these metrics you can demonstrate their ability to execute in unity and deliver results, which increases the perceived value of your company.

5.) BUZZ

Create buzz to get more top-of-mind awareness to target buyers, decision-makers, and transaction audiences combined. Creating buzz can be an effective way to increase awareness of your company among your target audience. To do this, you can leverage various marketing channels such as social media, email marketing, and content marketing to build excitement and generate interest in the transaction. By building buzz around the transaction, you can increase visibility, generate leads, and ultimately, attract potential buyers or investors.

Many of these topics are covered throughout this book, but seeing the consistent advice from other B2B software CMOs is also helpful.

Topics of Confusion

Marketing can be a complex and multifaceted discipline, and there are several topics that can be difficult for executives and investors to understand. I asked respondents in the same survey to share their opinions on the topics that they saw as most difficult to understand leading up to the transaction process. In order of popularity, the top five responses are as follows:

1.) LINKING BRAND AWARENESS TO QUARTERLY RESULTS

Building brand awareness is critical for the long-term success of a company, but it can be challenging to measure its impact on a quarterly basis, particularly when that is how revenue growth alone is evaluated. Investors and executives may struggle to understand the relationship between brand awareness and short-term financial metrics such as revenue and profit.

There are several strategies that you can use to gauge the impact and trending of brand-building efforts and the relationship to financial results. By tracking customer perception, tracking new website traffic as a proxy, measuring SOV and social media engagement, using attribution modeling and tracking conversion rate rises, and conducting sentiment research with key influencers, you can gain a better understanding of how brand efforts are influencing short-term results.

2.) THE TIME HORIZON FOR MARKETING TO HAVE AN IMPACT

We've talked about this a lot before. Marketing is a long-term investment, and it can take time for its impact to become evident. Executives and investors may struggle to understand the time horizon for marketing to have an impact and may be impatient to see results. Part of this is because many companies don't have the same CMO over years to see the results of the efforts before the strategy changes. However, if executives and investors understand the customer journey and what is needed to improve conversions at each stage, it's easier to get everyone onboard the long game that should be played with persistence, regardless of who comes and goes. By tracking conversion trending improvements over time, it will become clear what is or isn't working in each stage of the customer experience.

3.) APPRECIATING THE DIFFERENCE BETWEEN SALES CAPACITY AND EXECUTION AND EARLY PIPELINE DEVELOPMENT

When quarterly sales targets are not met, the reason that is instantly given in most cases is that there aren't enough at-bats for sales to deliver. The immediate implication is marketing isn't generating enough pipeline, which according to the respondents is not the core issue. While building a strong pipeline is critical for long-term success, companies also need to have the sales capacity and efficiency to close deals and generate revenue in the short term. Both elements are needed, but more pipeline is not always the main dependency.

4.) IMPROVING EBITDA WHILE ALSO EXPECTING ACCELERATED GROWTH

Companies may need to invest in marketing to achieve accelerated growth, but this can come at the expense of EBITDA. Executives and investors struggle to understand the balance between improving EBITDA and expecting accelerated growth.

5.) STAKEHOLDER UNDERSTANDING OF THE DIFFERENCE BETWEEN COMPANY AND PRODUCT POSITIONING

Executives, particularly those who are technologists, may struggle to understand the difference between company and product positioning. While product positioning focuses on the features and benefits of a specific product, company positioning focuses on the overall value proposition of the company based on what customers value and how it differentiates itself from competitors. Overall, the value of a company has to do with the company-level value proposition, not just its technology alone.

To address these challenges, CMOs and CEOs must align on the long-term benefits of marketing while also acknowledging the need for short-term results.

Biggest CEO Misperceptions— Respondent Verbatims

When asked what the biggest misperceptions by CEOs and investors were, the one that stood out was what the value marketing can deliver in a certain time frame. These quotes sum up the respondents' sentiments best:

"Founders, CEOs, and investors often expect faster results from marketing investments, but investments need to be aligned to the long game. They have a perspective of more traditional 'feed the funnel' lead volume style marketing, not the role that marketing can play today across the entire revenue process."

"Since most founders and CEOs I've worked with came from sales, they believe marketing value is primarily demand gen and the value is directly linked and exclusive to opportunity conversion. Lack of understanding related to the establishment of the broader content and conversation above the sales funnel."

"They think you can just sprinkle a little marketing on everything to drive growth and revenue and that it's just a cost center versus a value driver. It's on us to educate and come armed with the numbers, we own the sales and marketing alignment and shared goals, sales won't come knocking, you must drive this discipline."

"Investing in marketing today drives results tomorrow. There are things that need to be done to ensure alignment and turning on marketing won't produce results on day three."

"They think that marketing is just pretty pictures and clever noise."

"They think that marketing is easy."

Respondents were also asked to share their biggest challenge in the transaction process. Here are some of their responses:

"Trying to grow awareness and pipeline while significantly cutting program spend and head count."

"The challenge is to show the benefit of building the brand."

"The idea that you can provide a PE firm instant data when the company is new to marketing. Everything must be built first. Also, they don't understand how important messaging and positioning is to the business."

"Finance folks can often drive the process and don't understand marketing well enough to know where and when to insert it."

"Getting people to listen."

"Unrealistic expectations."

Finally, respondents were asked what one question they get repeatedly from their stakeholders that never goes away. The examples below were selected to represent the largest represented sentiments:

"What one program will give me the most pipeline?"

"If you hire one more marketing person, what will the impact be?"

"Why does everything cost so much?"

"How much longer until our brand is famous for recognition and recall?"

Advice from Industry Experts and Legendary CMOs

RICH ROGERS

Former marketing executive at Oracle, Symantec, SAP, Palo Alto Networks; global head of Startup Marketing Amazon Web Services (AWS)

"There are three things that define success:

First, the product must work and be something that people want to buy. Be brutally honest in making sure you have something that you can market. That means if you are going after a big market, you need to have a genuinely disruptive product.

Next, you need to have the right team that knows how to drive accountability. Get a good marketing leader who will help you be honest about where the gaps are and what needs to be done. Their primary job is to get the entire company behind the one-line sentence that says how you're different and why no customer can live without you and to get customers to evaluate your product. However, that will only work if you bring in a marketing leader who is both willing to do all the work to get alignment and drive accountability and who can operate as a peer and direct member of the leadership team. The whole team must operate together to align around a GTM that can succeed.

Finally, you are either profitable or you have a clear path to profitability as an independent business, and you can execute that plan. You won't get there if the CEO doesn't hold marketing and sales accountable, so execution accountability must come from the top down. I don't believe in handovers or interlocks; it's about executing the conversions at each stage, given the targets you set. It's simple: either you are jointly executing the goal or you are not.

There needs to be a belief that the marketing organization is a conversion function, not a helper or a service to anyone. Marketing is there to drive conversion through the entirety of the pipeline. There needs to be incentive systems where sales and marketing are measured against net new pipeline creation at a consistent close rate. Set targets and hold everyone accountable for that target so everyone knows where the new pipeline is coming from. For example, marketing creates 30 percent, sales creates 30 percent, and partners create 30 percent, and everything cascades from there. The targets are set, and every single marketing and salesperson has access to the CRM system and all the data, so everyone knows who is responsible for what and where everyone is at.

Marketing is sales at scale but only if you build it that way. They should be directly responsible for 30 percent of your pipeline in B2B. But for that to be true, you need to open up the entire year's worth of pipeline, look at all of it, and then jointly incentivize sales, marketing, and channels to work together to drive new business.

Where there's confusion during a transaction is with the transparency of the entire demand funnel. There is still too much nonsense and mystery around it because historically, sales has been allowed to drive quarterly forecasts and treat marketing and demand generation as separate or dependent functions, not part of a unified effort to drive results.

If you have all this, here are your priorities in order:

1. If you don't already have it, get your value proposition down to one sentence or less. It needs to state how you're different from everyone else and in a way that your target customer can't live without you.

2. Focus all your online, social, and demand generation efforts on contact discovery and all of your calls to action on driving evaluation and adoption of your product and skip all the unnecessary steps.

3. Drive marketing and sales alignment around legitimate pipeline creation, including shared targets that guarantee every salesperson is following up on every lead. Redesign your quarterly targets and CRM systems to instrument this.

4. Limit your awareness and social efforts to high-scale, low-cost mechanisms that reinforce your value proposition and drive all the above. Play up your differentiation or your unique position in the market."

HEIDI MELIN

Former CMO at Hyperion, Polycom, Taleo, Eloqua,
Plex, and Adobe Workfront (three of which were sold
to Oracle); current board member and advisor

"The modern CMO needs to look at the entire revenue process. They need to have strengths in brand, communications, and demand generation and think about how every tactic supports the revenue cycle from beginning to end. This can be a big *aha!* for growth or scale companies that may have predetermined ideas about marketing as a support function, only responsible for doing certain things or only driving leads.

Here's my advice: First, sales and marketing need to be aligned on objectives, even though the motions are different. The GTM is fragile until the marketing and sales leaders are aligned on the same outcomes and work together. Sales needs to focus on predictable revenue growth, and marketing needs to focus on account engagement all the way through the pipeline. It is also important to acknowledge that a sales leader may have a shorter-term lens on the business (current quarter), and the CMO should have a longer-term lens (current quarter plus one, current quarter plus two, or more). This difference in perspective is healthy but, when not acknowledged, can lead to misunderstandings or miscommunication.

Next, it's no longer about marketing qualified leads, and CEOs need to change their thinking about lead volume being the right measure for marketing. Today, it's about creating engagements within qualified accounts as customers go on their journey and how to leverage those engagements to move prospects through. Yesterday, it was about leads because we couldn't see what the leads were doing. Now we have the tools and technology to see what is happening in an account and measure it. By taking an account-based approach, we can track what each account is doing, which one has higher intent, and focus on accounts that have the highest probability of making it through the sales cycle. The technology is there, but a lot of companies aren't ready to use it or aren't thinking of it this way. Account-level engagement data is the most important tool we have today, and it's still not fully leveraged.

Also, there needs to be more education about the contribution marketing can have. It's different than it was ten years ago, but many CEOs and investors aren't fully aware. Marketing can make a big difference because now we have the data and technology to target the right buyers with right message and show quantitative results. Part of the problem is there isn't always a good CEO/CMO relationship, and CMOs can often be on their own. This can stem from CMOs needing to articulate what they are going to do and what they are not going to do, and those can be difficult conversations to have if a CEO doesn't have the right expectations about what can and can't be done well.

Growth is hard, and marketing must narrow down what the marketing team is going to do based on the business strategy, which is where the strategic trade-offs come in. You can be helpful here and there, but the CMO needs to know what they are ultimately held responsible for and where they can have the biggest impact. If it's a net new pipeline, for instance, there may be a trade-off with the focus and support on protecting the base and retention. These are hard conversations, especially for newer CMOs who don't like saying no. But in the end, there needs to be specificity in how marketing investment and resources are allocated and how success will be measured.

Finally, brand awareness efforts aren't often well understood or easy to quantify on a quarterly basis, but it's best to think of them as creating uplift for everything else and an effective way to take friction out of the buying process. If you can remove friction at the top of the pipeline, you can get more in the pipeline. If prospects have more affinity, fewer fall out of the pipeline. It's as simple as that. There are, of course, proxies to measure awareness, like unique web visits, unprompted engagement by an account on your target account list, share of voice, or analyst engagement."

....

SUE BARSAMIAN

Former senior GTM executive and general manager at Hewlett Packard Enterprise Software, Mercury Interactive, Critical Path, and Verity; current board member and strategic advisor to enterprise software and cybersecurity companies

Get Strategic Focus to Scale

"In technology companies it is common to hear the phrase 'you either build the product, you sell the product, or you support the people who build and sell.' Some may think this puts outsized importance on R&D and sales. There are other critical functions upstream that are foundational for continuous profitable growth and include having the challenging job of maintaining product market fit and establishing the optimal GTM segmentation model for growth motions that often define the focus for the entire company. Having a sound market and GTM strategy is critical, especially as you scale. Traditionally, these capabilities are delivered by a strong product management and product marketing team and help the company focus in harmony.

The rules of the jungle seem to be that the more success you enjoy, the more others also become interested in your category. So you may feel the squeeze from both ends—larger platform companies who want to claim your space and new start-up companies who want to offer what you do but faster and cheaper.

Now is the time to play both defense (defend your current ground) and offense (expand into new TAM, or total addressable market). New TAM will require new investment even with strong adjacency. If the SMB market is an adjacency, and your product is already being criticized as too complex by new start-ups, then investment in simplicity, a self-service PLG-like motion, and accelerated time to value is likely required. If the larger enterprise TAM is an adjacency, then investment in enterprise-ready functionality, security, and regulatory standards and a professional services team is likely required.

Making investment decisions and trade-offs to maintain product market fit while expanding TAM is a never-ending job. Companies stall or enter a downward spiral if this is not done right, so having the right strategic talent who can deliver the right GTM plan in your team is one of the most critical success factors for sustained profitable growth. Strong product/solution marketing defines the playbook for the rest of the company and is necessary for effective execution by other functions like demand generation and sales to connect the right product to the right customer in the right segment in the right geography at the right time. If done well, the rest of the company can execute against a clear playbook and drive friction-free growth. This playbook becomes even more important, and more challenging, as companies move from single-product to multiproduct companies that need to execute a land-and-expand set of activities.

Focus matters. A great PM/PMM team will deliver product market fit and the optimal GTM playbook for today's growth plan and run the experiments that will yield tomorrow's expansions.

Be Maniacal about Customer Experience

Organizational boundaries within companies are chasms that customers and prospects fall into.

If the baton passes from one function to another don't happen as planned, who notices besides the customer? If a customer doesn't successfully adopt your product, or stay educated on new capabilities as your offering evolves, who raises the alarm? Often, you don't discover a problem until it's too late and a frustrated customer has found another alternative.

Automating the customer journey from onboarding to adoption, support, education, community, and expansion is foundational for companies who want to enjoy best-in-class metrics for growth and retention. Today's customers have increasingly higher bars for time to value and process simplicity; they prefer a high-quality digital experience and easy access to real people when they need it. For companies, the investment in a digital customer experience will give you a comprehensive and consistent view of each customer, their engagement levels, and whether they are on track to fulfill their original purchase objectives. A great customer experience is a significant competitive differentiator these days, and increasing customer retention is one of the top levers for growth.

Instrument to Optimize

Sales and marketing is the largest operating expense line item in a company's P&L, usually surpassing R&D and far surpassing G&A (general and administrative). All companies are under pressure to improve profitability while driving growth, and the GTM team is a necessary target for efficiency. However, because of the complexity in GTM and the number of disparate functions that it spans, decisions about how to improve efficiency while driving growth are challenging and not without risk.

An investment in instrumentation and the right metrics framework can move these decisions from gut feel to fact based and help to de-risk the outcomes. Evolving a metrics framework into a true business management system is the master class. A great GTM business management system will include a full range of metrics for both productivity and efficiency across sales and marketing by segment and by geography. It will compare your performance to your plan, to your historical trends, and to best-in-class peers in the industry where possible. You will know your hot spots; you will better understand root cause issues and actionable steps to remediate. Companies are increasingly investing in roles like revenue operations or chief growth officers to look at GTM performance end to end and drive growth. Many companies underestimate the importance of a good business management system to set these roles up for success."

ROBIN MATLOCK

Former CMO of VMware; former senior executive at Imperva, McAfee, and Symantec; current board member and strategic advisor

Business Strategy versus Marketing Strategy

"It may seem like common sense, but I assure you it's harder than you'd think. Business strategy is always first. Before you try and take something to market, it's imperative to have defined your strategy, defined your competitive advantage, and articulated your ideal target customer. Even if these strategic elements are not perfectly validated, it's vital to do the work up front to outline your strategic direction and value long before you start amping up your position (and spend) in the market. Preserve precious capital by testing and targeting your theories before unleashing your marketing investment.

There is a tendency to lean on positioning and messaging as the means to navigate a lack of clarity on strategy and specifically product market fit. Sure, great positioning and messaging can capture the imagination of your audience, it can educate your prospects on your value, and good positioning and messaging can create a gap between you and your competition. But the fact is, you can't message your way out of a competitive battle if you're competing on the wrong battleground. To be successful, you must do the work, gain deep knowledge of your target customers, test and validate your theories, and make the hard decisions and trade-offs that feed into your broader GTM strategy.

The Power of Focus

Insight into your product market fit is vital. When you have clarity about who needs your product, why they need it, and what motivates them to buy it, that's when the magic begins. Often, companies cast too wide a net into the market, positioning their solution across multiple segments to multiple buyers for multiple use cases. This approach rarely works and often confuses the market, your buyer, and your partners. It's far more effective to invest the necessary time up front to define and validate through testing the customer segments that are the best match for the product, then focus execution (including marketing) on owning your sweet spot. You can expand over time from a position of strength and grow your TAM by going after new segments, new use cases, or new buyers. Without this focus, it's too easy to end up positioned as all things to all people, which is essentially the same as *no thing to no people*. At that point, it's hard to even get good feedback from the market about what is and isn't working. Focus on where you believe you have targeted, product market fit, and you will get clearer signals from the market relative to your offering and perceived value.

The reason leaders resist such a focused approach is because they don't want to miss out on market opportunity or be boxed in too narrowly. Ironically, a broad approach has the opposite effect: you end up missing out on what makes you special. Great vision and focused GTM are not in conflict. Owning a specific beachhead, or target market, doesn't make you small and narrow, nor does it lock you in to any specific market. We need to dispel this belief that focus limits TAM. Carve out a TAM you can own, position a broad vision, but execute with focus, then expand. Growing your TAM from a position of market share dominance is much more effective than spraying multiple markets and segments with a diluted value proposition and competing against multiple categories of competitors. It's a matter of timing and sequencing.

Marketing Metrics

Measurement is a pet peeve of mine, particularly in B2B marketing. Expectations and pressure on measurement are exceptionally high. There are unrealistic expectations of measuring the precise contribution each marketing dollar spent has on a specific dollar of revenue. It's not impossible; it's just cost prohibitive. If you wanted precise impact measures on every dollar spent, your research budget would dwarf your media budget. In complex selling environments, where a transaction takes months to land, customers engage with your brand dozens of times, and buying cycles are loaded with numerous stakeholders, it's just not that easy to boil down marketing spend to a specific cause and effect analysis. At some point, such granular measurement becomes cost prohibitive or, worse, manufactured.

A perfect example of the challenge of measuring precise marketing impact on revenue is branding. Translating specific brand investments into an accurate ROI benchmark is messy. The I part is easy; you know what you spend on branding. It's the R part that gets trickier. Being able to definitively tie a dollar of inbound revenue to a dollar of outbound branding spend is a costly road to travel. You are going to spend more time trying to calculate ROI and correlating it than on the paid placements themselves. This truth makes people very uncomfortable. It makes me uncomfortable. My recommendation is to measure precisely what you *can* measure, but don't manufacture causal relationships that are so loosely correlated they simply aren't defensible. It's important to be realistic about using proxy measures and not overengineer scientific correlations that gobble up disproportionate amounts of working budget for weak insights and bogus dashboards.

There is lots you can measure, and the more digital our interactions become, the better the insights. Focusing on engagement data, for example, is very effective in complex selling environments. If prospects are consuming your content, meeting with your teams, going to your events, cruising your website, they are highly engaged and far more likely to buy. So while you can't effectively pinpoint which web page pushed them over the edge, you can see a bigger picture that gives your profound insights into their readiness to buy.

CMO Tenure

While a simple Google search will reveal the average tenure of CMO's in the F500 is just over four years, when looking below the F500, the story is considerably different. In Silicon Valley, I believe two to three years is typical. Why do we turn over our CMO's so frequently? The CMO job is a tough one. CMO's are big spenders of capital, and yet their impact is very tricky to measure with precision. They must appease a broad range of stakeholders, who are often not aligned. As a CEO, you need to evaluate your team's performance with a keen eye. Lagging sales are not always attributable to poor execution on demand generation. Lack of awareness may be a result of poor marketing execution, but make sure your strategy and execution are aligned as a whole, and you aren't just looking for a quick fix to a deeper set of issues.

As a CEO, set your leadership team up for success. Make sure you offer your CMO an equal seat at the strategic table, both formally and informally. Decide what you want out of a CMO, be clear on priorities, focus on outcomes, and help align the leadership team to those common goals and outcomes. Every executive must do their part. Expect excellence from your CMO, which includes a compelling marketing strategy; excellent execution appropriate for your market, customer profile, and buying cycle; deep partnerships with internal stakeholders; and a firsthand understanding of customer needs and the markets they represent. On the other hand, if you are churning through CMOs and never seem satisfied, maybe there's something more to the situation."

JOHN ELLETT

Former B2B marketing executive; former marketing agency CEO; author; *Forbes* contributor; CEO at the Ellett Group CMO Accelerator

"The biggest challenge with B2B is that companies get so enamored with technology that they forget about the customer. You have to keep the customer at the center of the focus, and this becomes really important to create sustainable differentiation and long-term value. In the early stages, you need to think about what customer segment you have the best opportunity to satisfy, what problems your core audience is trying to solve, and what the benefit is as opposed to barfing a list of features. Companies need to bring customer empathy into how they engage with prospects and the market at large.

The key role a CMO needs to play for the company is as follows:

First, you must keep the customer at the center of all decisions and designing experiences that will distinguish you long term. The last thing you want is to get acquired and then experience churn.

Next, create a story from an empathetic customer's point of view. Anyone can create a spec sheet. What is the proposition you are uniquely set up to solve, and how are you different than everyone else? For getting ready for a transaction, you need a brand story with a compelling value proposition that is easy to understand, not a recital of the features of the product. You need to be able to briefly describe how you are uniquely positioned to solve problems that allow you to attract more customers and keep them.

Also, you need to have a systematic demand-creation approach. More buyers are on a self-directed journey to find solutions to their problems, and they are using a variety of different sources and tools to find information than they once did. So much of the buying process happens before they ever engage with a salesperson, and a lot of buyers would prefer to do it without a salesperson if possible, which has changed how B2B software transacts. Instead of being sold, it is being bought.

Today, you need a systematic set of engagements designed to deliver the right message, at the right time, to the right person. It's not about the sales pipeline; it's about the customer experience overall and how marketing, sales, and support all fit together to predictably drive demand over time. Some do it better than others, but the ones that do it well have created it based on helping customers buy in a digital motion, not helping salespeople sell in a high-touch motion.

Finally, I want to comment on the concept of product-led growth (PLG). The nomenclature of PLG is unfortunate because it puts all the emphasis on the product and not the customer experience. The fundamentals have been around for decades in the consumer space: make the product easy to try and buy is the simple idea. In SaaS, it's about designing an easy experience that people can try with minimal friction and tailoring the messages around their pain point and how you help them solve it.

What's central to the PLG strategy is the customer experience of trying and buying your product or service, not the product. The problem is that PLG assumes that if people knew how cool it was, they would buy it, but PLG is being driven more and more out of tech teams without understanding that there's this discipline called marketing that is designed to get people familiar with how cool products are. There's a danger in this PLG path people are on because it assumes it's entirely a product development-led model. This is especially true in founder-led firms, where technology is the DNA and ethos of the company. The code is important but can get overemphasized to the point that other parts of the success formula are underutilized or nonexistent. There needs to be an understanding of how all functions contribute to the ultimate customer-led buying experience."

JULIE PARRISH

Former CMO at NetApp, Checkpoint Software,
RedSeal; CMO at Corelight

"What's most important overall in marketing is to create a compelling company narrative for investors, focus on getting the basics right as these are often overlooked, create repeatable, scalable models early on, and align with sales and the rest of the company on agreed outcomes and metrics, not on activities and programs. As a rule, less is more since most early stage companies die from indigestion, not starvation.

Here's my advice leading up to a transaction: During the twelve to eighteen month run-up to the transaction, it is important to build a compelling narrative that captures the following:

- What is the TAM and SAM, and (a) is the market big enough to be interesting over time, (b) how crowded is the market today, and (c) what advantage will you have over competitors?

- Why people want what you have—what is the *right here, right now* problem you solve and have a cadre of easy-to-remember customer stories to support this?

- What kind of sustainable competitive advantage (IP, technology) do you have?

- Be able to tangibly demonstrate the health of your business: annual recurring revenue, burn to net annual recurring revenue ratio, customer acquisition trends, and customer retention.

- Understand where you win, why you win, and show proof that you are executing against a model, with core metrics such as time to rep productivity, percent of sales reps at/over quota, 4Q pipeline, number and size of deals per quarter, percentage of new, incremental, and annual recurring revenue.

Figure out how to quickly tell the above story to potential investors! Understand that investors are a specific audience that needs tailored messages and a story. In my opinion, this is one of the most important things that marketing can do in the lead-up to a transaction. Marketing can help figure out how to build the narrative and tell the story effectively.

In addition, make sure marketing is focused on creating repeatable, successful models that can be used as proof points of success in your narrative. Repeatable models can be more easily created if you focus on basics like target marketing, unique positioning and messaging, and alignment on both marketing and sales activation.

Here are some marketing basics that you must get right:

Have an ideal customer segment profile; it should be clear and detailed to include customer size, verticals, tech stacks, key pain points, etc. Then clearly articulate your positioning and messaging with proof points.

Create a buyer's journey so everyone understands who you're targeting, what their pain points are, where they go to get information, and how they experience the buying process.

Drive marketing and sales alignment through a joint sales funnel model that puts responsibilities and metrics in the appropriate places and aligns key demand efforts. However, don't over-rotate and measure marketing on revenue. This is almost always a flawed approach, in my opinion.

Create a marketing dashboard that groups outcomes into key areas such as awareness, familiarity, intent, and conversion."

· ·

SCOTT BRINKER

Marketing technologist and thought leader; editor at
ChiefMartec.com and platform ecosystem at HubSpot

"There has been a set of historical paradigms about how B2B marketing operates, but expectations are shifting, which is tied to the technology we are using and what we are now able to do with it. For example, there's been a shift in interest toward an account-based focus in sales. For us in marketing, we figured that out years ago, but there was no GTM process for how to operationalize that with sales, so everyone just remained stuck. By unifying the functions across a shared customer experience with the technology underneath it, we can finally execute on this.

There's been a rise in the last four years because a lot of SaaS companies realize they need to move more broadly to deliver a digital experience. You can't be a software company today and not understand how to instrument and optimize marketing funnels or automated sequences that can handle different segments and points of the buying cycle. Even if you are going for a pure product-led growth (PLG) model, you need to understand your customers and how they are influenced by a broader community. Today, people get information and advice from a complex network. Without technology, you can't instrument the network of connections and see the patterns that are driving intent and conversion.

Martech was originally on its own island, generating a lot of marketing data and insight. Now that data is starting to get smarter and integrate more broadly into how companies operate overall. Consequently, marketing is in a position to offer insights to help the company understand a broader set of signals. We can now get access to more useful data and operationalize insights to take actions that drive results.

Here's my top advice:

First, marketing is strategic, and it's a pillar of how your business runs. If you aren't treating your marketing function, marketing operations, and marketing technology as first-class pillars of how your business runs, it's a digital world now, and you will get left behind. If you are a software company, you can't escape the fact that you are a digital business; it's not a question. You have no choice. Your only choice is whether you want to be a good business or not. Once you recognize the value of the data and the technology-enabled customer experience it provides, it isn't some back-office supporting function anymore. That's a view that is decades old, and you must realize marketing is a strategic function.

Second, you must create a marketing organization that is change-ready and agile. It's not just about hitting a target; it's about building a set of skills that endure. The world is going through patterns of change, and market dynamics are such that the rate of change has accelerated. If I'm a CEO, the capability of my company needs to be good at change. So the marketing and sales organizations, the workflows, and the technology need to be adaptable to meet that challenge.

We have gotten relatively good at how we train salespeople, but we are still very bad at marketing enablement and taking advantage of new trends and new ways of thinking.

It's not about getting good marketing; it's about having people, processes, and technology that are good at adapting to whatever the market can throw at you. If you get really good at that, you will be better prepared than your competition to succeed.

Third, there's a litmus test for claiming to be customer-obsessed. Is your tendency to make long-term decisions that are good for customers or short-term decisions that are good for your company? Being customer-obsessed is not about putting customer in every internal memo and being done. You need to make decisions based on what is best for the customers over the long haul because your customer base is your value creation.

Today, the incentive structure is so focused on the short term that there is no advantage to making a longer-term decision to keep customers over time. If we are all striving for lifetime value (LTV) for customers, why are we so focused on short-term decisions that don't actually help achieve the LTV goals? It's easy to be customer centric when it is at no cost to you, but when it costs something (either money, time, or resources) and the answer is no, that's when you know the company does not have a customer-centric focus."

KIM WHITLER

Former CMO; author; *Forbes* contributing editor; currently professor at Darden School of Business, University of Virginia

"I recently completed some research talking with B2B leaders from one hundred companies to understand how marketing functions should be organized at different stages of growth (from Series A to Series E/IPO).

At the Series A stage, firms need a scrappy, roll-up-your-sleeves CMO who can create content and then pull together an investor presentation. However, as companies grow (Series B–D), firms need scale experts who are better equipped to reorganize to help the function become more structured and systematic. As firms mature further (Series E/IPO), the CMO needs to have the ability to lead a more sophisticated organization with more layers and a broader remit.

At this stage, the CMO job often grows beyond the skills of the incumbent in the role. If CMOs and CEOs are not on top of this, the CMO will be underprepared to manage the role. The advice I would provide investors and CEOs is to understand what stage of development your firm is in, to hire a CMO with the skill set that matches the requirements based on the stage of firm development (scrappy generalist early on, scale experts later, with structured and more sophisticated marketers at E/IPO). Also, be ready to develop your CMO so they are prepared for future growth. If CEOs are not on top of this, the CMO will be underprepared for the road ahead.

While this insight may seem obvious, it isn't.

Most CMOs believe their jobs are designed wrong, and the result is an exceptionally high turnover rate. The fact that CEOs are finding a disconnect between what they have and what they need is also an indication that CMO placements may not be well thought through. This research suggests that CEOs need to be more aware of the level of skills required and ensure their CMO is prepared to effectively perform and work as the company matures."

....

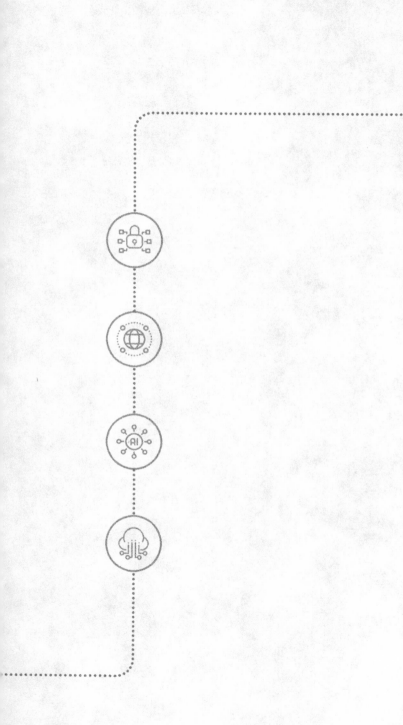

CONCLUSION

WE HAVE JUST been on a journey together exploring ways you can use marketing more strategically in your business to get the results you want and deserve. Marketing is more critical than ever to small and midsize B2B software companies because of the complex nature of the modern digital experience, rapidly evolving customer expectations, the explosion of the software industry, and the economic pressures from competitors and investors. My goal for this book is to help you understand how you can unleash hidden value in your company and gain a competitive advantage by using the five principles to get the Power of Surge.

In the beginning of this book, I made the following promises:

- I would provide advice based on proven methods that are practical, immediately actionable, and risk-free.

- You would walk away with a prescriptive approach for how to use marketing to unlock hidden value for your company that investors will care about, particularly if a transaction is in your future.

- You would finish this book with a clear idea of what a marketing strategy looks like and what you can expect from a modern marketing engine.

- You would have a clearer idea of what kind of CMO you need and how to keep them.

- You would know what situations, decisions, and dangerous assumptions to avoid.

- You would gain insights and perspectives from CMOs across the B2B industry in addition to my own.

A fundamental idea of this book is that unless you are a market leader today or are on your way in the next two years, there are two probable factors that require deep consideration: facing financial headwinds and participating in a transaction. With this being the case, you and your CMO need to be aligned on a strategy so you can get the growth and valuation benefits in time for it to matter. Downturns have taught us that companies that prioritize customer experience, digital modernization, and strategic brand positioning perform better through tough times and are more attractive to multiple buyers, so planning for those inevitabilities is prudent.

The digital-first world requires you to adapt or risk falling behind because of rapid technological advances and changes to buyer behavior that are shifting business dynamics every moment. Therefore, a sound marketing strategy is the only way to keep up with the speed, scope, and scale of digital today, and random, tactical marketing programs in this environment can often do more harm than good.

B2B technology buyers are becoming more like consumers, wanting to interact with companies when, where, and how they want. Organizations that differentiate themselves based on the customer experience and align their business operations with the customer journey have statistically predictable success rates and create a valuable competitive moat for themselves. Today, a B2B brand's positioning affects adoption and conversion rates and thus growth and market share. B2B companies rarely combine effective brand positioning with sales activation, so doing it well in combination can give them a significant advantage. As more software companies enter the market, organizations with this integrated approach will grow faster, make more money, and be forgiven for imperfect software products and services.

We now have a new definition of B2B marketing. Technical buyers and customers expect B2B software companies to engage digitally in our connected world. Today's marketing creates meaningful customer relationships through compelling, always-on experiences that increase business value through a complex web of technologies and interactions that provide a seamless, engaging customer experience.

We explored why the customer journey is no longer linear but is instead interconnected and complex and has upended traditional GTM models and sales motions because interactions are becoming more digital. These changes require a whole new perspective on marketing and how it can help you drive business value.

> **Are you cruising or are you racing to win?**

If you believe you are racing, then you need a marketing approach to match your intention, and you can get there using the five Power of Surge principles outlined below:

S – STRATEGY
Know yourself and commit to a course.

It's critical to have a crystal clear idea about your business situation, where you honestly sit in the market competitively, and what customer segments best fit with what you can deliver. Only with an honest, informed assessment of your situation can you hope to succeed. Yet this fundamental principle can be elusive while chasing growth. With a sober view of your situation, priorities become obvious. With careful consideration of your options and a commitment to your course, it's easier to determine where and how to focus to achieve your goals, even if it means walking away from ambitious opportunities that salespeople are excited about.

U – UNITY
Create radical unity for aligned execution.

The best leadership is unified around one mission and strategy and tightly aligned to a set of metrics that drive accountability and execution. There must be organizational discipline at the top to provide structure and order, while each functional commander is given discretion and decision authority that allows for flexibility, innovation, and variation based on their unique situational awareness. Radical unity is the shared mission, but there should be tightly aligned command and delegated authority at the point of action.

R - REPUTATION

Define your unique advantage and consistently deliver on it.

To compete successfully, you must identify the right context in which to compete, capitalize on your strengths in a compelling way, and position yourself advantageously in relation to the other alternatives. Just as important is to consistently deliver on your promises to your customers, building a lasting trust in your company that keeps them coming back and referring you to others. By positioning yourself strategically, you have a better chance of creating momentum and building a valuable brand reputation in the market.

G - GAINS

Unlock hidden value in new ways.

Company visions should be ambitious, but when goals are set too high or gains are seen as only coming from a maniacal focus on sales execution, you may miss achieving gains from hidden corners of your company that are otherwise just sitting there idle. By expecting and collecting gains as small victories in many places, such as in marketing, you might create new streams of profit and value that may surprise you. By rewarding small wins in many places, your people will build both confidence and desire to win.

E - EFFICIENCY

Move swiftly and effectively and with impact.

Speed and efficiency are essential to take advantage of opportunities as they arise. It's no longer about getting to market; it's about getting to the right person at the right time with the right message through the right methods that matter. Precision targeting, agile execution, and meaningful engagement can only be done if you have a clean foundation for process, data, and accountability.

With a little planning, you can avoid the slow and painful barnacle buildup and have the speed and agility of a company three to four times your size with legacy technology and fixed methods. Modern processes, talent, functions, and a tech stack are needed to create efficiency and scale. Following best practices with the right modern tech stack improves success and ROI measurement, and it also helps your company focus on what customers care about.

> **Smooth sailing toward a successful endgame requires smart investing, sound leadership, and avoidance of dead reckonings that can take you off course.**

While there are some broad investment guidelines, deciding what to invest in marketing depends on your business situation, what you are trying to achieve across the customer life cycle, and how much time you have. Whether you have a million dollars or one, you need a marketing plan that matches your business strategy and customer journey. Simply using a percentage of revenue and a competitor spending can be misleading, so don't fall into this trap.

Most CMOs agree that there are many ways to spend money, but it really comes down to where you are starting from. Foundational marketing, like your digital stack and always-on activities, are the dial tone for being open for business and will always cost money. If you have this in place, you can spend more in targeted areas to create consistent execution and market momentum. It's easier to start with a focus on the foundation because you will spend money on it either way, in the beginning to get it right or a lot more later to make up for lost time or clean up the mess made by years of bad operational discipline. If you always take the view that marketing is an investment in helping customers achieve their goals faster or better as they try, buy, and use your solutions, it's easy to see where to prioritize funding.

Finding and keeping a great CMO is about knowing what you need and getting aligned on strategy, trust, and communication and setting realistic expectations. If you get a great CMO (or plan to develop one), you have a role in their success, so it's best to start with clear expectations and a shared vision. Also, consider your business when hiring a CMO, as different business models require different skills. Be aware that the CMO-CEO gap of grief hinders execution, and you can gain an advantage over your competitors by taking actions to close this gap.

Dead reckonings are decisions that seem right in the beginning but can lead you astray. To stay on track and achieve your goals, make these organizational decisions mindfully: PLG model, CRO structure, and BDR reporting lines. Every modern software company should strive for the PLG model, but for most, it's an evolution, not a revolution. Consider how PLG models affect modern marketing and traditional ideas about sales. If you intend to put marketing under a CRO, be aware of the risks and long-term impact. If your business is moving toward a digital-first commercial software model, you may want to consider a career CMO instead. Putting BDR/SDR teams under marketing means you can finally give marketing a number!

Finally, we saw many common themes emerge from the advice of other legendary CMOs and GTM leaders. Strategy is seen as a major gap; however, market segmentation, positioning, and focusing on what's most important when making difficult decisions, are the key ingredients to a winning strategy. Having unity across marketing, sales, and customer success is also critical and requires a shared view of the customer journey, shared accountability, and full transparency. Instrumenting your business using modern technology, a unified workflow, and integrated, customer-focused methods will determine success or failure in the very near term. New dynamics require a shift away from old marketing paradigms and depend on marketing being a more strategic function for B2B software companies serious about winning.

This book outlines how you can harness the power of your existing resources and the current conditions to work in your favor to create the surge in business value you want. Now that we've navigated the complexities of the digital landscape, evolving customer expectations, and the competitive pressures of the software industry, you can immediately use the Power of Surge to help chart a better course to your destination starting today.

Consider this not just a conclusion but a launchpad. In the business of B2B software, where the stakes are high, where every decision matters, the Power of Surge can be used to help you manage uncharted waters. The digital-first world is like an ocean, it demands adaptation, and your marketing strategy can be your vessel that helps you not just survive a passage, but triumph in your current race.

As you proceed, remember that the Power of Surge remains your steadfast companion, guiding you toward growth, value creation, and market leadership. May your journey be marked by strategic clarity, radical unity, and the ability to manage storms and take advantage of the conditions to create your own forward momentum as you surge toward your final destination.

Finally, remember that sound and swift execution starts with you. It begins with your willingness to look at your situation from a new perspective, given your ambitious goals. When you wish to achieve remarkable outcomes, you must consider alternative paths to what worked for you in the past.

> **70 percent of the earth is water, yet nearly every map we use in our everyday life shows mostly land.**

When I made the decision to take on a circumnavigation, I looked at a map of the planet realizing for the first time in my life that most of it is water and coastline. The map was never wrong, but how I was looking at it limited my perspective and beliefs about what was possible for me. Suddenly, how I looked at achieving goals and managing risk was different as limiting beliefs melted away and the seriousness of the endeavor became crystal clear. Priorities had new fidelity and purpose was now a word with substance.

When you look at a map every day that shows you land, you can't help but cling to its meandering paths, sprawling roadways, and tidy burial plots. When suddenly that map becomes a chart of oceans and waterways you can't help but wonder why you didn't see it earlier and can't wait to step off the cliff of comfort and dive into a sea of possibilities.

This may be a lot of philosophy for a business book, but my deepest hope if you have gotten this far is that you can look at your own business situation and see the possibilities in a new way. Remember, the most profound lessons lie beneath the surface. Embrace change not as a tempest to endure, but as a tide guiding you toward new horizons. By adopting a new mindset, you'll ride the waves of change, discovering uncharted opportunities and unlocking the boundless potential for personal and professional growth. Truthfully, none of this is hard if you turn your perspective to the open spaces and quit looking at the land masses in between.

Fair winds for now.

How inappropriate to call this planet
Earth, when it is clearly *Ocean*.

—ARTHUR C. CLARKE

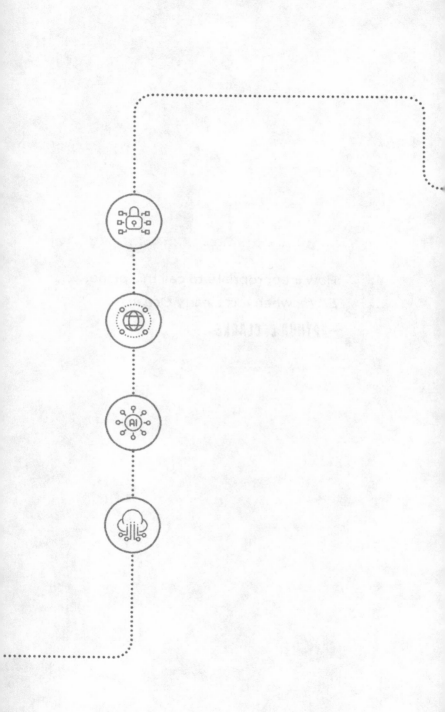

HOLLY ROLLO has three decades in the business-to-business (B2B) technology industry with a focus on transforming and repositioning brands facing pivotal moments, including turnarounds, hypergrowth, carve-outs, and pre- or postequity transactions. Her focus is to help ambitious B2B software businesses create meaningful value for their customers and investors through impactful GTM strategies designed for the digital-first era. Holly is currently the founder and CEO of Surge Strategies, a strategic advisory firm.

As the former chief marketing officer and senior vice president at RSA, Holly helped lead the successful carve-out from Dell in 2020. Prior to that, Ms. Rollo served as CMO at Fortinet and SumTotal Systems, a Vista Equity Partners company, which was later acquired by Skillsoft. She has held executive positions at FireEye, which grew from $5 billion to $13 billion market cap during her tenure; SuccessFactors, which was acquired by SAP for $3.4 billion; Cisco, leading the SME cloud market strategy; and at SAP, where she helped drive the GTM transformation into the SME market with its first cloud-based ERP platform. She spearheaded repositioning for Sybase, later acquired by SAP for $5.8 billion; helped drive the utility-computing product strategy at Veritas, later acquired by Symantec for $13.5 billion; and co-led post-acquisition strategic planning at IBM/Tivoli. She has also supported major brand repositioning strategies for various clients on the agency side.

Holly's teams have been honored to receive awards for ROI and digital transformation. She has contributed to publications such as *Harvard Business Review* and *Forbes* and has been a keynote speaker at numerous large-scale industry events.

She holds multiple board and advisory roles in both the public and private sector. She is a mentor and an advocate for young women in technology and graduated with honors from Santa Clara University.

Printed in the USA
CPSIA information can be obtained
at www.ICGtesting.com
JSHW020317070924
69343JS00003B/15

9 781642 258110